OXFORD MONOGRAPHS ON MUSIC

BURGUNDIAN COURT SONG IN THE
TIME OF BINCHOIS

Burgundian Court Song
in the
Time of Binchois

The Anonymous *Chansons* of
El Escorial, MS V.III.24

WALTER H. KEMP

CLARENDON PRESS · OXFORD
1990

Oxford University Press, Walton Street, Oxford OX2 6DP
Oxford   New York   Toronto
Delhi   Bombay   Calcutta   Madras   Karachi
Petaling Jaya   Singapore   Hong Kong   Tokyo
Nairobi   Dar es Salaam   Cape Town
Melbourne   Auckland
and associated companies in
Berlin   Ibadan

Oxford is a trade mark of Oxford University Press

Published in the United States
by Oxford University Press, New York

© Walter H. Kemp 1990

British Library Cataloguing in Publication Data
Kemp, Walter H., 1938–
Burgundian court song in the time of
Binchois: the anonymous chansons of El
Escorial, Ms V. III 24.—(Oxford monographs
on music)
1. France (Kingdom) Burgundy. Court music,
1430–1453
I. Title
780'.880621
ISBN 0–19–816135–2

Library of Congress Cataloging in Publication Data
Kemp, Walter H., 1938–
Burgundian court song in the time of Binchois : the anonymous
chansons of El Escorial, Ms V. III 24. / Walter H. Kemp.
(Oxford monographs on music)
Bibliography: Includes index.
1. Music—France—Burgundy—15th century—History and criticism.
2. Chanson, Polyphonic.   3. Chanson, Polyphonic—Analysis,
appreciation.   4. Binchois, Gilles, 1400 (ca.)—1460.   I. Title.
II. Series.
ML2627.7.B9K45   1989   784.3'00944'4—dc 19   88–32228
ISBN 0–19–816135–2

Set by Latimer Trend & Company Limited

Printed in Great Britain by
St Edmundsbury Press Ltd
Bury St Edmunds, Suffolk

TO THE MEMORY OF MY PARENTS

Preface

THE *chansonnier* El Escorial, Biblioteca del Monasterio MS. V.III.24 preserves some of the most significant examples of the craft of fifteenth-century Franco-Flemish court song. Its chief fame has been as a prime resource for studying the secular repertoire of Binchois. Although only one of the manuscript's sixty-two pieces carries an ascription specifically naming Binchois as the song-maker, concordant sources have enabled a total of nineteen songs in this collection to be attributed to him. Thirty-four songs, of which twenty-nine are *unica*, have no scribal attribution, and so this corpus of material is of an interest equal to that of the Binchois ascriptions. Linking these two principal bodies of repertoire are certain identifiable musical features which distinguish Binchois's style, and which isolate particular anonymous pieces to be proposed as belonging either to the Binchois canon or to a 'school of Binchois'. It is clear that, while the *chanson* at the court of Duke Philip the Good of Burgundy continued medieval forms and functions, the idiom did possess enough scope for a strong creative personality to assert itself. The first part of this book will explore the extent to which Binchois's markedly individual musical style can reveal more fully his contribution to the mix of traditions that was the Franco-Flemish style in which he was engaged. In the second part the factors which related the *chanson*'s character and expression to its nurturing environment will be considered as the songs are placed within the context of the courts in whose service they were made.

Before we address issues concerning authorship and sociology of Burgundian *chansons* in the Escorial Manuscript V.III.24 (hereafter called *EscA*), it would be useful to review some of the basic details about the source itself. The parchment manuscript, large octavo 16 × 25 cm, was written in black notation with red colouration. It comprises eight gatherings, each of four double leaves placed within each other. The foliation 1–62 was added in the nineteenth century, and although it does not take into account two missing leaves the system is retained here because all modern studies employ it. Further details on the physical make-up of the manuscript may be found in the commentary by Wolfgang Rehm published with a facsimile edition (*Codex Escorial: Chansonnier* (*Documenta Musicologica*, zweite Reihe: Handschriften-Faksimiles, 2; Kassel: Bärenreiter, 1958)). The flaws in this facsimile publication make accurate transcription impossible without careful scrutiny of the original source:

1. Omitted note: fo. 16ʳ, Contratenor, third note *d* of the second liga-
ture in colouration.

2. Omitted note: fo. [40ᵛ], Cantus, two minims *f*, *f*, after what should
                           be the second *Ligatura cum opposita proprietate*.

3. Wrong value: fo. [46ᵛ], penultimate note should be a semiminim,
                           not a minim.

4. Missing *punctus* in
   Cantus: (*a*) fo. 7ᵛ (*CMM* 77/4 m. 20);
                           (*b*) fo. [43ʳ] (*CMM* 77/20 m. 12);
                           (*c*) fo. 26ʳ (*Rehm* 5 m. 14).

5. Missing letter: fo. [43ᵛ], should read 'Encontre', as in MS, not
                           'ncontre'.

6. General technical
   problem: differentiation between the intended qualities of red
                           made by Scribes A and B not reproduced, likewise
                           original blue capitals.

Two scribes made the collection. Scribe A was responsible for twenty-eight songs, notated on a six-line staff and ordered alphabetically: *EscA* 26–8, 30–9, 41–55. He knew a slightly earlier repertoire than his fellow scribe, copying eleven of the fourteen songs in major prolation, including Fontaine's 'J'ayme bien' with Contratenor Trompette, Binchois's 'De plus en plus', and nine anonymous pieces. He seems to have had a special knowledge of a localized Burgundian court practice: notating both the Contratenor Trompette added to Fontaine's *chanson* and the two versions of Binchois's 'Dueil angoisseus'; he provided fourteen anonymous pieces, twelve of which are *unica*; his apparent exposure to a north-north-eastern repertoire resulted in the inclusion of two Middle Dutch songs. He seems to have been quite familiar with French spelling, grammar, graphic forms, and poetic structure. He established the affinity between the contents of this collection and those concordant manuscripts in Rome, Strasbourg, and Munich: the songs which he copied represent four of the six concordances with *R*, four of the seven with *Str*, and six of the seven with *MüEm*. Eleven songs by Binchois are his work; of the fourteen anonymous pieces we shall attribute to Binchois on stylistic grounds, *EscA* 27, 34, 38, and 54 are in his hand; he copied all five of the songs we shall attribute to a 'school of Binchois'—*EscA* 33, 36, 46, 49, and 52.

Scribe B notated thirty-four songs, using a five-line staff for the first twenty-four songs in the manuscript and a six-line staff for the concluding seven songs; his songs are not in alphabetical order; his interpolation of *EscA* 29 interrupts Scribe A's alphabetical sequence, but a second interpolation, *EscA* 40, continues the order properly. Because of these interpolations, his use of the remaining six-line staves for *EscA* 56–62, and the omission of capital letters for which space had been provided, it may be assumed that Scribe B did his work after Scribe A. This opinion is reinforced by observing the repertoire he copied. All but three of the songs are in perfect *tempus* (*EscA* 1, 14, 18), hence, if we agree with Besseler and Hamm, the major part of such a repertoire would be *c*.1430 or after. Whereas Scribe A seems to have been familiar with a group of songs specific to Binchois's court setting, Scribe B cast his net wider: he notated one song each by Dunstable, Merques, and Vide, all five attributed Dufay works including three with the written ascription 'G. du ✠ Y', and the three *rondeaux* we shall attribute to a 'school of Dufay'. Like Scribe A, Scribe B's contribution was closely related to a particular concordant manuscript tradition; he notated ten of the fourteen songs concordant between this *chansonnier* and O. The composers represented in Scribe B's list are customarily admitted to the Burgundian orbit, although there is no conclusive proof they operated within it. The chances that a meeting between Dunstable and Binchois took place have improved since the former has been found residing in Normandy; Dufay himself may have sojourned in Laon 1424–6, and held livings in Laon, Cambrai, Bruges, and Tournai, but he did not come into full residence at Cambrai until 1440 and in general there is no evidence he was actually a musician at court; the Nicholas de Merques recorded as singer in the Council of Basle between 1433 and 1463 came from Arras; only for Vide is there documentary evidence of Burgundian court service: listed as *valet de chambre* (1423) and secretary (1428), he disappeared from pay records after 1433. It is instructive to note here also that, unlike Scribe A, Scribe B made quite a few textual errors, and seems to have been uncomfortable with the spelling of aurally transmitted words, rendering certain sounds in the manner of north-north-eastern France: in Dunstable's 'Puis que m'amour' there is 'sartain' (*EscA* 5) for 'certain' (*Tr* 88), in Dufay's 'Porray je avoir' there is 'entcheulx' (*EscA* 25) for 'ainchois' (O, *PR*). Again, while Scribe A was meticulous in rendering this scriptorial nicety, Scribe B was inconsistent with his treatment of the second person plural pronoun ('vo'/'vo?'). It would appear that the Escorial *chansonnier* is a compilation of two manuscript traditions within the field of Burgundian court song, each scribe making his peculiar contribution. This is so even for the ascribed Binchois pieces, those also in O being exclusive of the others, as may be seen in Table 1; Table 2 enumerates the concordant sources of other named composers in the collection; neither Table lists *contrafacta* or instrumental arrangements.

What binds together the idiosyncratic contributions of the Escorial *chansonnier*'s two scribes is their common acknowledgement of the pre-eminence of Binchois's works and style. As we shall see, what is known of his career reflects the nature of this manuscript's contents: birth at Mons (*c.*1400), early training and practice at St Waudru and Lille, and possibly in service to at least one member of the English government in France, William de la Pole (1420s)—these formative experiences in the first three decades of the century can be traced in the interplay of French and English traits in his early *chansons*. By 1430 his role in the chapel choir of Philip the Good had begun, from which he would retire in 1453; habitually paired with Dufay, at this time he might have crossed the latter's path on one occasion only—in 1434. It was Binchois who was the Burgundian court composer, whose fifty-four attributed songs (and there are at least about twenty other probable attributions) earned him in the memory of Ockeghem the accolade of 'le

TABLE 1. EscA *Binchois Ascriptions in Concordant MSS*

EscA Scribe No.		BU	EscB	Luc	Mü	MüEm	O	PC	PR	R	Str	Tr 87	Tr 92
3	B		x		x					x			
7	B				x					x			
9	B											x	
11	B				x								
15	B											x	
16	B	x					x					x	
17	B						x						
21	B						x						
26	A										x		x
28	A		x		x	x	x			x			
30	A			x									
32	A					x						x	
35	A					x							
37	A		x	x	x	x				x			
39	A						x						
41	A		x							x	x		
47	A						x		x				
51	A										x		
53	A				x					x			
Canon		1	4	1	6	4	6	1	1	6	3	4	1
Total		1	6	1	9	7	28	6	3	12	5	6	1

TABLE 2. *Other* EscA *Ascriptions in Concordant MSS*

Composer	EscA No.	Scribe	BL	O	PR	Str	Tr 88	Tr 90
Dufay	13	B		x				x
	24	B		x				
	25	B		x	x	x		
	57	B		x		x		
	60	B		x				
Dunstable	5	B					x	
Fontaine	50	A	x	x				
de Merques	22	B					x	
Vide	6	B		x				

père de joyeuseté'. The career, output, and prestige of Binchois were the living parallel to the chronology, content, and importance of that most valuable document of Burgundian court song *c.*1430–45, the Escorial MS. V.III.24.

For a more detailed account of the literature and description of the manuscript, together with inventory and notes, the reader is referred to the present author's 'The

Manuscript Escorial V.III.24', *MD* 30 (1976), 97–129. The material of this book is derived from the author's doctoral dissertation, 'The Burgundian Chanson in the Fifteenth Century, with special reference to the anonymous chansons in the MS Escorial V.III.24 and related sources' (2 vols.; Oxford, 1972), volume ii, Parts 2 and 4. In conjunction with the present book, one should consult the author's edition of the anonymous *chansons: Anonymous Pieces in the Chansonnier El Escorial, Biblioteca del Monasterio, Cod. V.III.24, CMM* 77 (Stuttgart: American Institute of Musicology, Hänssler-Verlag, 1980) in which are included variant readings in concordant manuscripts. Errors in previously published editions of ascribed and anonymous songs are listed in Volume II of the dissertation, pp. 6–12, and scribal errors in the manuscript itself are given on pp. 19–21; see also *MD* 30 (1976). A small number of emendations to the poetry and music as they appear in the *CMM* edition are listed in Appendix 4 of this book. Appendix 1 is an inventory of the manuscript; in Appendix 2 are catalogued the anonymous *chansons* and their proposed attributions; the verse structure of the songs with French texts is surveyed in Appendix 3.

It is a pleasure to record thanks to those who advanced this work. My residence in Oxford was supported by a Canada Council Pre-Doctoral Fellowship; study of sources at the Bibliothèque nationale, Paris, was facilitated by a grant from Exeter College, Oxford. Respect and gratitude are owed to my doctoral supervisor 1963–5, the late Dr Frank Ll. Harrison; to Dr Frederick Sternfeld for his sustaining encouragement; to Dr Cecil H. Clough, School of History, University of Liverpool, for instruction, example, and friendship; to Miss Elizabeth Rutson, Fellow of St Anne's College, Oxford, for her unselfish advice in the preparation of the poems; to David Fallows, Senior Lecturer in Music, University of Manchester, for his interest and helpful comments; and to Thomas J. McGary, Nazareth College, NY, for permission to cite transcriptions from his dissertation. During the recent revision of my thesis material preparatory to the publication of this book the work of Mr Dennis Slavin has begun to emerge, and I would like to thank him for sharing with me the text of his paper delivered at the Fiftieth Annual Meeting of the American Musicological Society, Philadelphia, 1984, 'Binchois and Escorial A'; Slavin's codicological studies will provide firm evidence for ascription from a field of investigation other than the analytical, and represents a very promising next stage of ascriptive research. My sincere appreciation is extended to Bruce Phillips and David Blackwell for their patient guidance of this project through the press. A twenty-five-year association with Escorial MS V.III.24 has been shared with my wife Valda, who as typist has been 'dame sans per'.

W. H. K.

Halifax,
Nova Scotia 1989

Contents

✠

Abbreviations

Concordant MS Sources

BL	Bologna, Civico Museo Bibliografico Musicale, Codex Q 15 (*olim* Lic. Mus. 37)
BLib	London, British Library, Add. 34360
BU	Bologna, Biblioteca Universitaria, Codex 2216
EscB	El Escorial, Biblioteca del Monasterio, MS IV.a. 24
Harl	London, British Library, Harley 1512
Jard	*Le Jardin de Plaisance et Fleur de Rhétorique.* Facsimile edition of 1501 print, Société des anciens textes français (Paris, 1910), vol. ii
Luc	Lucca, Archivo di Stato, Mancini Codex 29
Mü	Munich, Bayerische Staatsbibliothek, Mus. MS 3192
MüBux	Munich, Bayerische Staatsbibliothek, Mus. MS 3725 (The Buxheim Organ Book)
MüEm	Munich, Bayerische Staatsbibliothek, Mus. MS Clm 14274 (St Emmeram)
O	Oxford, Bodleian Library, Canonici misc. 213
PC	Paris, Bibliothèque nationale, nouv. acq. fr., 4379
PR	Paris, Bibliothèque nationale, nouv. acq. fr., 6771 (Codex Reina)
R	Rome, Città del Vaticano, Biblioteca Apost. Vaticana, Cod. Urb. lat. 1411
Rit	London, British Library, Add. 5665 (Ritson's MS)
Roh	*Die Liederhandschrift des Cardinals de Rohan,* ed. Martin Löpelmann, Gesellschaft für romanische Literatur, 4 (Göttingen, 1923); from the MS Berlin, Staatliche Museen (Kupferstichkabinett), 78 B 17 (Hamilton 674)
Str	Strasburg, Bibliothèque de la ville, MS 222.C.22
Tit	London, British Library, Cotton Titus A XXVI
Tr	Trento, Castello del Buon Consiglio, MSS. 87, 88, 90, 92
TrC	Cambridge, Trinity College, MS R.3.20

Secondary Sources

Acta Mus	*Acta Musicologica*
AfMw	*Archiv für Musikwissenschaft*
CMM	*Corpus Mensurabilis Musicae*
CSM	*Corpus Scriptorum de Musica*
EETS	Early English Text Society
JAMS	*Journal of the American Musicological Society*
MB	*Musica Britannica*
MD	*Musica Disiplina*
MGG	*Die Musik in Geschichte und Gegenwart*
ML	*Music and Letters*
MQ	*The Musical Quarterly*

PMLA	*Publications of the Modern Language Association*
PRMA	*Proceedings of the Royal Musical Association*
RBM	*Revue belge de Musicologie*
Rehm	Rehm, *Die Chansons von Gilles Binchois*
TLS	*The Times Literary Supplement*
ZfMw	*Zeitschrift für Musikwissenschaft*

Li diex d'Amors lors m'encharja,
tot issi com vos oroiz ja,
mot a mot ses comandemenz.
Bien les devise cist romanz;
qui amer veut, or i entende,
que li romanz des or amende.
Des or le fet bon escouter,
s'il est qui le sache conter,
car la fin dou songe est mout bele
et la matire en est novele.
Qui dou songe la fin ora,
je vos di bien que il porra
des jeus d'Amors assez aprendre,
puis que il veille tant atendre
que je die et que j'encomance
dou songe la senefiance.

Guillaume de Lorris,
Le Roman de la Rose,
ll. 2055–70

PART ONE

The Anonymous Chansons: *Analysis and Ascription*

Introduction

THE music of Escorial MS V.III.24 is divided between a significant number of anonymous *unica*, no doubt of locally specific familiarity, and a collection of favourite songs by the song-makers who had established some larger reputation. The composers represented, the strong family ties among the principal concordant manuscripts, the use of certain north-north-eastern textual peculiarities, and the presence of Middle Dutch songs reinforce Besseler's opinion that it is a Burgundian document written about the fourth decade of the century.[1]

The stylistic elements of court *chansons* during the reign of Philip the Good are well known. The relationship between the structure of a poem and its musical setting, the interplay of linear, vertical, and rhythmic procedures, and the resulting textures, have been codified successfully into models and formulae whose norms have become connotative of a 'Burgundian' quality, even if the source and exact nature of certain techniques such as 'fauxbourdon' and the English 'guise' are not yet closed questions.[2]

Twentieth-century scholarship has confirmed the estimation of fifteenth-century musicians themselves, that Binchois and Dufay were the masters of Burgundian secular song. The initial antiquarian inquiries of Haberl, Closson, *et al.* had their fruition in complete editions of these composers edited by Rehm and Besseler. Information compiled since the 1930s, of which the publications by Marix were the foundation, is being enriched by the continuing archival research accomplished by our own generation of musicologists such as Fallows and Wright; newly corrected editions are in progress. The predecessors, teachers, and lesser contemporaries of Binchois and Dufay have become accessible through the volumes of Reaney's *Early Fifteenth Century Music*. Composers whom their modern editors confess were very minor today have their place in libraries.[3] Unattributed works are achieving printed status.[4]

[1] Besseler, art. 'Escorial Liederbücher', *MGG* iii (1954), cols. 1520–3.

[2] See Thibault, art. 'Chanson II. Chanson von ca. 1420 bis ca. 1520', *MGG* ii (1952), cols. 1046–54, and its extensive bibliography, as well as the bibliographies of appropriate articles ('Binchois', 'Burgundy', 'Dufay', etc.) in *MGG* and *New Grove*; see also Fallows's study of Dufay for *The Master Musicians Series*. The growing list of recorded Burgundian repertoire now includes an edition of the complete secular music of Dufay performed by The Medieval Ensemble of London.

[3] Such as Gülke (ed.), *Johannes Pullois: Opera Omnia* (CMM 41).

[4] Kottick (ed.), *The Unica in the Chansonnier Cordiforme* (CMM 42); Reaney (ed.). *Anonymous Chansons from the MS Oxford, Bodleian Library, Canonici Misc. 213* (CMM 11. iv); Wilkins (ed.), *A 15th-Century Repertory from the Codex Reina* (CMM 37). See also Burstyn, 'Power's *Anima Mea* and Binchois's *De plus en plus*: A Study in Musical Relationships', *MD* 30 (1976), 55–72, and two articles by David Fallows, 'English Song Repertories of the Mid-Fifteenth Century'. *PRMA* 103 (1976–7). esp. 71–6, and 'Words and Music in Two English Songs of the Mid-15th Century: Charles d'Orléans and John Lydgate', *Early Music* 5 (1977), 38–43.

Unfortunately the master composers have been gratuitously assigned unascribed songs by editors, without reference to systematic comparison of styles with which to validate the proposed ascription.[5] Attribution is a very important task. The larger the available number of anonymous pieces, the more rigorous should be our criteria for distinguishing their attributive characteristics.

The chief purpose of this analytical study was to establish stylistic criteria by which the unascribed works might be attributed more knowledgeably. Examination of their cadences and mensuration reconfirms the manuscript's date of compilation as *c.*1430–45. The postulation of an Anglo-Burgundian style is supported by various rhythmic and triadic patterns in the *rondeau* melodies. The twenty-five songs may be separated into four Texture Groups, that give rise to certain implications for making decisions in performance practice.

Six procedures peculiar to Binchois may be isolated:

1. Contratenor final iambic rhythm ♩ ♩ on a repeated pitch;
2. rhythmic pattern ♫♩ involving lower auxiliary note;
3. Cantus structural rhythmic order ♩ ♩. ♪ ;
4. systematic imitation;
5. 'English' triadic figure, and melodic rhyme;
6. Cantus late-dropping third.

Nine anonymous songs possess two or more of these traits, and an additional five songs contain active employment of one of them. Thus, in a manuscript already recognized as a reliable source for his music, fourteen additional *chansons* may be proposed for the *opera attribuenda* of Binchois.[6]

[5] For example, 'Depuis le congié que je pris' (*EscA* 10) and 'Je cuidoye estre conforté' (*EscA* 49) are wishfully ascribed to Binchois by Rehm without stylistic evidence (*Nachwort* to facsimile edition of *EscA*, n. 18). Reaney has made rather tenuous attributions for the anonymous pieces of MS O; his ascription to Binchois of 'Soyés loyal à vo povoir', *EscA* 56 (*CMM* 11. iv, p. xvi), is not completely convincing in the light of the examination of this piece in a succeeding chapter of this book. For more on these attributions see Fallows's article on Binchois in *New Grove*, ii. 709–22.

[6] In his article on Binchois for *New Grove*, ii. 715 and 721, Fallows has kindly cited certain elements of this present study as convincing and also has listed the titles of the attributed pieces presented in my dissertation. The potential for attribution was not dealt with in either of the other two dissertations on the Escorial Chansonnier; Shipley (MA, West Virginia) offers a transcription and commentary; McGary (Ph.D., Cincinnati), in addition to a transcription, makes 'an historical-analytical evaluation', his treatment of the musical materials employing a statistical apparatus.

1

The Rondeaux *For Three Voices: Cadences*

CADENCES have been a dependable source of guidance to musicologists seeking to delineate the progress of vertical organization during the transition from linear to bass-oriented patterns.[1] The final cadences of the twenty-five *rondeaux* under consideration in this chapter reflect the situation of the Escorial MS V.III.24 collection as a whole within the chronology of fifteenth-century sound-structure.

The harmonic sonority of the Escorial collection is relatively traditional, with some conservative practices. Within the sixty-two pieces there are only three final passages that suggest an advance along the new path toward bass-governed disposition of cadential progressions. 'Or ne sçay je que devenir' (*EscA* 20, *CMM* 77/10) is the only anonymous song in the final cadence of which is foreshadowed the perfect-fifth descent in the lowest sounding voice from which would be developed the V–I authentic cadence formula of later practice. In such a progression the Cantus and Tenor reverse their traditional roles in discant-style final cadences, the Tenor ascending to the final note, meeting the Cantus (or discant voice) which descends to the unison, the Contratenor dropping from a third below the Tenor to the octave below (Ex. 1).[2] It is curious that this final cadence, like those of Binchois's 'Adieu, jusques je vous revoye' (*EscA* 30, *Rehm* 2) and Dufay's 'Estrinez moy') (*EscA* 60, *CMM* 1. vi/58), Example 2a and b respectively, involves a delayed fall onto the final sound by at least one voice. Possibly the arrangement of the voices was to reinforce the broadening effect created by the 'extra' beat. The final cadence of 'Or ne sçay que devenir' is the sole exception to the two-voice frame of $\frac{7}{2}$–$\frac{8}{1}$ adhered to in plain or ornamented formulae over several centuries of

---

[1] See Reese, *Music in the Renaissance*, 44–8; Besseler, *Bourdon und Fauxbourdon*, ch. 2 (with chart p. 37); Wienpahl 'The Evolutionary Significance of the 15th century Cadential Formulae', *Journal of Music Theory*, 4 (1960), 131–52; Hamm, 'The Motets of Lionel Power', in Powers (ed.), *Studies in Music History: Essays for Oliver Strunk*, 130–3; McGary, 'Partial Signature Implications in the Escorial Manuscript V.III.24', *Music Review* 40 (1979), 77–89; Mahrt, 'Guillaume Dufay's Chansons in the Phrygian Mode', *Studies in Music from the University of Western Ontario*, 5 (1980), 81–98.

[2] 'Si autem tenor discantus formulam assumpserit capiat discantus speciem tenoris commeando cum tenor: aut ex tertia in unisonum stante penultima contratenoris in tertia sub tenore'. (Leipzig Anonymous, *Introductorium musicae* (*c.*1500), cited in Riemann, *History of Music Theory* (trans. Haggh, and hereafter denoted Riemann–Haggh), 272–3 and n. 71). Rules for the perfect-fifth descent of the Contratenor *Bassus* had been given by Gulielmus Monachus (*c.*1480), but there the Cantus was in its discant cadence position a sixth above the Tenor on the penultimate *concentus*, the Contratenor a fourth above; see Gulielmus Monachus, *De preceptis artis musicae*, ed. Seay (CSM xi), 4; also cited in Bush, 'The Recognition of Chordal Formation by Early Music Theorists', *MQ* 32 (1946), 230–1).

discanting. The Contratenor preserves the $\frac{8}{5}$ *concentus* of perfect consonances which had been the required starting- and finishing-points of a discant: 'Qui veult faire bon deschant, il doibt commenchier et finir par acort parfait, c'est à scavoir par unisson, quinte ou double'.[3] Apart from that of 'Or ne sçay', the final cadences of the anonymous three-voice *rondeaux* are various versions of the two principal types employed in the first half of the century: the 'doubled leading-tone' cadence and the 'octave-leap' cadence.

Ex. 1

Ex. 2

(a)

(b)

---

[3] From *Tractatus de discantu*, Anonymous XIII of Coussemaker, *Scriptorum de musica medii aevi*, iii. 497; cited in Riemann–Haggh, 102, *inter alia*.

The cadential 'octave leap' of the Contratenor from a fourth below the Tenor to a fifth above was an early employment of the under-fifth as a means of cadence organization. Its systematic use in combination with the discanting cadence-frame was the accepted evasion of consecutive fifths, even if not avoiding their audible presence. There is such a passage in 'Qui ne veroist' by the early fifteenth-century Cambrai musician Loqueville (Ex. 3).[4] From a survey of polyphony 1400–60 it has been shown that, of the material examined, the 'octave-leap' type accounted for 22.4 per cent of final cadences and was primarily Burgundian.[5] With specific reference to individual repertoires, it can be found that Binchois employed the 'octave-leap' final cadence twenty-seven times out of fifty-five songs (49.09 per cent), Dufay twelve times out of seventy-four (16.22 per cent).[6]

Ex. 3

Loqueville, 'Qui ne veroist', mm. 16 - 19

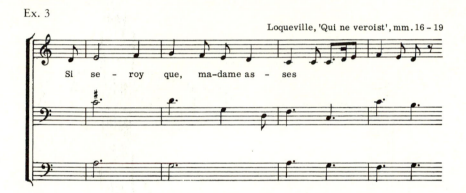

Si se - roy   que,   ma–dame as - ses

Group One (*a*) (Ex. 4) comprises the 'octave-leap' cadence with three ornamentations of the 'under-third' formula. Notice the strong dissonance factor of the cadence in 'Belle, esse dont vostre plaisir' (*EscA* 33, *CMM* 77/15). Group One (*b*) has the same type with the $\frac{7-8}{2-1}$ frame. Again notice the dissonance factors, in 'Helas! ma dame, qu'ay je fait' (*EscA* 43, *CMM* 77/21). Group One (*c*) is a very important subdivision of this cadence type. The 'under-third' Cantus is used, in three different ornamental formulae, but what separates these cadences from those of Group One (*a*) is the imperfection of the final breve in the Contratenor to produce an iambic repetition on the fifth. This rhythmic tag, always in *tempus perfectum*, is not found in any of the seventy-four French secular songs by Dufay authenticated by Besseler. However, in the fifty-five collected *chansons* of Binchois it appears at the conclusion of nine songs: *Rehm* 1, 2, 7, 9, 10, 19, 36, 50, 54. Only the first two are not preceded by the Contratenor's octave leap. Four of the nine songs are part of the Escorial collection: 'Je ne fai tousjours que penser' (*EscA* 3, *Rehm* 17), 'Adieu, adieu, mon joieulx souvenir' (*EscA* 28, *Rehm* 1), 'Adieu, jusques

[4] *CMM* 11. iii, 2. See Franchinus Gafurius, *Practica musicae* (1496), cited in Riemann—Haggh, 289–90.

[5] Wienpahl, 'Evolutionary Significance', 132 ff.

[6] Binchois: *Rehm* 19, 25, 27, 50 (*EscA* 3, 16, 53, 37), 3, 4, 6, 7, 8, 9, 10, 13, 16, 18, 23, 29, 30, 35, 36, 37, 41, 43, 45, 49, 51, 52, 54; Dufay: *CMM* I. vi/69 (*EscA* 57), 46, 64, 65, 66, 70, 71, 74, 79, 80, 81, 83.

Ex. 4

Cadence Group One (a)

Cadence Group One (b)

Cadence Group One (c)

je vous revoye' (*EscA* 30, *Rehm* 2), and 'Dueil angoisseus' (*EscA* 37, *Rehm* 50). All these cadences employ some ornamented version of the 'under-third' Cantus. Since there is no other notated secular repertoire ending with this iambic tag, the songs in Group One (*c*) may be put forward as three works attributable to Binchois.[7]

One cadence should be observed, as being a subspecies of Group One. The close of 'Je n'atens plus de resconfort' (*EscA* 29, *CMM* 77/13) effects a slowing down of the work by the addition of an extra measure, highlighting the leading-tone in the Cantus (Ex. 5*a*). The Contratenor leaps up a (major) seventh, reminiscent of Tapissier and his contemporaries (Ex. 5*b*).[8]

Ex. 5

(a)   *EscA* 29

(b)   Fabri, 'Gloria'

Group Two (Ex. 6) comprises two presentations of the 'doubled leading-tone' final cadence, Group Two (*b*) consisting of seven conclusions where the 'under-third' of the Cantus ornament is duplicated by the Contratenor a fourth below. Notice that of the thirteen cadences in Group Two there are eight different treatments of the 'under-third' cadence; only 'Tous desplaisirs' (*EscA* 8, *CMM* 77/ 4) and 'Bien viengnant' (*EscA* 34, *CMM* 77/16) have similar conclusions. In Group Two (*a*) the 'under-third' is touched upon as an ornament before the leading-tone

---

[7] One earlier example is available, from 'J'aim. Qui?' by Paullet (*CMM* 11, ii, 102).

[8] Final cadence of a 'Gloria' by Tomas Fabri Scolaris Tapissier (*CMM* 11. i, 82); for similar cadences by Johannes Tapissier himself see ibid. 67, 69, 71, and 72.

Ex. 6

Cadence Group Two (a)

Cadence Group Two (b)

in 'Lune tresbelle' (*EscA* 23, *CMM* 77/11), the lower auxiliary is doubled by the Contratenor in 'Mon coeur avoeque vous s'en va' (*EscA* 54, *CMM* 77/28), and where the plain 'doubled leading-tone' procedure is used in 'Jamais ne quiers avoir liesse' (*EscA* 45, *CMM* 77/23) the Tenor performs its own ornamental 'escaped' dissonance in the new English-influenced consonant style.[9]

The conclusion measures of 'Loez soit Dieu' (*EscA* 52, *CMM* 77/27) are rigid *fauxbourdon*. The Cantus is a free-composed cantus firmus; a fourth below in *fauxbourdon* the Contratenor strictly parallels the decorative coloration of the *supranus* cadential formula.[10]

Although the cadential figures in the Cantus have a decorative quality, they are propulsive elements that beautify the skeletal linear closes of discant tradition. Bence Szabolcsi has called them 'vagrant formulae', to swing the lyric arc along— patterns of dynamic ornamentation.[11] The suave line-by-line periodization upon which the *chanson*-style of this era depended for its characteristic curve of melody and clarity of phrase was achieved by confluence of lines in a consciously-wrought rhythmic expression. The more cultivated the concentration of that rhythmic expression, the more subtle the interplay of syncopation and dissonance, which in continued practice would increase the concern for agreement between the horizontal and vertical aspects in later fifteenth-century composition and theory. Putnam Aldrich wrote that, although cadences 'are primarily rhythmic phenomena', in a well-wrought work 'the rhythmic articulations are reinforced and clarified by appropriate harmonic movement'.[12] By engaging in an incipient balance in the inter-activity of line and *concentus* the early fifteenth-century composers and the Burgundians made their cadences the focus of an evolving artistic interest. Without this interest in colouring the frame-closes, the makers of *chansons* had recourse to nothing but the skeletal clichés of functional periodicity, a periodicity of which Curt Sachs had implied the weakness: 'an almost obtrusive neatness . . . so that the whole appears to be trimly parcelled out'.[13]

The conclusion of 'Soyés loyal à vo povoir' (*EscA* 56, *CMM* 77/30) has been omitted until this point in the discussion, as it well illustrates the more progressive collaboration of rhythmic and vertical orders by which the more colourful *chanson*

---

[9] What few dissonances are in Dunstable *et al.* are primarily melodic ornaments in 'changing' and 'escape' notes, his innovation being 'purging of dissonances' from harmony: the 'frisque concordance' celebrated by Martin le Franc. (See Bukofzer, 'English Church Music of the Fifteenth Century', in Hughes and Abraham (eds.), *Ars Nova and the Renaissance, 1300–1450*, *The New Oxford History of Music*, iii. 185.)

[10] 'Contra vero dicitur sicut supranus, accipiendo quartam subtus supranum quae venit esse quinta et tertia supra tenorem. Iste enim modus communiter faulxbordon appellatur. . . .' (Gulielmus Monachus, *De preceptis artis musicae*, 38–9; example edited in Manfred Bukofzer, *Geschichte des englischen Diskants und des Fauxbourdons*, Ex. 14); '. . . quum tenor et cantus procedunt per unam aut plures sextas: tunc vox media sc. contratenor quartam semper sub cantu tenebit: tertiam semper ad tenorem observans in acutam. Huius modi autem contrapunctum cantores 'ad Faulxbourdon' appellant . . .' (Franchinus Gafurius, *Practica Musicae* (1496), III. v, as cited in Bukofzer, *Geschichte des englischen Diskants*, 83).

[11] Szabolcsi, *A History of Melody*, 251–2.

[12] Aldrich, 'An Approach to the Analysis of Renaissance Music', *Music Review*, 3 (1969), 7.

[13] Sachs, *The Commonwealth of Art*, 105.

cadence could be distinguished (Ex. 7). The dissonance on the second beat of the measure resolves to the standard penultimate *concentus* $\frac{\sharp 7}{\frac{\sharp 4}{2}}$ in the Dorian 'doubled leading-tone' cadence. The Contratenor, however, continues by paralleling the Cantus a third below: in tonal terms, producing a progression V (second inversion)– II (raised third)–I. This cadence was a minority type, according to Wienpahl, who gives as example the conclusion of Vide's 'Il m'est si grief' (Ex. 8);[14] the version he cites is that of MS O, fo. 77^r, not that of *EscA* 6.

Ex. 7

Ex. 8

Vide, 'Il m'est si grief'

The only cadence of this type in the Escorial collection is that of 'Soyés loyal', our Example 7. Occurrences of this progression, from late fourteenth-century French 'mannered' notation to the Burgundy of Binchois and Dufay, are catalogued in the next four examples. Notice how the disguisings of the pattern by rhythm (Ex. 10*c*) and by dissonance (Exx. 9*c*, 10*b*) are cleared by the time of Binchois and Dufay. Only in this latter group is the dissonance of the seventh present, a figure already

14 Wienpahl, 'Evolutionary Significance', 135.

seen in the Bodleian Library version of the Vide *chanson*; compare Example 8 with Examples 11*b*, and 12*a*, *b*.[15] Traditions of local practice might be implied, for these four songs are collected in fascs. 3 and 4 of MS. O (fos. 77ᵛ, 44ᵛ, 49ᵛ, and 30ᵛ, respectively).

Ex. 9

anon, late fourteenth-century French
(*a*) *Virelai*, 'Or sus' (*CMM* 53. i/212)
(*b*) *Virelai*, 'Contre le temps' (*CMM* 36, 26)
(*c*) *Ballade*, 'A gré d'amours' (*CMM* 36, 11)

Ex. 10

early fifteenth century.
(*a*) Cesaris, 'Mon seul voloir' (*CMM* 11. i/26)
(*b*) Charité, 'Jusques a tant' (*CMM* 11. ii/21)
(*c*) Haucourt, 'Se doit il pleust' (*CMM* 11. ii/36)
(*d*) anon., 'Quant si loing' (*CMM* 37/30)

---

[15] See also the final cadences of two Binchois *opera attribuenda*: 'Comme femme desconfortée' (*Rehm* 56) and 'Va tost mon amoureux desir' (*Rehm* 59).

Ex. 11

Dufay.
(*a*) 'Bien doy' (m. 13) (*CMM* 1. vi/20)
(*b*) 'Bon jour' (*CMM* 1. vi/59)
(*c*) 'Je triomphe' (*CMM* 1. vi/72)

Ex. 12

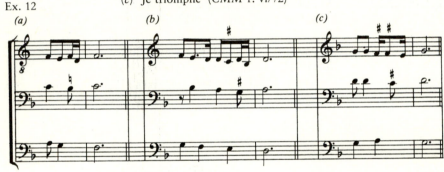

Binchois.
(*a*) 'Joyeus penser' (*Rehm* 21)
(*b*) 'Nous vous verens' (*Rehm* 33)
(*c*) 'Mon coeur chante' (m. 15) (*Rehm* 29)

None of the thirteen cadences in the four examples above has the Cantus cadential pattern of 'Soyés loyal'. Charles Hamm distinguished it an 'English figure' because it was a characteristic of English music after 1410.[16] Its appearances stretch from the Old Hall manuscript into the generation of Bedingham.[17] 'Risky

---

[16] Hamm, 'The Motets of Lionel Power', 131.
[17] Hamm, 'A Group of Anonymous English Pieces in Trent 87', *ML* 41 (1960), 212. In this study the pattern

in the Cantus is accepted as the 'English' figure even if not conveyed in triplet form

Thus even though it is true that in its triplet form 'Dunstaple uses it rather rarely at cadences, and never at the end of a piece' (Bent, *Dunstaple*, 27), the pitch series delivered by one of the above two rhythmic shapes is a trademark of his cadences, found eleven times in the first twenty-four pages of Bukofzer's edition. On 'Puisque m'amour' see Bent, *Dunstaple*, 86–7.

though it may seem to suggest the nationality of an anonymous piece on the basis of a short, apparently insignificant turn of the melody, it must be pointed out that it is almost impossible to find this English figure in compositions known to be by non-English composers'.[18] This is incorrect; in another publication Hamm pointed out two mid-cadences in *chansons* by Dufay: 'Or pleust à Dieu' and 'Porray je avoir vostre merchi'.[19] These are *EscA* 24 and 25. They are the only French secular songs by Dufay to employ the figure.

The 'English figure' appears in the Escorial pieces five more times. Final cadences in 'Liesse m'a mandé salut' (*EscA* 16) and 'Dueil angoisseus' (*EscA* 37) show that Binchois knew this little melodic idiom; 'Se je souspire' (*Rehm* 39) is his only other song to have it. Nicholas de Merques uses it in 'Las! comment porraye avoir joye' (*EscA* 22). And, as might be expected, it is a feature of *EscA* 5, 'Puis que m'amour', by Dunstable. The penultimate cadence of 'Jugiés se je doy joye avoir' (*EscA* 62, *CMM* 77/34), at the conclusion of the texted material, joins it to 'Soyés loyal', *EscA* 56: a pair of anonymous works under English influence.

Outside the Escorial manuscript's repertoire the 'English figure' appears once: in a song by Franchois Lebertoul, who is known to have been attached to the choir of Cambrai Cathedral, 1409–10.[20]

Example 13 catalogues these 'English figure' cadences.

Eight appearances in one relatively small collection is quite suggestive. With the exception of the popular 'Dueil angoisseus' they were notated by the second of the manuscript's two copyists, Scribe B.[21] They are unique in the repertoires of the major composers—the only two examples by Dufay, two out of the three by Binchois. The particular scribe's awareness of English music is suggested not only by the inclusion of Dunstable's song; the Escorial collection indicates his knowledge of six other works (plus 'Dueil angoisseus', *EscA* 37, Scribe A) into which is adopted an ingredient of English melodic flavour. Here is manuscript evidence of a direct Anglo-Burgundian stylistic encounter. Literary evidence for a very decided English manner of religious musical practice is afforded by the 'Bourgeois de Paris', who recorded that at the burial of the Duchess of Bedford (1432) 'the English sang most movingly by themselves in the fashion of their own country ('seullement les Angloys en la guise du pais moult piteusement')'.[22] The newness of what Martin le Franc in his *Le Champion des Dames* praised as the 'nouvelle pratique'—'la contenance Angloise'—and the prior use in insular music of the cadential pattern under discussion show that Dufay and Binchois learned

---

[18] Hamm, 'A Group of Anonymous English Pieces in Trent 87', *ML* 41 (1960), 212. For a quarrel over the nationality of this music see the Trowell–Hamm correspondence in *ML* 42 (1961), 96–7, 295–6; Hamm later acknowledged Trowell's corrections in his article 'A Catalogue of Anonymous English Music in Fifteenth-Century Continental Manuscripts', *MD* 22 (1968), 53 n. 72.

[19] Hamm, *A Chronology*, 118.

[20] Wright, 'Lebertoul', *New Grove*, x. 578.

[21] For more details on the individual work of the two copyists see Kemp, 'The Manuscript Escorial V.III.24', *MD* 30 (1976), 100–1, 104–9.

[22] Shirley, trans., *A Parisian Journal: 1405–1449*, 282.

Ex. 13

(*a*) Lebertoul, 'Depuis un peu (*CMM* 11. ii/43)
(*b*) Dunstable, 'Puis que m'amour' (*EscA* 5, *MB* viii 55)
(*c*) Mercques, 'Las! comment porraye' (*EscA* 22)
(*d*) Dufay, 'Or pleust' (*EscA* 24, *CMM* 1. vi/60)
(*e*) Dufay, 'Porray je avoir' (*EscA* 25, *CMM* 1. vi/33)
(*f*) Binchois, 'Liesse' (*EscA* 16, *Rehm* 25)
(*g*) Binchois, 'Dueil angoisseus' (*EscA* 37, *Rehm* 50)
(*h*) Binchois, 'Se je souspire' (*Rehm* 39)
(*i*) anon., 'Jugiés' (*EscA* 62, *CMM* 77/34)

from the English style in an immediate cross-channel influence.[23] Thanks to the archival research of Andrew Wathey, John Dunstable has been found in residence in Normandy, as a 'serviteur et familier domestique' of Humphrey Duke of Gloucester.[24] No means of contact between Dunstable and the two Burgundian master musicians is assured as yet. The anonymous 'Soyés loyal' (*EscA* 56) and 'Jugiés se je doy joye avoir' (*EscA* 62) were products of Burgundian alignment with English practice, but it is obvious that solely on the basis of the cadential 'English figure' the songs could be ascribed equally to Dufay or Binchois, both composers having used the pattern.

To review, the final cadences of the anonymous *rondeaux* are a small but symptomatic representation of the traditions that contributed to the centralizing stylistic activity of Burgundian music during the first half of the fifteenth century. They would confirm the compilation of the repertoire as being *c.*1435–45. Various combinations of consonance and melody activate the 'double leading-tone' cadence, ranging from the strict parallelism of *fauxbourdon* to the distinctively English practice of 'escaped' dissonance in the Tenor. One cadence, the progression $\frac{6\ 8}{\sharp 4{-}5}$ in Continental use since the fourteenth century, had its Cantus graced by the $2\ 1$ so-called 'English figure'. The 'octave-leap' cadence sought interest in melodic variety, spiced by the occasional dissonance. Two behavioural peculiarities exhibited by the Contratenor look back to Burgundian court composers of earlier decades in the century—the iambic repetition on the final breve, and the upward leap of the seventh; pieces with these direct links with Burgundian practice may be ascribed to Binchois. Looking in the other direction, three songs (4.84 per cent of the collection) closed with the progression V–I, an adumbration of more advanced sound-structures.

Of greater importance, the final cadences carry fingerprints of personal or national styles which allow relationships to be established with attributed works in this and other manuscripts.

---

[23] On *Le Champion des Dames* and its musical testimony see Kenney, *Walter Frye and the Contenance Angloise*, ch. 1; Hamm, *A Chronology*, 95–100. The event that could have brought together Dufay and Binchois, and possibly permitted the famous illumination of this pair to be executed, was the wedding of Louis de Savoie and Anne de Lusignan of Cyprus, Feb. 1434 (Wright, 'Dufay at Cambrai: Discoveries and Revisions', *JAMS* 28 (1975), 180; discussion amplified by Fallows, *Dufay*, 36–42. See Hamm, *A Chronology*, 100, for corroborative English notational practices taken over by Dufay and Binchois).

[24] Wathey, 'Dunstable in France', *ML* 67 (1986), 1–36.

2

The Rondeaux *for Three Voices: Melody*

WHEN seeking traits within the general style of the Burgundian *chansons* as represented in the Escorial MS V.III.24, it is rare to find one so definitive as to preclude any doubt as to its composer or national source. One such distinctive fingerprint of Binchois has been discovered: the iambic repeated fifth in the Contratenor at the conclusion of a song. There is a second such fingerprint in this repertoire, also rhythmic and entirely unique to the style of Binchois.

The final cadences of 'Mon coeur avoeque vous s'en va' (*EscA* 54, CMM 77/28) and 'Va t'en, mon désir gracieux' (*EscA* 61, CMM 77/33) (Ex. 14*a* and *b*) have a division of the first half of the Semibreve into two Semiminims and a Minim. When Dufay employs the rhythm in his secular music it is almost always in a scale design, the second semiminim being a passing note.[1] The same is true for the few occurrences of the rhythm in Reaney's early fifteenth-century collection.[2] But with Binchois the rhythm is an auxiliary note pattern, used the same way as at the conclusion of 'Mon coeur' and 'Va t'en'. In Example 15 are catalogued the three cadences in the Binchois canon using this figure, from 'Adieu, jusques je vous revoye' (*Rehm* 2), 'C'est assez' (*Rehm* 11), and 'Je ne pouroye' (*Rehm* 20). 'Je ne pouroye' also has the rhythmic figure at m. 13; it appears in 'Ay, doulourex' (*Rehm* 9, m. 21), 'Mon seul et souverain desir' (*Rehm* 31, m. 3), 'Rendre me vieng' (*Rehm*

Ex. 14

---

[1] CMM I. vi/14, 'Je me complains', m. 3; 22 'De ma haulte', m. 39 (Contratenor); 72 'Je triomphe', m. 2 (Contratenor), m. 4, m. 22 (Contratenor); a few other rhythm patterns are employed, but only twice as an auxiliary: 24 'Malheureulx cueur', m. 17 (Contratenor), and the final cadence of 'Je triomphe'.

[2] Adam, 'Tout a coup', R. Gallo and Francus de Insula, 'Je ne vis pas', Johannes Le Grant, 'Qui tollis' and 'Et in spiritum', Passet de Tornaco, 'Si me fault', and Gilet Velut, 'Un petit oyselet' (CMM 11. ii, 1, 25, 79, 87, 101–2, 119–21).

Ex. 15

(a)   Binchois, 'Adieu, jusques', mm. 34 – 5

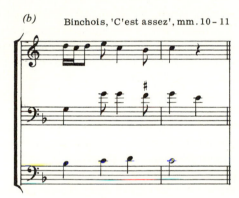

(b)   Binchois, 'C'est assez', mm. 10 – 11

(c)   Binchois, 'Je ne pouroye', mm. 34 – 5

38, m. 5, Contratenor), and 'Se je souspire' (*Rehm* 39, m. 41). Three of these seven pieces by Binchois are in the Escorial collection: 'Mon seul et souverain desir' (*EscA* 21, *Rehm* 31), 'Adieu, jusques je vous revoye' (*EscA* 30, *Rehm* 2), and 'C'est assez pour morir de dueil' (*EscA* 35, *Rehm* 11).

There are eight anonymous three-voice *rondeaux* in Escorial MS V.III.24 that have this rhythmic turn, all in the auxiliary note pattern. In addition to the final cadences of 'Mon coeur' and 'Va t'en', it appears at mid-cadences in the following:

EscA 10 (*CMM* 77/5)	m. 7	
EscA 14 (*CMM* 77/7)	11	
EscA 23 (*CMM* 77/11)	14	
EscA 34 (*CMM* 77/16)	12 (Contratenor), 15	
EscA 38 (*CMM* 77/18)	14, 15	
EscA 59 (*CMM* 77/32)	1 (Contratenor), 5, 8	

The pattern is definitely a musical, not an individual scribal trait, because 'Bien viengnant' (*EscA* 34) and 'De ceste joieuse advenue' (*EscA* 38) were the copy of Scribe A; the rest, Scribe B's work. We already have assigned two of these eight *rondeaux* to the *opera attribuenda* of Binchois, by virtue of their final iambic Contratenor: 'Le tresorire de bonté' (*EscA* 14) and 'De ceste joieuse advenue' (*EscA* 38); this double conviction prompts us to add the six other pieces to the list: *EscA* 10, 23, 34, 54, 59, and 61.

In the preceding chapter a distinctive 'English figure' was seen to be very active in the Escorial manuscript. There are several other features of Burgundian *chanson* melody which indicate English influence. Triadic motifs, escaped dissonances, and an idiom in which the Cantus rises a fourth over a static Tenor are all common features of English discant technique that impregnate thoroughly the Continental craft and make separate quotations unnecessary.[3]

The descending triadic motif

must be remarked upon here, because although it is common stock in Continental song throughout the century its employment by Binchois and Dufay—like that of Hamm's 'English figure'—is preserved chiefly through the Escorial Chansonnier.[4] Its four chief appearances among the fifty-five authentic songs by Binchois are in this manuscript: 'Vostre alée' (*EscA* 11, *Rehm* 46) and 'De plus en plus' (*EscA* 39, *Rehm* 12) as the opening idea, 'Adieu, adieu' (*EscA* 28, *Rehm* 1) mm. 2–3, and

---

[3] For melodic figures common to English and Continental music see Kenney, *Walter Frye and the Contenance Angloise*, 178–84, supplemented by Hamm, 'A Catalogue of Anonymous English Music in Fifteenth-Century Continental Manuscripts', *MD* 22 (1968), 58–9. Unfortunately, Kenney made no chronological distinction between the earlier carols of the Trinity Roll (contemporary with Binchois) and those of later collections; thus examples from British Library Egerton MS 3307 ('Illuxit leticia', 'St. Thomas honor we', 'Princeps serenissime') are most likely to be of a stylistic heritage common with Burgundy, rather than a source of Continental idioms.

[4] Some English examples in Kenney, *Walter Frye*, 180; for triadic patterns in Dunstable's works see

'Jamais tant' (*EscA* 47, *Rehm* 17) mm. 15–16 (source for transcription necessarily from O). Twice Dufay made it a feature of his melody: 'Belle, vueilliés vostre mercy donner' (*CMM* I. vi/47) and 'Or pleust à Dieu (*CMM* I. vi/60). The latter is *EscA* 24, already noted as being under English influence because it has the 'English figure' in m. 15. The descending triad is very apparent in *EscA* 5, Dunstable's 'Puis que m'amour'; the triad has three plain appearances and is traceable in three other phrases. Both plain and ornamented presentations of the descending triad in Dunstable's 'Puis que m'amour' are concisely stated, succinct motifs divorced from each other by rests (Ex. 16).

Ex. 16

This also applies to those of Binchois—as has been noted, in the same collection. Example 17*a, b, c* (from 'Vostre alée' (*EscA* 11), 'De plus en plus' (*EscA* 39), and 'Jamais tant' (*EscA* 47)) are isolated units without linear extension, as in the Dunstable. Example 17*d*, the opening phrase of 'Adieu, adieu' (*EscA* 28) arches over a triad in the English consonant manner, the figure of mm. 2–3 proceeding to

Ex. 17

(a)

(b)

(c)

Bent, *Dunstaple*, 32–4. Two early fifteenth-century Burgundian examples of a melody in which a descending triad is followed by a linear ascent may be found in Grenon's 'Je suy defait', source O, fo. 32ᵛ (*CMM* 11.vii, 3):

(d)   *EscA* 28, mm. 1 – 6

the cadence a fourth below; the typical English discant rising fourth over a static Tenor constitutes m. 2.[5]

The difference in Cantus techniques between Binchois and Dufay is immediately apparent when comparing Example 17 to Dufay's use of the descending triadic motif, first in 'Or pleust à Dieu' (*EscA* 24, *CMM* I. vi/60), then in 'Belle, vueilliés' (*CMM* I. vi/47). The motif in 'Or pleust à Dieu' is used in a similar modal position to Binchois's 'Adieu, adieu' (*EscA* 28), but is continued to spin a phrase (Ex. 18). 'Belle, vueilliés' combines English triadic play with a spun line of Italianate flavour, especially in the inevitable progress to minims in every phrase (Ex. 19).

Ex. 18

                                                                        EscA 24, mm. 1 – 6

Or ___ pleust à ___ Dieu _ qu'a son ___ plai - sir

Ex. 19

          Dufay, 'Belle, vueilliés vostre mercy donner', mm. 11 – 17

Bel - le,   vueil - lés vo   -   stre _____   mer -

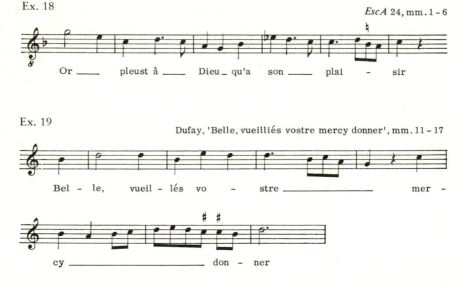

cy _____ don - ner

Remembering the pithy mottoes of Binchois contrasted with the spinning phrases of Dufay, we examine two anonymous *rondeaux* in the collection that have the descending triadic motif (others will be dealt with in future discussion of imitative *chansons* and of *ballades*). The last phrase of 'Depuis le congié que je pris' (*EscA* 10, *CMM* 77/5) has its text set to the motif used in the same modal position as Binchois's 'Adieu, adieu' (*EscA* 28); it is not really spun out, as in Dufay's 'Or pleust à Dieu' (*EscA* 24), because the final melisma in the Cantus is a purposeful melodic rhyme with the close of the third line of text (mm. 23 ff.) (Ex.

⁵ Kenney, *Walter Frye*, 183.

20). The same procedure is evident at the close of 'Bien viegnant' (*EscA* 34, *CMM* 77/16). The final melisma opens with the descending triadic motif (m. 19) and moves towards the cadence. Again, however, this is not Dufay's *Fortspinnung*; it is a rhyme with the mid-close, mm. 10–11, introduced—or padded—by the triadic cliché (Ex. 21).

Ex. 20

EscA 10, mm. 31–5

Que   cest   des   re - bel - lez le _____ pris.

Ex. 21

EscA 34, mm. 19–21

[né -   -   -   -   -   e]

The undeveloped appearance of their motif and the similar employment of it would persuade us to place 'Depuis le congié' (*EscA* 10) and 'Bien viengnant' (*EscA* 34) in a 'school of Binchois', as concerns the adoption of this English melodic idiom. This affords the second stylistic indication that these two songs belong to Binchois, again a satisfying conclusion. Securing them in the Binchois fold is the observation that the rhyme secured in both pieces between the final cadence and a preceding phrase does not occur in the French-texted songs ascribed to Dufay. Melodic rhyme was fashioned by Binchois in one other early song, 'Triste plaisir', dated by Rehm 1420–5; the rhyming last two lines (Ex. *22b*) use an idea set

Ex. 22

(a)

(b)

Ris en plou - rant sou-ve-nir ob - - lieux

M'a - com - pag - nent _ com - bien que sen le soy - e.

up in the opening textless measures (Ex. 22*a*).[6]

The triadic curve of Dufay's opening phrases, and occasionally some of Binchois's (as in 'Adieu, adieu', *EscA* 28, Ex. 17), is a gift of Dunstable and his English contemporaries often remarked upon (Ex. 23).

The shorter melodic spans in the Continental *chansons* whose style is represented by the music attributed to Dunstable and Binchois have their English counterparts in the fifteenth-century carol. Manfred Bukofzer pointed out similarities between these two contemporary bodies of song: lines of 'pristine simplicity' were at once smooth (owing to the consistent use of patterns built around reiterated notes) and disjunct (in progression), the whole borne by a vigorous rhythm.[7] The chronological evolution from major prolation to perfect *tempus* of both the Burgundian *chanson* and the English carol was simultaneous, resulting in an

---

[6] *Rehm* 45, source O, fo. 56ᵛ. Poem by Alain Chartier. This is the song with which the poet Jean Regnier consoled himself when a prisoner, captured on a secret mission for the Duke of Burgundy (1432): *Les fortunes et adversitiez de Jean Regnier*, 154, from Champion, *Histoire poétique du quinzième siècle*, i. 232 ff., as cited in Marix, *Histoire de la musique et des musiciens de la cour de Bourgogne sous le règne de Philippe le Bon, 1420–1467*, 186–7. Regnier's version had a few *varia*, but even so could have been sung to the Binchois tune.

[7] Bukofzer, *Studies in Medieval and Renaissance Music*, 166–9.

Ex. 23

Dunstable, 'Quam pulcra es', mm. 1 – 9

identical set of shifting $\frac{6}{8}/\frac{3}{4}$ patterns.[8] To Bukofzer the parallel stylistic change was 'all the more surprising as there is no direct contact between the forms'.[9]

There is a relationship between the melodic style of the carol and several pieces in the Escorial collection. 'Loez soit Dieu' (*EscA* 52, CMM 77/27) is the third anonymous *rondeau* in the collection to exhibit clearly English triadic influences in its melody (q.v. m. 13). There is a close resemblance to its opening phrase in two carols: the Burden of 'There is no rose' and the Verse of 'Alma redemptoris mater' (Ex. 24).[10] These carols are Nos. 3 and 13 of the Trinity Roll, the manuscript which 'certainly imparts the polyphonic carol in the earliest known stage of development', and was written about the same time as the Escorial MS. V.III.24, *c*.1440.[11]

Ex. 24

(a)

Lo - ez   soit Dieux des ___ biens de ___ ly

(b)

There is   no   Rose of ___ such   vir - tue

(c)

As   I   lay up – on ___ a ___ night

[8] ibid. 164–6.

[9] ibid. 166. The question of such possible contacts is taken up by Fallows, 'English Song Repertories of the Mid-Fifteenth Century', *PRMA* 103 (1976–7), 61–79.

[10] Ed. Stevens, *Mediaeval Carols* (MB iv), Nos. 14 and 4, pp. 10, 3.

[11] Bukofzer, *Studies in Medieval and Renaissance Music*, 166: more on Cambridge, Trinity College, ms O.3.58, in *MB* iv, 125.

In later fifteenth-century carols some of the English idioms which had become essential elements of Continental melodic style occurred not only copiously by themselves but even simultaneously (Ex. 25).[12] Most interesting are the carols contained in *Rit*, where also was notated a duo on the Tenor of Binchois's 'Vostre tres doulx regart plaisant' (*EscA* 7, *Rehm* 43). In several of these carols the semibreves are frequently subdivided, the first half expressed in two semiminims to produce the rhythmic turn on the lower auxiliary note which we have already discovered to be a Binchois fingerprint.[13]

Ex. 25

Smert & Trouluffe, 'O clavis David', mm. 52-5

O   Da - vid

Through correlations such as these, evidence is weighted heavily in favour of a series of direct Anglo-Burgundian musical encounters, both in the formative period of Burgundian style and in the later reciprocal return of Continental craft to England.[14] Composers who knew Burgundian power in Paris and English power in France, and who subsequently served the courts and ecclesiastical institutions of Philip the Good, had no need for any intermediate Italian sojourn in which to temper the new style.[15] The more exclusively Anglo-Burgundian these encounters can be defined, the more they confirm Wathey's limitation of the Continental

---

[12] *MB* iv, No. 91, p. 79.

[13] *MB* iv, Nos. 86, 90, 103; collected last quarter of the century. For a discussion of the improvisatory textless duet on the Tenor of Binchois's 'Vostre tres doulx' see Kemp, ' "Votre trey dowce": A Duo for Dancing', *ML* 60 (1979), 37–44, in which a case is presented for its being the first part of a *basse danse mineur*.

[14] In the initial decades of the century English and French musicians traded ideas not only of craft but also on the purposes to which the craft might be put. For example, the English (Cooke, Damett) had begun to adopt Continental *chanson* style for the composition of antiphons, and by the third decade Binchois, de Salinis, *et al.* also applied it to antiphons. Thus during the first half of the century the style, used as a vehicle for sacred texts, was being matured simultaneously by England's Dunstable and Power and by Burgundy's Binchois (Harrison, *Music in Medieval Britain*, 297–303).

[15] Some claim that Italian theoretical rules and modal practice, transmitted in Italian manuscripts and through the Italian offices of men like Ciconia, brought about fauxbourdon and the 'English' consonant guide; see *L'Ars Nova: Recueil d'études sur la musique du XIVᵉ siècle, Les Colloques de Wégimont*, ii (1955), 176–80, 209–12; also Kenney, *Walter Frye*, 7–10. Still there is no adequate explanation, if there was an Anglo-Italian musical intercourse, and notwithstanding the appearance of English songs in Italian manuscripts, why there is no reference to English composers and singers in Italy (Trowell, 'Some English Contemporaries of Dunstable', *PRMA* 81 (1955), 81–2). Dunstable's patron, Duke Humphrey of Gloucester, had followers filled with the spirit of Italian Humanism, and their presence at Rome, Florence, and Ferrara could have transmitted English music to the scribes of these cities; see Wathey, 'Dunstable in France', *ML* 67 (1986), 29–30.

effectiveness of 'La Contenance Angloise': 'The *Champion des dames* was an impeccably Burgundian text, with its own audience, preoccupations and ends; the view of English music it retails forms a discrete and coherent part of the musical contacts specifically between England and Burgundy.'[16]

. Binchois's 'De plus en plus' (*EscA* 39, *Rehm* 12) is the only song in the Binchois canon (there are none in the Dufay list) to open with a texted phrase on a single pick-up note (Ex. 26). This is quite characteristic of English carols, but appears only once more in this collection: the anonymous 'Loez soit Dieu' (*EscA* 52, *CMM* 77/27), which by its opening phrase already has been declared under English influence. Rehm dated 'De plus en plus' *c.*1425, the time of Binchois's reported service to the Duke of Suffolk. Another song Rehm placed at that period was the *ballade* 'Je loe amours', which also opens with a descending triad (Ex. 27).[17]

Ex. 26

De   plus   en   plus _____   se re -   nou - vel - le

Ex. 27

Je loe a - mours   et   ma da - me mer - cy

Measures 25–7 of 'Je loe amours' (Ex. 28*a*) duplicate, in the hemiola rhythm of notational coloration, a melodic pattern of 'Loez soit Dieu', mm. 8–11 (Ex. 28*b*). It occurs again, in iambics, mm. 40–1. This ascending pattern is fairly rare. No other song ascribed to Binchois has it. Coutreman built part of a *rondeau* melody with it, 'Vayle que vayle', a *rondeau* unusual in its triadic explorations. (Ex. 29).[18] For

Ex. 28
(a)

(b)

Et   se — ly   pry   pour — plus — d'es - pa   -   -   ce

---

[16] Wathey, 'Dunstable in France', 2.
[17] *Rehm* 52, source O, fo. 88'; for Rehm's chronology see p. 13* of his edition.
[18] *CMM* 11. ii, 21–2; cf. p. iii.

Ex. 29

Coutreman, 'Vayle que vayle', mm. 9 - 12

Trop re - doub - ter ____ fayt a - mer ____ sans par - ti - e

et en dou - leur _____

Ex. 30

(a)

EscA 25, mm. 2 - 6

Por - ray je a - voir vos - tre mer ____ ____ chi

(b)

Dufay, 'Je donne a tous', mm. 8 - 13

Pour e - stri - nes u ____ ne sous - sy ____ e ____

Dufay its ascent was cast in a lyric curve which, like the Coutreman extract, shows the composer to be concerned with length and shape of line rather than pungency of motif (Ex. 30).[19] Haucourt's 'Je demande ma bienvenue' is closer in its simplicity to Binchois patterns, repeated in 'Loez soit Dieu' (*EscA* 52). It is such a skeletal version of what Binchois could clothe in more lyric and harmonious fashion that the melody deserves to be quoted in full (Ex. 31).[20]

Ex. 31

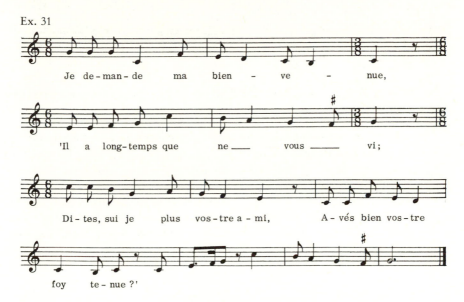

Je de-man-de   ma   bien - ve - nue,

'Il   a   long-temps que   ne ___ vous ___ vi;

Di - tes, sui je   plus   vos-tre a - mi,   A - vés bien vos-tre

foy   te - nue ?'

The anonymous 'Belle, esse dont vostre plaisir' (*EscA* 33, *CMM* 77/15) has the ascending pattern in its textless conclusion, and in 'Cuid'on que je poille castaingnes' (*EscA* 36, *CMM* 77/17) it is set to the last line of the text, mm. 14–18 (Ex. 32). This recalls the manner of Binchois, Coutreman, and Haucourt, and could make the idea a French melodic idiom. In a more extended phrase, its pitch-order stressing the shape of a broken common chord, it receives a smoother sound as the underlaid phrase for line 2 of 'Je n'atens plus de resconfort' (*EscA* 29, *CMM* 77/13) and line 3 of 'Soyés loyal' (*EscA* 56, *CMM* 77/30), both anonymous (Ex. 33).

Ex. 32

Tou - tes   joi - es   me   sont   es - train - gnes.

Thus it has again been demonstrated that the Escorial MS V. III.24 is a record of the Anglo-Burgundian musical alliance. 'Loez soit Dieu' (*EscA* 52) and several

---

[19] Opening of 'Porray je avoir' (*EscA* 25, *CMM* 1. vi/33), and *rondeau*, 'Je donne a tous les amoureux', mm. 8–13, *CMM* I. vi/52, source O, fo. 77ʳ.

[20] *CMM* 11. ii, 38–9.

Ex. 33

(a)

Je   ne   me ___ fais ___ plus de ___ rien ___ fort

(b)

Bien   brief ___ mon a - my ___ gra - ci - eux

other *chansons* probably qualify for the Binchois canon and others at least pertain
to its milieu.

The Cantus clichés of Burgundian song were for the most part expressed in three
rhythmic figures of the perfect breve: ♩♩♩, ♩♩.♪, ♩.♫ (♩.♩♪). From these
expressions of the newly established *tempus perfectum* was wrought the fresh
cantabile melody of Continental song.[21]

It is unusual to find a song so rich in the embroidery of its Cantus by these figures
as the anonymous 'Adieu, ma tresbelle maistresse' (*EscA* 27, *CMM* 77/12). The
variety of rhythmic figures makes it a notable melody (see Figure 1 and Ex. 34).

FIGURE 1

Ex. 34

[21] On 'Kantabile Ligaturen' (♩♩. ♪ etc.) see Besseler, *Bourdon und Fauxbourdon*, 129–31.

The rhythmic figure ♩ ♩. ♪ was not particularly favoured by Dufay in his secular music. He recognised its basic ♩ ♩ pattern as possessing the property of working against his favoured principle of lyrical extension. Thus for the smoother phrases of 'Craindre vous veul' (*EscA* 13, *CMM* I. vi/61) he used this pattern only twice, at the last internal cadences. In all he put it to significant use in only ten songs: *EscA* 24 ('Or pleust à Dieu'), 25 ('Porray je avoir vostre merchi'), 57 (Las! que feraye?), 60 ('Estrinez moy'), and six others (*CMM* I.vi/32, 51, 53, 55, 62, 67). Binchois, however, seems to have enjoyed this rhythmic figure. Out of forty ascribed *rondeaux*, in only seven did he employ it as an integral part of the Cantus line: *Rehm* 29 and 31 in ○|**1**, *Rehm* 6, 13, 18, 24, and 33 in ℂ|.

In seven of the *EscA* three-voiced anonymous *rondeaux* the figure ♩ ♩. ♪ is noticeably functional. The first phase of 'Lune tresbelle' (*EscA* 23, *CMM* 77/11) and the last phase of 'Cuid'on queje poille castaingnes' (*EscA* 36, *CMM* 77/17) (Ex. 35a and b) are a simple exposition of the idea. A general reliance upon this rhythmic figure is the air of 'Je cuidoye estre conforté' (*EscA* 49, *CMM* 77/26) and 'Mon coeur avoeque vous s'en va' (*EscA* 54, *CMM* 77/28). From perpetual repetition of the pattern in 'Le tresorire de bonté (*EscA* 14, *CMM* 77/7) (Ex. 36a), 'Soyés loyal' (*EscA* 56, *CMM* 77/30), and 'L'onneur de vous' (*EscA* 58, *CMM* 77/ 31) (Ex. 36b) springs the rhetorical and expressive life of the melodies.

Ex. 35
(a)

(b)

Ex. 36

(a)

(b)

Once again *EscA* 14, 23, 36, and 54 are identified with Binchois's habits of craft. *EscA* 49, 56, and 58 are demonstrated as being linked with his style.

3

The Rondeaux *for Three Voices: Mensuration, Texture, and Performance Practice*

IT is possible to propose a chronology for the works of a fifteenth-century composer by grouping them on the basis of mensural practice.[1] Charles Hamm's criteria for his chronological study of mensuration in Dufay's compositions may be applied to the anonymous pieces of the Escorial MS V.III.24. Because the delimitations of Hamm's groupings were drawn from periods of Dufay's personal history they must be slightly loosened when applied to songs of unascribed authorship; the lack of mensuration signs and notational complexities in this particular manuscript requires fewer categories. However, the chief guidelines remain (Table 1).

Category One corresponds to Hamm's Group 1, wherein ₵ and ○ are used as basic mensurations. In each mensuration, movement in the Cantus is in semibreves and minims: there are no semiminims. The three anonymous *rondeaux* in the Escorial collection that fit this category are in mensuration ○ .

TABLE 1. *Chronology of Anonymous* Rondeaux *by Mensural Practice*

Group One (–1424)	
○	
EscA 8, 27, 42	

Group Two (*c.*1424–30)	
₵	○
EscA 1, 33, 36, 43, 48, 52	*EscA* 45, 58

Group Three (1425–)
○
EscA 10, 14, 19, 20, 23, 29, 34, 38
49, 54, 56, 59, 61, 62

[1] Hamm, *A Chronology of the Works of Guillaume Dufay, Based on a Study of Mensural Practice*.

The second group is also drawn from Hamm's thesis. Basic mensurations are ¢ and ○. The movement in ¢ is in semibreves and minims, but shifts to breves and semibreves in ○. Flagged semiminims are used regularly in ¢, only occasionally in ○. The six anonymous pieces in ¢ among the twenty-five *rondeaux* under discussion qualify for this category. Of these, 'Se mon cuer à hault entrepris' (*EscA* 1, *CMM* 77/1), 'Cuid'on que je poille castaingnes' (*EscA* 36, *CMM* 77/17), and 'J'ay mains espoir d'avoir joye' (*EscA* 48, *CMM* 77/25) have flagged semiminims restricted to the Cantus; there are none in the Tenor of 'Loez soit Dieu' (*EscA* 52, *CMM* 77/27). Two songs in ○ qualify. 'Jamais ne quiers avoir liesse' (*EscA* 45, *CMM* 77/23) has no semiminims, but a Cantus progressing to a rhythmic movement of breves and semibreves. There is one measure of two flagged semiminims in 'L'onneur de vous, dame sans per' (*EscA* 58, *CMM* 77/31).

Group Three accounts for all the rest of the three-voice anonymous *rondeaux*. The basic mensuration is exclusively   . There is an increased use of semiminims, which are now coloured. 'Bien viengnant, ma tresredoubtée' (*EscA* 34, *CMM* 77/16) has two coloured semiminims in the Cantus, and two flagged semiminims in the Contratenor. Hamm placed Dufay's 'Craindre vous veul' (*EscA* 13, *CMM* I. vi/61), 'Or pleust à Dieu' (*EscA* 24, *CMM* I. vi/60), 'Porray je avoir' (*EscA* 25, *CMM* I. vi/33) and 'Las! que feraye?' (*EscA* 57, *CMM* vi/69) in this category, his Group 7; Dufay's 'Estrinez moy' (*EscA* 60, *CMM* I. vi/58) was in his Group 2.

With Group Three any attempt to place the anonymous *rondeaux* in more exact chronological order breaks down. The date 1433 chosen for the equivalent period in Hamm's Dufay chronology was predicated on the theory that his exposure to English influences came at this time.[2] In the preceding chapters of this book many of the anonymous *rondeaux* discussed have been connected closely to English practices and also to those of Binchois. Binchois's opportunities to acquire English idioms were opened to him sooner than to Dufay, who had to experiment with them as accepted practices rather than actively absorb them as did Binchois. Sylvia Kenney has made this comparison significant:

> that the rigid form of fauxbourdon plays a smaller role in the works of Binchois, whose contact with English composers was more direct and more lasting than Dufay's. The consonant, contrapuntal style of English music was assimilated more completely in the early works of Binchois, and it is in his music, rather than in Dufay's that the importance of the English element in the formulation of the Netherlands style can best be understood and evaluated.[3]

On grounds of mensuration no valid chronological assertions can be made about the anonymous pieces other than those in Groups One and Two. The approximately two decades covered by Group Three must have their component repertoires revealed by those individual traits of melodic style, those intervallic and rhythmic idioms which are recognizable features of ascribed works or of pieces under English influence. In this regard our application of Hamm's thesis has proved fruitful, in

---

[2] ibid. 94 ff.

[3] Kenney, *Walter Frye and the Contenance Angloise*, 187. Binchois could have become familiar with English style before Dufay's return from Italy; see Fallows, 'Binchois', *New Grove*, ii. 712.

that only 'Adieu, ma tresbelle maistresse' (*EscA* 27, *CMM* 77/12), 'Cuid'on que je poille castaingnes' (*EscA* 36, *CMM* 77/17), 'Loez soit Dieu' (*EscA* 52, *CMM* 77/27), and 'L'onneur de vous, dame sans per' (*EscA* 58, *CMM* 77/31) of Groups One and Two had been categorized on the basis of rhythmic or melodic style.

The textures of the twenty five anonymous *rondeaux* may be divided into four groups. Into Group One are gathered songs in an early fifteenth-century style, of which 'Belle, esse dont vostre plaisir' (*EscA* 33, *CMM* 77/15) is the best example. There is a full texture of three equally busy voices, which in some studies is called 'conductus-style'—an anachronism best avoided. The voices intermittently cross. The texted first half of each phrase has all voices in rhythmic concordance, although only the Cantus is texted (Ex. 37). *Chansons* of this texture have been preserved either with all voices texted or, like 'Belle, esse dont vostre plaisir', with text only in the Cantus. The following ascribed pieces are in MS O: Cantus texted, rhythmic concordance with Tenor, Contratenor, or both—Coutreman, 'Vaylle que vaylle' (fo. 50ᵛ), G. Le Grant, 'Pour l'amour' (fo. 94ʳ), 'Ma chiere mestresse' (fos. 96ᵛ–97ʳ), Raulin de Vaux, 'Savés pour quoy' (fo. 121ᵛ) (Ex. 38*a*), Reson, 'Il est temps' (fo. 53ᵛ); three voices texted—Francus de Insula, 'L'aultre jour' (fo. 97ᵛ and *BL*, fo. 91ᵛ), G. Le Grant, 'Or avant' (fos. 111ᵛ–112ʳ), J. Le Grant, 'Entre vous' (fo. 30ʳ), Malbecque, 'Ma volenté', 'Dieu vous doinct bon jour' (Ex. 38*b*), and 'Ouvrés vostre huys' (fos. 47ʳ–49ʳ).[4] Reaney would ascribe the anonymous 'Espris d'amour' (fo. 125ʳ) to Binchois because of its imitative textless opening,[5] but the common rhythms of the three texted voices are of more note in the context of this discussion. There are three relevant songs in the fifteenth-century repertoire of the Codex Reina (source *PR*): Grenon, 'La plus jolie' (fos. 91ᵛ–92ʳ and O, fo. 87ᵛ), anonymous, 'Amis, vous n'estes pas usé (fo. 103ʳ) and 'Il est venus' (fos. 118ᵛ–19ʳ).[6]

Dufay composed over a dozen pieces with multiple text underlay, but in a different style—often imitative. Closest to the style of 'Belle' are 'J'ay mis mon cuer

Ex. 37

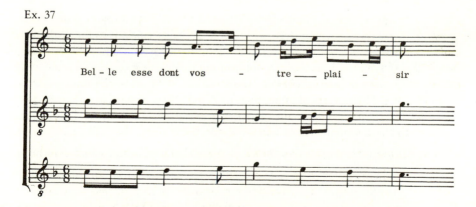

Bel - le esse dont vos - tre ___ plai - sir

---

[4] *CMM* 11.ii, 21, 49, 104, 105, 24, 50, 73, 94–6.
[5] *CMM* 11. iv, p. xiii, 28.
[6] *CMM* 37/3, 18, 25; the Grenon is also in *CMM* 11. vii, 2.

Ex. 38

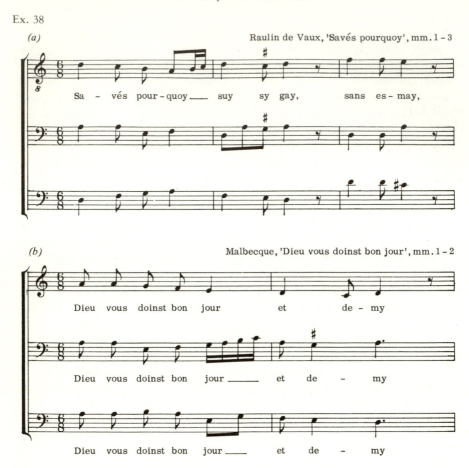

(a)   Raulin de Vaux, 'Savés pourquoy', mm. 1 – 3

Sa - vés pour - quoy ___ suy sy gay,   sans es - may,

(b)   Malbecque, 'Dieu vous doinst bon jour', mm. 1 – 2

Dieu vous doinst bon jour   et   de - my

Dieu vous doinst bon jour ___   et de — my

Dieu vous doinst bon jour ___   et de — my

et ma pensée' (*CMM* I. vi/13, source O, fo. 126ʳ) and 'J'atendray tant qu'il voul playra' (*CMM* I. vi/42, source O, fo. 51ʳ) (Ex. 39). The ascriptions to Binchois have only two songs with more than the Cantus underlaid. 'Amoureux suy' (*Rehm* 6, source O, fo. 82ʳ) is a duo over a Contratenor, of Italian flavour. The first two phrases of 'Joyeux penser' (*Rehm* 21, source O, fo. 49ᵛ) are in the same style as 'Belle' (Ex. 40). The vertical organization of 'Belle' is less stereotyped than that of Binchois–Dufay songs. The final cadence is quite 'un-English' in its dissonance, even though the dissonance is caused by the florid upper voice.[7] The cadence at m. 9 sounds the infrequent *concentus* $\frac{8}{6}$, a vertical combination which had been approved by theory for over a century, although isolated from any structurally functional progression: 'It is sweet when a sixth be placed in one contrapuntal voice and the other at the octave, in which position they shall be consonant

---

[7] Against dissonance in discant see the diatribe by Jacobus de Liège, cited in Kenney, *Walter Frye*, 96–7.

Ex. 39

Ex. 40

Ex. 41

without the Tenor [being a third apart]'.[8] These vertical traits, plus the smooth way
in which the rising figure 'x'—remarked upon earlier—is incorporated in the lyric
flow, suggest that 'Belle, esse dont vostre plaisir' is part of the French repertoire that
Reaney has published in his edition of early fifteenth-century music (Ex. 41).

'J'ay mains espoir d'avoir joye' (*EscA* 48, *CMM* 77/25) belongs to Group One
also. Despite the more agile intervals of the Contratenor and crossing of line among
the three voices, the rhythmic concordance maintained allows complete textual
underlay (Ex. 42).[9] Crossing of voices likewise qualifies 'Loez soit Dieu' (*EscA* 52,
CMM 77/27) for membership in this group.[10]

Ex. 42

The texture represented by Group Two also depends upon equality of voices.
Instead of vertical simultaneity the three songs of this group have imitation among
the voices occurring at the beginning of phrases. The phrases are now in the *tempus
perfectum* of the new *cantabile chanson*.

Scattered moments of imitation may be found in the music of several Burgundian composers. It was Dufay who advanced the art by his use of canon, five
chansons being built on this device: 'Entre vous', 'Resvelons nous'/'Alons', 'Je ne
puis plus'/'Unde veniet', 'Par droit', and 'Puisque vous estez campieur' (*CMM* I. vi/
26, 28, 29, 43, 81). Partial imitation (that is, not every phrase imitated) appears in
the course of seventeen other songs, including 'Porray je avoir vostre merchi' (*EscA*

---

[8] 'Et dulce quod potest, poni est quando quinta ponitur in uno contrapunctu et in alio decima, quia
quamvis tenor taceret, illi duo contrapunctus insimul concordarentur sine tenore, quia esset sexta':

Ars discantus per Johannem de Muris (Coussemaker, *Scriptorum de musica medii aevi*, iii. 93), cited in
Riemann–Haggh, 230–1, and Bush, 'The Recognition of Chordal Formation by Early Music Theorists',
MQ 32 (1946), 228.
[9] Its syllabic underlay brings 'J'ay mains espoir' (*EscA* 48, *CMM* 77/25) close to what Besseler
described as 'punkthafte Melodie' in *Bourdon und Fauxbourdon*, 129, cf. 124.
[10] A single treatise, Anonymous XI, *Ars contratenoris* (mid-fifteenth century), states that the
Contratenor may move above the Discant, in which case it is a Contradiscant (Riemann–Haggh, 245).

25, *CMM* I. vi/33). Two songs by Binchois, 'Plains de plours' (*EscA* 17, *Rehm* 34) and 'Margarite, fleur de valeur' (*EscA* 53, *Rehm* 27), likewise have imitation of a single phrase. The hints of imitation in 'Les tres doulx jeux' (*Rehm* 24) and 'Seule esgarée' (*Rehm* 42) are not related to the Cantus melody. 'Files a marier' (*Rehm* 55) is an imitative dialogue over a textless Contratenor. Only one other secular song ascribed to Binchois has imitation, 'Vostre alée me desplait tant', (*EscA* 11, *Rehm* 46). Unlike any of Dufay's songs involving imitation, this latter piece has each of its five texted phrases and the concluding textless passage open with exact imitation. The order of entry is invariably Contratenor–Cantus–Tenor. Imitation is at the unison. This pervasive imitative counterpoint anticipates the 'points' of the polyphonists of the Netherlands School. It is true that 'since the piece is a *rondeau*, the form of the composition does not derive from the imitation, as does that of the later works referred to; rather, the imitation decorates the form'.[11] Nevertheless the accumulation of these twenty-four head-motif entries during the performance of the complete *rondeau* must have afforded a striking effect (Ex. 43).

Ex. 43

Vos-tre a - lé - e   me   des - plait ＿＿＿＿ tant

Apart from the unique 'Files a marier', what little imitative work Binchois put into his secular music was recorded in the Escorial collection. His systematic application of this technique in 'Vostre alée' definitely separates his processes from Dufay's equally systematic but canonic approach to the same object: a texture constituted of equally important voices.

In 'Depuis le congié que je pris' (*EscA* 10, *CMM* 77/5) the last phrase is introduced imitatively. This descending triad, the semibreve rhythmic snap of its Cantus, and the rhyming close already have been discussed. This could be the third *chanson* by Binchois in this manuscript to demonstrate partial imitation.

'Tous desplaisirs m'en sont prochains' (*EscA* 8, *CMM* 77/4) and 'Je n'atens plus

[11] Reese, *Music in the Renaissance*, 88; cf. 56, for partial imitation in songs by Dufay. For an earlier *chanson* with imitative opening, by Do. Vala (source *BU*, fo. 56ʳ), see von Ficker, 'The Transition on the Continent', in *The New Oxford History of Music*, iii. 153: 'Belle, bonne' and 'Dame excellent' by Baude Cordier, in *CMM* 11.i/9, 12; 'A son plaisir' and 'De bien amer' by Fontaine (source *O*, fos. 88ᵛ and 100ᵛ respectively).

de resconfort' (*EscA* 29, *CMM* 77/13) have not been isolated so far in this study as possessing any traits of Binchois's style. They now may be placed within his influence, because both employ systematic imitation. In 'Tous desplaisirs' each phrase is exposed by having its Cantus melody anticipated in the Tenor. Three-voice imitation opens the song, in the order Contratenor–Tenor–Cantus. Before the Cantus enters with phrase three, the textless voices pair in thirds on its theme (mm. 13–15) (Ex. 44). 'Je n'atens plus' opens in a manner similar to Dufay's 'Navré je sui d'un dart penetratif' (*CMM* I. vi/34), the only secular song in which Dufay disconnected the triadic head-motto from the ensuing lyric arch, a melodic procedure more common to Binchois (Ex. 45). In 'Je n'atens plus' the imitative entries are at the unison, and occur in the following order:

Phrase 1: Ct,   C,   T
        2: T,   C,   Ct
        3: Ct,   T,   C
        4: Ct,   T   C
        5: Ct,   C,   T

Ex. 44

Ex. 45

(a)

(b)

The concluding textless passage, unlike 'Vostre alée', does not begin with imitation. This *rondeau* is an interesting blend of English melodic idiom, systematic counterpoint, and early fifteenth-century cadential structure.

Group Three comprises the majority of these anonymous *rondeaux*, and would do so for the majority of any collection of Burgundian *chansons* at this time. These are the pieces in the familiar 'ballade style' texture, prevalent since the French Ars Nova: a lyric line, over two (generally textless) crossing lines. The Contratenors exhibit varying degrees of activity, from a strict paralleling of the Cantus a fourth below to a disjunct leaping approximating the 'trompette' style (e.g. 'Bien viengnant' (*EscA* 34, *CMM* 77/16) and 'L'onneur de vous' (*EscA* 58, *CMM* 77/ 31)). The Tenors either have a movement in breves or are in fairly equal rhythmic concordance with the Cantus.

Group Four crosses over from the style of such pieces as 'Bien viengnant' and 'L'onneur de vous' into a texture in which the Cantus and Tenor provide a self-sufficient frame and the Contratenor leaps about with rhythmic energy.[12] 'Le tresorire de bonté' (*EscA* 14, *CMM* 77/7) and 'Cuid'on que je poille castaingnes' (*EscA* 36, *CMM* 77/17) have Contratenors whose motifs are of the 'trompette' type.

TABLE 2. *The Textures of the Anonymous* Rondeaux

Group One: equal-voice texture by rhythmic concordance; possibly all texted.
EscA 33, 48, 52

Group Two: equal-voice texture by imitation.
EscA 8, 10, 29

Group Three: lyric Cantus over two textless crossing voices.
EscA 1, 19, 20, 23, 27, 34, 38, 42, 43, 45, 49, 54, 58, 61

Group Four: Cantus–Tenor frame; very active Contratenor.
EscA 14, 36, 59, 62

The *rondeau* omitted from Table 2 is 'Soyés loyal à vo povoir' (*EscA* 56, *CMM* 77/30). Its cadential structure has been cited in Chapter 1, both for the 'English figure' in the Cantus and for its less usual vertical progression. It is made up of so varied a set of elements that it is difficult to classify. The melody has very well-defined modal areas in which it moves: first the upper, then the lower, then the full octave. This is a feature of Dufay's melodic design that is not found systematically employed in the Escorial collection outside those pieces ascribed to him.[13] Nevertheless we have shown the melody to be based upon a rhythmic figure that

---

[12] Not yet the rhythmically equivalent action of the Discant–Tenor pair, established by mid-century; described by Kenney, *Walter Frye*, 156. For earlier examples of this texture see three songs by Grenon, *CMM* 11. vii, 1, 4, 5.

[13] See Treitler, 'Tone System in the Secular Works of Guillaume Dufay', *JAMS* 18 (1965), 144 ff.; 'L'onneur de vous' (*EscA* 58, *CMM* 77/31) is the only anonymous song in which this procedure is approximated.

was chiefly Binchois's. What is most curious is the mixture of textures. The 'ballade style' predominates, but at mm. 16–18 there is a spaced texture with staggered non-imitative entries. Occasionally the Contratenor is exceptionally agile in French 'trompette' style; at other times it is in fairly slow rhythmic concordance with the other voices. In the textless conclusion the Cantus and Tenor voices cross. This hybrid piece is indicative of the flux of stylistic forces at work on the Continent *c*.1425–35, a reflection of the action and reaction of politics at the courts in which it was performed.

Analytical observation, such as the identification of four distinctive texture groups within a body of twenty-five *rondeaux*, gives to musicians of today the opportunity to achieve a historically valid performance based not only on evidence from iconography, literature, and organology, but also on the testimony of the music itself.

The *chansons* included in Texture Group One could have been given an unaccompanied vocal performance, the lyrics made 'delectables et embellies par la melodie et les teneurs, trebles et contreteneurs du chant . . .'.[14] Singers taking the second and third parts, untexted in the manuscript, would have been as aware of the required underlay as was the performer of the Cantus line to which the other voices were rhythmically concordant—hence the scribe felt it necessary to record the text only for this one, melodic voice. Polytextual songs, like 'Par tous'/'Cheluy' (*EscA* 4, *CMM* 77/3), of necessity would have been notated with precise text underlay.[15]

Evidence for an exclusively vocal interpretation may be seen in the depiction of the four vocalists at the Burgundian court's open-air festivities in the painting attributed to Van Eyck, as well as in scenes of musical diversion passed within the Garden of Love.[16] The privacy of chamber, bower, and enclosed garden would have been enhanced by an unaccompanied consort of vocalists, one singer to a part. If recorder, organ, and/or plucked instrument(s) joined in, their gentle sonorities would have been in support of the voices; they would not have been equal partners.[17]

[14] Eustache Deschamps, *L'Art de Dictier*, in *Œuvres Complètes*, vi, 272.

[15] For polytextual *chansons* by Cesaris see *CMM* 11. i, 19 (two voices, each with its own poem), 22 and 24 (two voices, each with its own poem, with untexted Tenor). Dufay's 'Je vous pri'/'Ma tres douce amie'/'Tant que mon argent' has a partially texted Tenor, alluding to various phrases in the other voices (*CMM* I. vi/25) The greater number of *rondeaux* by Dufay have text underlaid in all voices.

[16] Besseler, 'Die Besetzung der Chanson im 15. Jahrhundert', in International Society for Musical Research, *Report of the Fifth Congress (Utrecht, 1952)*, 65–72. The copy of the painting titled 'La Chasse du duc de Bourgogne' at Versailles (Musée du Chateau, MV 5423) is reproduced by, amongst others: (colour), Fowler, *The Age of Plantagenet and Valois*, 87, Bowles, *Musikleben im 15. Jahrhundert*, 91; (black and white), *MGG* ii, Plate 17, *New Grove* iii, 467; (detail of vocal quartet), *MGG* iii, Plate 21; (detail, copy in the Musée de Dijon, of singer with roll of music, Binchois?), *New Grove* ii. 710.

[17] Various combinations of voice and 'soft' instruments for modern performance of fifteenth-century song are suggested in McGee, *Medieval and Renaissance Music: A Performer's Guide*, 75–6, 97–9, and 120–1.

The acoustics of the banqueting hall would have been less conducive to an intelligible delivery of a polyphonic song fully texted in every voice. A separation of timbres would have been required to preserve the linear quality of the *rondeaux* in Texture Groups Two and Three. Supporters of the multi-instrumental performance of *chansons* have favoured contrasting colour-lines: the texted Cantus doubled with a monodic instrument, the lower pair of textless voices played by at least two other instruments of a different sound quality.[18] Such hypothetical performance practices were derived from literary sources, too often of an extravagant imagination. Mixed vocal–instrumental ensembles are not a feature of the historical accounts of Burgundian court culture. Even strictly instrumental arrangements were rarely recorded; one such occasion occurred in 1454, when Philip the Good, passing through the territory of the Count of Württemberg, gave a series of *dons* to minstrels including one who played 'chansons a sa trompette'.[19]

An exclusively vocal performance of the *chansons* should be accepted. Clarity of line may be obtained from children's voices just as well as from dissimilar instruments. A child's vocal quality, like that of the male alto in whose range also much of the repertoire lies, is edgy or nasal enough in timbre to perform successfully those *rondeaux* of Texture Group Two in which a texture of 'ballade style' is disguised at the opening of each phrase by pervasive imitation. These songs, the voices of which are in equality, would lose their linear interplay if sounded, let us say, by three recorders; a clearer line would result from a texted voice sung with two vocalizing voices, the Tenor and Contratenor perhaps also singing the initial words of the imitated text. The *rondeau* 'A l'aventure va Gauvain' by Cesaris indicates that this hypothesis has some foundation in actual practice.[20] Alternating with textless passages and a 'ballade-style' texture, lines 2, 6, 8, 10, and 14 have texted imitation in the Tenor and Contratenor, the lines reverting immediately thereafter to a slower untexted music (Ex. 46). Reaney went only half-way in explaining this practice: 'One can imagine the instrumentalists singing instead of playing this bar in the tenor and contratenor. Evidently wind instruments are not in use here. If they were, the players would not have time to replace their instruments in their mouths after singing.'[21] Far better to welcome this as evidence of an *à trois* vocal rendition of the whole song, the texted phase interrupting vocalized vowels. If vocalization was ideal for imitative textures, as suggested by the Cesaris song, there should be no reason not to agree that it was a way of performing the textless Tenors and Contratenors in general. In those passages where the three voices were textless,

---

[18] Bowles, 'Musical Instruments at the Medieval Banquet', *RBM* 12 (1958), 49–51.

[19] Marix, *Histoire de la musique et des musiciens de la cour de Bourgogne sons le règne de Philippe le Bon, 1420–1467*, 72–3. Besseler (*Bourdon und Fauxbourdon*, 190) printed a three-voice Spanish work in 'ballade-style' scored for *alta* winds. See Marix, *Histoire*, 101–3, Bowles, 'Instruments at the Court of Burgundy (1363–1467)', *The Galpin Society Journal*, 6 (1953), 48, and the same author's 'Unterscheidung der Instrumente Buisine, Cor, Trompe und Trompette', *AfMw* 18 (1961), 69.

[20] *CMM* 11. i, 21 (source O, fos. 109ᵛ–110ʳ).

[21] *CMM* 11. i, p. ii. This hypothesis would explain the texted incipits of the imitated phrase three of Binchois's 'Margarite, fleur de valeur' as notated in *EscA* 53.

Ex. 46   Cesaris, 'A l'aventure', mm. 10 - 16

vocal melismatic passages would have been as effective as comparable practices in the music of the family of man, from Gaelic mouth-music to pop 'scat'-singing.[22]

Boys' voices had sufficient carrying power even at a party so gargantuan as the Feast of the Pheasant (Lille, 17 February 1454), 'si haulte, si solempnelle et si pompeuse, que je cuide que de aige d'homme vivant n'a poinct esté faict la pareille'.[23] In this effusive and rapturous account by Philip the Good's secretary Jehan de Molesme it was reported that there came into the hall 'un cerf blanc sur lequel estoit un ensfant qui chantoit moult bien et mélodieusement, et le cerf lui tenoit la teneur'. Neither here nor in the passage devoted to the elephant with Holy Church in the tower does the writer mention the title of the song; his real interest is in quoting the Ducal Oath 'de mot à mot'. Chroniclers more directly concerned with the trappings of festivals described the clothing and accoutrements of the 'cherf merveilleusement grant et bel' and the singer, who was twelve years old. 'Et à l'entrée de la salle commencha ledit enfant le dessus d'une chanson, moult hault et cler et ledit cherf lui tenoit la teneur sans avoir autre personne, sy non l'enfant et l'artifice du cherf, et nommoit-on la chanchon qu'ilz disoient: *Je ne vis oncques la pareille*.'[24] This often-quoted description is cited here again to remind us of two

---

[22] Harrison also drew such analogies not only for secular song but also for the vocalization of sacred pieces composed in *chanson* style ('Tradition and Innovation in Instrumental Usage, 1100–1450', LaRue (ed.) *Aspects of Medieval and Renaissance Music: A Birthday Offering to Gustave Reese*, 328–9).

[23] 'Lettre de maître Jehan de Molesme, secrétaire du duc de Bourgogne, Philippe le Bon, aux maire et échevins de Dijon, relative à un entrements (ou *fête à table*) donné par le duc a Lille' [opened and read before the mayor and council, Monday 3 Mar. 1453], in Champollion-Figeac, *Documents historiques inédits tirés des collections manuscrites de la Bibliothèque nationale et des archives ou des bibliothèques des départements*, iv. 457–62.

[24] Mathieu d'Escouchy, *Chronique*, ed. du Fresne de Beaucourt, ii. 146–7; cited in Marix, *Histoire*, 37–41. Olivier de la Marche, as edited in his *Mémoires*, ed. Beaune and d'Arbaumont, ii. 340–94, wrote that 'ledit cherf lui chanta la teneur'. For a digest of the eighteen *entremetz* of the Feast see Gallo, *Music of the Middle Ages*, ii. 102–7. He mistakenly identified the 'child' as a girl, but has correctly removed the picturesque pasty-pie of yore! He translates *pasté* as 'fort'. One meaning of *paté* passing into nineteenth- and twentieth-century usage was that it referred to a round fortification offering shelter in flooded terrain

points. First, that the child's voice was evidently very apt for the spacious scene: it was 'moult hault et cler'. Second, that the writer stresses the Tenor to have been sung by a soloist 'sans avoir autre personne', quite a feat under those circumstances since the line was rather active.[25]

At the Feast of the Pheasant a church was erected in which were four singers 'qui y chantoient et jouoient d'orgues'. There were 'trois petis enfans d'église et ung teneur' who sang 'une tres doulce chansson'.[26] Four years later the comte de Foix entertained the ambassadors of the King of Bohemia (Tours, 22 December 1457) and mounted a similar spectacle:

There was a large castle, with four turrets. In addition there was a main central tower, in which there were four windows. In each window was the face of a young maiden with her long tresses hanging down in such a way that only her face and hair could be seen. Within the main tower were six children, singing with such art that the song seemed to proceed from the mouths of the maidens.[27]

Children's voices would not have been as muffled as those of adults singing behind stage walls; it is evident that women were not encouraged to sing in public shows.[28] Another occasion when children sang a secular song was recorded. On Monday and Tuesday 20–1 January 1449, Philip the Good heard morning Mass, when the Cambrai scribe Jean le Robert recorded that the ducal chapel 'canta et discanta bien legierement'. On Tuesday after dinner, 'deux petits enfants' of the chapel 'canterent une canchonette de lequelle un de ses Gentils Hommes tint le teneure et loy volentiers'.[29]

---

or at a site surrounded by water (Imbs, *Trésor de la langue française*, xii. 1160). Another use of *paté*, again in defensive fortification, was to donate a platform bordered by a parapet acting as a covering in front of the stronghold's portal (Littré, *Dictionnaire de la langue française*, v. 1540). If the *pasté* of the Feast was a platform—and this fits with its medieval/Renaissance definition as a desk (as listed in Godefroy, *Dictionnaire de l'ancienne langue française et de tous ses dialectes du IXe au XVe siècles*, and in Huguet, *Dictionnaire de la langue française du seizième siècle*, v. 676)—then this was simply a fifteenth-century version of equipment common to show business right up to the portable stands used in modern outdoor 'rock' concerts and folk festivals. If it was a round tower, or fort rising out of water, this would agree with the description written by Jehan de Molesme: 'Au milieu avoirt une grosse rochemoult bien faicte, autour de laquelle avoit chasteaux et forteresses, et au dessus de laditte roche avoit le personnage d'un enfant tout nud qui pissait eau roze' (Champollion-Figeac, *Documents historiques*, iv. 457–62). See also n. 27.

[25] *CMM* 1. vi/91, attributed to Dufay and (far less likely) Binchois; see Kenney, *Walter Frye*, 157–8. Singing a *son* on horseback was a part of the lore of Old French Literature (Page, 'Music and Chivalric Fiction in France 1150–1300', *PRMA* 3 (1984–5), 25–6, but singing a polyphonic part inside a 'hobby-stag' would have been quite another matter.

[26] Mathieu d'Escouchy, cited by Marix, *Histoire*, 38. This particlar chronicler was not actually present at the banquet; see Doutrepoint, *La Littérature française à la cour des ducs de Bourgogne*, 106 ff. and 356 ff.

[27] My translation from Marix, *Histoire*, 86; cited from Chastellain, *Chronique*, iii. 375. For a translation from further contemporary descriptions of these entertainments see Vaughan, *Philip the Good*, 348.

[28] One exception is the lady in service to the Duchess of Burgundy who sang with the two blind *vielle* players and a lutenist at the Feast of the Pheasant. This interlude and a previous song for two voices and lute are the only accompanied vocal music reported at the Feast; however, it is commonly agreed there is no proof that these songs were not monophonic.

[29] Marix, *Histoire*, 67 (cited from Dupont, *Histoire ecclásiastique et civile de la vile de Cambrai, ii*, pp. xvi–xxi).

From these documents it is evident that there was purely vocal interpretation distinguished by acoustical clarity: a mature voice on the Tenor with the keener timbre of the boys' voices over it. There is no mention of a Contratenor part. This supports what may be deduced from the manuscript sources, that within the large number of 'ballade-style' songs, and progressing to the frame texture of Group Four, the Cantus and Tenor could form a self-sufficient duet. Some songs have been preserved in two different arrangements, the notes of a two-voice setting revised just enough to provide a satisfactory rhythmic and consonant structure to make a convincing three-voice song.[30] It is also known that several different Contratenors could be set to the given duo. The songs by Vide and Fontaine notated in the Escorial Chansonnier are a case in point.[31] The performers would have known their rules sufficiently to make the small adjustments required to accommodate the presence in their midst that day of a more agile vocalist who excelled in leaps and syncopation.

A different motivation prompted the added voice to combine the lower notes of a given Tenor and Contratenor to produce a new line, resulting in a continuous melodic span of the vertical elements separating the two lower voices in 'ballade style', a line predominantly of perfect intervals.[32] This fourteenth-century practice was carried into the fifteenth, giving to the music much more energy and sense of progression. The *Solus contratenor* on fo. 38[r] of 'Dueil angoisseus' (*EscA* 37, *Rehm* 50) acts as a reduction of the other two Contratenors provided.[33]

In another context (see n. 8) we noted an example from the *Ars discantus per Joannem de Muris*, describing a 'sweet' *concentus* of three voices, abstracted from any functional progression. Progression is the role of the pair of discanting voices. The Contratenor must be understood not as a progressive line but as a series of separate vertical sound-structures enriched. This explains much of the intervallic nature of early fifteenth-century Contratenors. They are rhythmic activations (often syncopated patterns on only one or two notes) of convenient vertical expansions of the self-sufficient discanting Cantus–Tenor frame. The 'octave-leap' cadence is the simplest example.[34]

An analogous technique within the context of English improvised discant demanded a singer skilled in changing sights, above or below the Tenor. He had to sing an extremely jagged line, supplying the missing note in the *concentus*, and therefore he must have possessed a wide vocal range. By definition he was a bass:

---

[30] See my article, 'A Chanson for Two Voices by Cesaris, *Mon seul voloir*', MD 20 (1966), 47–56.

[31] Whereas *EscA* 50 had a different Contratenor in MS *BL*, the song was recorded in M5 O as a duo, without Contratenor. Such scribal practices heighten interest in the performer of Contratenor parts as a skilled improviser. The duo versions appear in the earlier manuscripts; see Kenney, *Walter Frye*, 164–5.

[32] See Besseler, *Bourdon und Fauxbourdon*, 92–6; Davis, 'The Solus Tenor in the 14th and15th Centuries', *Acta Mus.* 39 (1967), 44–64; Salop, 'Jacob Obrecht and the Early Development of Harmonic Polyphony', *JAMS* 17 (1964), 288–94.

[33] As suggested in *Rehm*, p. 11*; discussion of the *secunda pars* of 'Deuil angoisseus' in Davis, 'The Solus Tenor', 48–50. See the comparative edition of the three Contratenors, *Rehm*, 73.

[34] Crocker, 'Discant, Counterpoint, and Harmony', *JAMS* 15(1962), 13–15. On a suggested progress from a complementary to an obligatory vocal *Contratenor* see Hughes, 'Some Notes on the Early Fifteenth-Century Contratenor', *ML* 50 (1969), 376–87.

'Also a man that hath a low voyce may syng a countertenor in-stede of a mene, ffor whan the tenor is hye the countertenor may be low, and whan the tenor is low than the countertenor may be the mene'.[35] There is no reason to suppose that a good *menestrel de bouche*, specializing in virtuoso Contratenor parts, could not have drawn with his performance of Example 47 from the Chansonnier Cordiforme or the deeper conclusion of 'J'ayme bien' (*EscA* 50) the same appreciative response from his (admittedly quite different) auditors than could an English *basso profundo* with 'Many brave hearts are asleep in the deep'![36]

Ex. 47   anon., 'Quant du dire adieu', mm. 12 - 14

In the performance of Burgundian repertoire the leaps over perfect intervals by the *solus tenor*, and the masking of discant progressions by an active Contratenor unconcerned with linear movement, produced a bounding voice-part whose frequent fanfare-like passages were connotative enough to be cultivated into a distinct idiom. This idiom was considered peculiarly French, hence the title of the anonymous *Tuba gallicalis*. It was vocal.

Trumpetum est cantus mensuralis per quatuor choros procedens in quo quilibet suo fungens officio in cantando via sua cantacionis directa progreditur sed quartus obviat omnibus voce sonora aliquantulum rauca in modum tube gallicane sine hoc quod alicui, faciat suo occurrsu caccofoniam seu malam et dissidentem sonoritatem.[37]

[35] The so-called 'Pseudo-Chilston', British Library Lansdowne MS 763, XVI, ed. Meech, 'Three Musical Treatises in English from a Fifteenth-Century Manuscript', *Speculum*, 10 (1935), 261; cited by Bukofzer, *Geschichte des englischen Diskants und des Fauxbourdons nach den theoretischen Quellen*, 149 and Kenney, *Walter Frye*, 118 (cf. 128).

[36] Ex. 47 from a *bergerette*, 'Quant du dire adieu me souvient' (*CMM* 42, 18); further examples of deep Contratenors in Besseler, *Bourdon und Fauxbourdon*, 46, 49. In court records apparently the classification 'menestrel de bouche' specifically designated a vocalist, who functioned within a secular setting. For materials from documents relating to the reign of Philip the Bold and John the Fearless see Wright, *Music at the Court of Burgundy, 1364–1419: A Documentary History*, 27–8; drawn upon by Greene, 'The Schools of Minstrelsy and the Choir-School Tradition', *Studies in Music from the University of Western Ontario*, 2 (1977), 33.

[37] Riess, 'Pauli Paulirini de Praga Tractatus de Musica (etwa 1460)', *ZfMw* 7 (1925), 261.

If lines especially created in this idiom were intended specifically for an instrument there would have been no need to denote them '*ad modum* tubae'; the 'Contra-tenor trompette' of 'J'ayme bien' must be interpreted in the same logical way.[38] What we have here is late medieval picture-music, reproducing natural and concrete sounds in vocal terms.[39]

The likelihood of exclusively vocal performances of Valois court songs was a supposition in the 1960s.[40] It is satisfying to observe since then the growing interest among researchers and performers alike in this practice. In fact, in recent years it has become 'trendy' to the point of being dubbed the 'new secular *a cappella* heresy'.[41] Christopher Page set the pace with his inferences drawn from *L'Art de Dictier et de Fere Chançons* (1392) by Eustache Deschamps.[42] Craig Wright[43] and David Fallows[44] subsequently presented archival materials which could accelerate accep-tance of this option, for, lively or not, an option was what it must have been.[45] To propose today that the untexted lower lines could be vocalized no longer seems a 'wild suggestion'.[46] If it can be proposed that even the longer durations of the Tenor part could be activated with reiterated notes by harpers,[47] there is no reason to doubt that with their repeated syllables singers could achieve the same activation, perhaps even in imitation of the sound of the harp: another form of 'ad modum' vocalization![48]

[38] It was not possible to play such lines on the slide trumpet; perhaps the Burgundian S-shaped trumpet was not a 'slide' but a 'claret' trumpet; probably the music was not intended for a brass instrument at all. For this progression of opinion see Harrison, 'Tradition and Innovation', 331–2; Sachs, 'Chromatic Trumpets in the Renaissance', *MQ* 36 (1950), 62–6; Downey, 'The Renaissance Slide Trumpet: Fact or fiction?', *Early Music*, 12 (1984), 26–32; Höfler, 'Der "Trompette de Menetrels" und sein Instrument: Zur Revision eines bekannten Themas', *Tijdschrift van de Vereniging vor Neder-landse Muziekgeschiedenis*, 29 (1979), 92–132.

[39] Harrison, 'Tradition and Innovation', 331.

[40] As in Harrison,'Tradition and Innovation', 332. This thinking shaped the interpretation of the analytical material on textures in this Chapter, the core of which had been formulated during the preparation of the author's dissertation; for once, continuing research has strengthened a hypothesis rather than discarding it.

[41] Brown, review of Page's recording *The Castle of Fair Welcome, Early Music*, 15 (1987), 278.

[42] Page, 'Machaut's "pupil" Deschamps on the Performance of Music: Voices or Instruments in the 14th-Century Chanson', *Early Music*, 5 (1977), 484–91.

[43] 'Voices and Instruments in the Art Music of Northern France during the 15th Century: a Conspectus', in International Musicological Society, *Report of the Twelfth Conference, Berkeley, 1977*, ed. Heartz and Wade, 643–9.

[44] 'Specific Information on the Ensembles for Composed Polyphony, 1400–1474', in Boorman (ed.), *Studies in the Performance of Late Mediaeval Music*, 109–59, esp. 131–44.

[45] On keeping options open we must agree with the cautions made by Leech-Wilkinson in his review of Boorman's *Studies* (*Early Music History*, 4. 353), that a 'best performance' may have meant a locale-specific ensemble.

[46] Fallows, 'Specific Information', 132; see Brown, 'The Trecento Harp', in Boorman (ed.), *Studies*, 589.

[47] As instructed, it would appear, by Senleches; see the article 'Harp', *The New Grove Dictionary of Musical Instruments*, ii. 136–7.

[48] In harp/lute duos, possibly such as those of the Faenza Codex, the harp's comparative limitations would restrict it to the Tenor part (McGee, 'Instruments and the Faenza Codex', *Early Music*, 14 (1986), 483). Given that the harp was also the best instrument to execute the skipping intervals and what McGee calls the 'stop-and-go' sections of the Contratenor (*Medieval and Renaissance Music: a Performer's Guide*, 98–9, 120–1), is it possible that the highly trained singer alluded to above and the

Until we learn more about the true performance situation of the Valois court singer, particularly, as Wright has advised, in regard to the *rotulus* from which the pieces were actually sung,[49] we must go back to that evidence supplied by the polyphonic textures of the music which was the basis for the hypotheses of twenty years ago. The four texture groups into which we divided the anonymous *rondeaux* of the Escorial MS V.III.24 illustrate the statement by Deschamps that a piece 'may be sung with the voice in an artistic way without words'.[50] Harrison's idea may be asserted even more firmly: for all lines of the Burgundian *chanson* the 'normal possibility' was vocalization.[51]

Frank

accomplished harper, who could read music (McGee, 'Instruments', 484), were one and the same? Is this the meaning of Binchois holding *his* instrument in the miniature, because he was the creative virtuoso of supported vocalise and supporting plucked instrumental colour?

[49] Wright, 'Voices and Instruments', 644.

[50] '... chanter and par voix et fort art, sanz parole'; trans. Page, 'Machaut's "Pupil"', 488–9.

[51] Harrison, 'Tradition and Innovation', 332.

4

Other Rondeaux, *the* Ballades, *and the* Middle Dutch Songs

As a result of the analysis of the twenty-five anonymous *rondeaux* reported in the preceding chapters, there may be established within the repertoire definite criteria for stylistic subdivisions and tools for attribution. Analytical exposition of the remaining nine anonymous songs thus may be more concise.

Other Rondeaux

EscA 4, 'Par tous/Cheluy' (*CMM* 77/3): mensuration: Group Two, ℭ with flagged semiminims.

Duos of two equally important voices did not achieve much attention and quickly died out of fashion, judging from the few that have been preserved. Double *rondeaux* such as this piece, with a specific text in each voice, account for only three of the eleven such duos in fascicles 5–8 of MS O; two are anonymous (O, fo. 83ʳ and fo. 92ʳ), and one is by Cesaris (fo. 84ᵛ); there is one in fascicle 3, fo. 35ʳ by Reson.[1]

The duos by Cesaris and Reson generally are in rhythmic concordance, preserve the norms of consonance, cross frequently, and interchange the roles of discant–tenor in cadential progressions. The phrases are well marked, and the Cesaris has separate textless passages. Like the anonymous duo on fo. 92ʳ, the first two phrases of the Reson display double counterpoint (Ex. 48).

The duo 'Par tous'/'Cheluy' proceeds in a different manner. Clarity of text is assured by presenting the texted portion of one voice in counterpoint with an untexted passage in the other. There is a moment of dissonance, second semibreve of m. 12. Although the voices cross, there is no doubt that the line beginning 'Par tous' is the upper of the two. Its melody is more coloured, and the voice 'Cheluy' is assigned the role of Tenor fundament at the cadences. A three-note pattern is played with in the upper voice, made up of the successive intervals of a second and

---

[1] Anonymous, 'Puis que vous plet'/'Pour ton present' (*CMM* 11. iv, 1) and 'Je ne vous ose regarder'/'Laysiés Dangier' (*CMM* 11. iv, 39); Cesaris, 'Pour la douleur'/'Qui dolente' (*CMM* 11. i, 19), previously edited in Danneman, *Die Spätgotische Musiktradition in Frankreich und Burgund vor dem Auftretens Dufays*, 136; Reson, 'Ce rondelet'/'Le dieu d'amours', (*CMM* 11. ii, 105) previously edited Stainer and Stainer, *Dufay and his Contemporaries*, 185. There are two double-texted duets in Paris, Bib. Nat., nouv. acq. fr. 4917, fos. 1ᵛ–2ʳ.

Ex. 48

Reson, 'Ce rondelet'/'Le dieu d'amours', mm. 1–6

Ce ron - de - let je vous ____ en - voy - e Pour

Le dieu d'a - mours si vous l'o - troy - - e Et

con - so - la - ti - on de joy - - e

vous en doint par - fait - te ____ soy - e

Ex. 49

Par tous lez a - lans de ____ par la

Che - luy qui vous re - mer - chi -

A vous me fais re - comman - der,

ra   De par moy vous fait sa - lu - er,

a third; the pattern appears nine times (Ex. 49). Overlapping of the two lines at cadences increases as the song proceeds, impairing the definition of phrase essential to Burgundian style.

EscA 46, 'Je n'ay quelque cause de joye' (*CMM* 77/24): mensuration: Group Two, with flagged semiminims.

This is an example of the syllable delivery that Besseler termed 'punkthafte Melodie'. There is one textless passage, two melismas. The single noteworthy feature of this Cantus is the unusual musical unity, brought about by the rhyming cadences of lines 3 and 6, and the setting of the octosyllabic line 5 to the identical music of line 2: four syllables plus melisma (Fig. 2, Ex. 50).

<u>Musical scheme</u>   <u>Verse scheme</u>

l. 1, 8 syll. + melisma   a
l. 2, 4 syll. + melisma   a
l. 3, 8 syll.   b
⌢   ⌢
l. 4, 4 syll.   b
Interlude
l. 5, 8 syll.   a
l. 6, 8 syll.   b

Exact Duplication   Cadence Rhyme

FIGURE 2

Ex. 50

Je n'ay quel-que cau - se de__ joye; ____

__ Ou que je soye   Mon-tre sam-

blant d'es - tre joi - eulx   Je ris des __ yeux

Quant le plus au cuer__

il   m'a – noy   –   e,   Da-me, par   qui j'ai tous mes ___ deulx.

EscA 40, 'En bonne foy' (*CMM* 77/19): mensuration: Group Three, ○ with coloured semiminims.

The architectonic design of the Cantus is very clear. The first two phrases present a tonally balanced valency that is well articulated (Ex. 51).[2] Clarity is heightened by a static passage on V (mm. 12–13), similar to static triadic measures in English as well as Burgundian pieces (Ex. 52).

Ex. 51

Ex. 52

(a)   *EscA* 40, mm. 12 – 13

[2] Hoppin has noted the striking frequency 'with which the tonal center of a composition was unequivocally established during the first few measures', and goes on to describe what is duplicated in 'En bonne foy': opening on the home level, cadencing through the level of the fifth ultimately to the tonic, in balanced phrases. The 'growing tendency to begin with I is symptomatic of an even greater concern for making the tonality immediately apparent', and is demonstrated by a table of secular works which shows an increase in tonal clarity of 29 per cent from Machaut to the repertoire of Reaney's edition ('Tonal Organization in Music Before the Renaissance', in Glowacki (ed.), *Paul A. Pisk: Essays in his Honor*, 25–37, esp. 25–7). Only when the complete structure is taken into account, whether *à 2, à 3*, or more, can such a 'tonal' view be accepted, in so doing reinforcing the theory of Treitler in which Dufay's secular pieces (melodies and total structure) articulate definite areas of the scale system: a melodic craft which is akin to that of *EscA* 40 (Treitler, 'Tone System in the Secular Works of Guillaume Dufay', *JAMS* 18 (1965), 144 ff.); see also ch. 3 n. 13. Tonality in Dufay's *chansons* is discussed further by Marggraf, 'Tonalität und Harmonik in der französischen Chanson zwischen Machaut und Dufay', *AfMw* 23 (1966), 27–31.

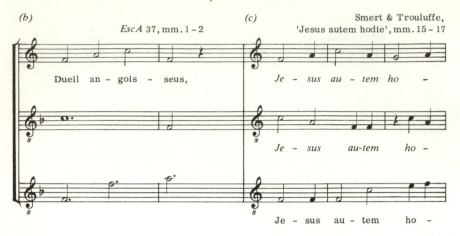

(b)

EscA 37, mm. 1 - 2

Dueil an - gois - seus,

(c)   Smert & Trouluffe,
'Jesus autem hodie', mm. 15 - 17

Je - sus au - tem ho -

Je - sus au-tem ho -

Je - sus au - tem ho -

English idioms form much of the Cantus line. The repeated note in measure 2 and the several patterns based on a descending third are amongst those figures characteristic of English music linked with Burgundian melody.[3] Most indicative is the presence of the 'English figure', at the penultimate cadence, mm. 16–17 (Ex. 53). The Cantus is unusually expressive in its nine cadential formulae.

Ex. 53

The voices cross when making the first cadence, m. 3. The rhythmic equivalence of the voices is very apparent, in the active setting of lines 2 and 4 and in the vocalization, mm. 14–15. This piece would seem to be a self-sufficient duo, progressing toward the mid-century type of discant–tenor song. It is strongly under English melodic influence, but the individual idioms are woven together into strands, instead of being featured in repetitive motifs as in Binchois. By this, its tonal architecture, long lines, and imitation at an interval other than the unison, we would be persuaded to assign it to the school of Dufay rather than to that of Binchois.

EscA 44, 'Helas! je n'ose descouvrir' (*CMM* 77/22): mensuration: Group Two, ¢ with flagged semiminims.

---

[3] Kenney, *Walter Frye and the Contenance Angloise*, 178–81. Example 52*c* is from Rit, fos. 40ᵛ–41ʳ (*MB* IV, No. 108, p. 97).

A frame of little remark. Five out of six cadences use the same variant of the 'under-third' type. The opening phrase and the escaped dissonance in the Cantus, mm. 14–15, are traces of English guise. The Cantus rhythm depends upon the iambic division of the semibreve. These traits might suggest the school of Binchois, but they are the only features worth noting. Unlike the duo 'En bonne foy' (*EscA* 40), this piece requires a Contratenor to make it particularly interesting.

The Ballades

EscA 2, 'Je vous salue, ma maistresse' (*CMM* 77/2): mensuration: Group Three ○ with coloured semiminims

Musical Form:

I Stollen	II Abgesang	
A₁ A₂ A₁ A₂	B	R ‖
ouvert clos		

The texture is 'ballade style', but with the Refrain introduced by pervasive imitation at the unison; order of entries Contra–texted Cantus–Tenor: typical Binchois procedure. The piece has the two rhythmic idioms we established as characteristic of Binchois: the pattern ♫♩ with lower auxiliary note (Cantus, mm. 13 and 24), and the Contratenor iambic repeated fifth at the final 'octave-leap' cadence.

Three cadences have the Contratenor in strict parallel at the under-fourth (mm. 9–10, 13–14, 24–5). It is interesting to note that elision of phrases occurs, mm. 5–6, between lines 1 and 2 (3 and 4), giving stronger unity to the *prima pars*. The cadence at mm. 17–18 has the Cantus decorate below the Tenor, the Contratenor effecting a triadic root (Ex 54). The last phrase has a well-wrought Cantus span, ranging a tenth, building on Binchois's favourite rhythmic order (Ex. 55).

Ex. 54

ri - ans — yeux

Ex. 55

et   me fist __ vo-stre,__ si m'ait __ Dieux. _____

On the stylistic bases already employed in this study, this *ballade* very readily can be added to the canon of Binchois's works.[4]

EscA 12, 'Je ne porroye plus durer' (*CMM* 77/6): mensuration: Group Three, ○ with coloured semiminims.

Musical Form:

I Stollen   II Abgesang

A₁ A₂ :‖   B   R(= A₂)

The texture is 'ballade style', with an overall quality of uniformity among the voices: the Cantus line is not very coloured, nor the Contratenor active. The final cadence is an 'octave leap', with under-fourth parallel of the Cantus at two mid-cadences. At those measures, 3–4, 20–1, the composer duplicated his material in preparation for the required repetition of mm. 5–10 for the Refrain.

The activated triad sounding through the voices at mm. 4 and 21 is a symptom of the English influence, as is the dropping third in the Cantus, m. 17 (Ex. 56).

Ex. 56

Besseler drew attention to the late melodic third, indicative that it was from the years of change, *c.* 1430; the work with which he demonstrated this was *EscA* 30, 'Adieu jusques je vous revoye' by Binchois, where the late third appears three times:

---

[4] During the printing stage of this book evidence has been published that the poet of 'Je vous salue' was none other than Binchois's reputed patron William de la Pole, Duke of Suffolk, a discovery which David Fallows kindly links with my ascription on musical grounds to 'strengthen the likelihood that the music is indeed by Binchois' (review of Boffey, *Manuscripts of English Courtly Love Lyrics in the Later Middle Ages*, *Journal of the Royal Musical Association*, 112/1 (1987), 132–3).

mm. 9, 15, 25.[5] *EscA* 3, 'Je ne fai tousjours que penser' by Binchois, has one. Four other secular songs by Binchois, and four by Dufay, have the idiom.[6] The Binchois fingerprint, ♫♩ with lower auxiliary, appears at the first cadence, m. 3. This *ballade* too may be added to the catalogue of his works.

EscA 18, 'Puis que fortune m'est si dure' (*CMM* 77/8): mensuration: unusual, ¢ with coloured semiminims.

Musical Form: as in *EscA* 12

Again the penultimate cadence rhymes with that of line 1, preparing the repetition of material for the Refrain. The texture is 'ballade style', with little rhythmic variation among the voices, especially between the textless pair. All but one of the cadences imply a II–I progression, the other (mm. 9–10) V–I. Iambic patterns of the subdivided semibreve are the rhythmic feature of the Cantus in every phase. No other features mark this *ballade* as pertaining to the style of any particular composer.[7]

The Middle Dutch Songs

EscA 31, 'Al eerbaerheit weinsch ic voort an' (*CMM* 77/14): mensuration: Group Two, ¢ with flagged semiminims.

EscA 55, 'Ope es in minnen groot ghenuecht' (*CMM* 77/29): mensuration: Group two, ¢ with flagged semiminims.

The texture of *EscA* 31 is 'ballade style', with a skipping Contratenor. An 'octave-leap' cadence concludes a work of strong cadential quality, marked by descending intervals of the fourth and fifth in the Contratenor (mm. 1–2, 3–4, 8–9, 10–11, 21–2) and a hidden descending fourth in the sounding bass line, mm. 12–13.

The tonal scheme of *EscA* 55 is also quite clear. The textless prelude's Cantus is a fine articulation of the Lydian major triad and the balanced use of upper-fifth and under-fourth areas. All but two cadences provide a V–I structure. The Contratenor serves as a harmonic bass, V–I, mm. 13–15.

The texture of *EscA* 55 alternates between 'ballade style' and three-voiced rhythmic concordance, the latter at the texted lines 1, 2, and 4. There is a greater use of semiminim passage-work than in other songs of this collection, particularly in the Cantus figurations both of the interlude between text lines 2 and 3 and of the textless conclusion. The Contratenor does not contribute to a pan-consonant sound as in the rest of the manuscript. It works as a pair with the Tenor, in rhythm

---

[5] Besseler, *Bourdon und Fauxbourdon*, 56–7.

[6] *Rehm* 7, 21, 48; *CMM* 1. vi/17, 52, 62; *Rehm* 9 (twice) and *CMM* 1. vi/31 each have the rhythmic figure in a pattern of escaped dissonance.

[7] The two types of musical Ballade Form in the ascribed works of Binchois break down as follows: *ouvert* and *clos*, new Refrain (*Rehm* 49, 52, 53, 54), identical close of *Stollen* and *Abgesang* (Rehm 48, 50 (*EscA* 37, 51)).

and in consonance; the lines frequently cross. With the Cantus it is frequently dissatisfying: in accented dissonance (mm. 1, 3, 6, 7, 9, 11, 16), passing dissonance (mm. 10, 17), and parallel octaves (mm. 6, 11, 14). By its mixed texture, its rapid passage work and dissonance, *EscA* 55 should be considered the earlier of the two songs.

Unlike the French-texted songs of the collection, each of the Middle Dutch pair seems to aim at a melodic unity beyond the exploitation of cliché patterns. The texted phrases of *EscA* 31 are unified by a rhythmic series, presenting a standard three-note syllabic opening, followed by a hemiola, and concluding in a cadential formula of different quantities (Fig. 3).

Trisyllable	Hemiola	Cadence

Al   eer-baer- heit weinsch ic voort an,

Ghe-nucht so - laes enn   vroylicheit,

Om een ghe -zicht van reinicheit,

Dat man vul-pri - sen niet en can.

FIGURE 3

The melodic unity of *EscA* 55 is found in the pitches used for the texted lines. Lines 1–4 are restricted to the range of a fourth, with similar progressions in the arc. Line 5 is expanded in range to a fifth, with no similarity to the other four in shape (Ex. 57).

Ex. 57

Both songs are framed by a self-contained textless prelude and conclusion. Hemiola is featured in both preludes and in the conclusion of *EscA* 31. Each has a textless interlude. Of the twenty-five three-voice anonymous *rondeaux* only 'Le tresorire de bonté' (*EscA* 14, *CMM* 77/7) has both textless prelude and conclusion. Binchois's forty-six ascribed *rondeaux* include twelve with textless preludes, seventeen with conclusions; of these only four have both, none of which are in the Escorial manuscript.[8] Of fifty-eight songs with French texts by Dufay, ten have textless preludes, twenty-six have textless conclusions. Eight have both; as was the case with the four Binchois pieces, none of these are in the Escorial collection; they are considered by Besseler to date fairly early in Dufay's career.[9] In the framed *chansons* of Binchois and Dufay the width of frame is quite substantial, for example Dufay's 'He, compaignons' with eight measures on both sides plus final note. No further conclusion can be drawn from these observations, relevant to the two Middle Dutch songs *EscA* 31 and 55, save that they would seem to be confirmed as being among the earlier items of the manuscript.

The careful choice of melodic patterns, the tonal tendencies, the external frame: these the anonymous musician(s) employed to create two songs with a singularly fine sense of structure.

---

[8] *Rehm* 9, 26, 39, 43.
[9] *CMM* 1. vi/27, 30, 39, 44, 46, 47, 49, 51.

5

A New Binchois Repertoire

THE thirty-four anonymous songs of the manuscript Escorial V.III.24 have been divided into groups, according to the organization of their cadences, mensuration, and texture. The co-operation between horizontal and vertical elements at cadence points has been demonstrated to be representative of various procedures followed by Burgundian composers in Binchois's time. The groupings by mensuration and texture would appear not only to be valid in themselves but also to be complementary. For example, the songs deemed to have been created earlier, by virtue of the rhythmic concordance of their voices, belong to the ₵ of Mensuration Group Two (c.1424–30). Probing more deeply we have isolated melodic, rhythmic, and structural characteristics by which, having documented their presence in the ascribed works of Binchois and Dufay, we may assign the anonymous songs in which they were employed to the very separate styles exhibited by those two master composers. By observing idioms of melody and consonance it has been possible to identify a body of songs as a product of the Anglo-French musical *entente*. A new corpus of attributions to Binchois has been proposed.

These attributions, based solely upon musical evidence, are supported by an examination of the indices of concordant sources. For example, the anonymous 'Adieu, ma tresbelle maistresse' (*EscA* 27, *CMM* 77/12) has been attributed to Binchois on the basis of its Contratenor rhythm in the final breve. It is the only *chanson* in this collection concordant with the manuscript Munich, Bayerische Staatsbibliothek, Mus. MS Clm 14274 (*MüEm*) that is not ascribed to Binchois. It is found therein as a sacred *contrafactum*, like Binchois's 'Adieu, mes tresbelles amours' (*EscA* 26, *Rehm* 5) and 'C'est assez pour morir de dueil' (*EscA* 35, *Rehm* 11). In the Escorial *Chansonnier* it is placed between two Binchois pieces which are also in the Munich source. A second instance of an assured ascription to Binchois founded upon manuscript order and concordance is 'Depuis le congié que je pris' (*EscA* 10, *CMM* 77/5). It, too, was notated between two Binchois songs, 'Se la belle n'a le voloir' (*EscA* 9, *Rehm* 41) being concordant with Trent Codex 87 and 'Vostre alée me desplait tant' (*EscA* 11, *Rehm* 46) with Munich, Bayerische Staatsbibliothek, Mus. MS 3192 (*Mü*), fos. 13ᵛ–14ʳ. 'Depuis le congié que je pris' (*EscA* 10) has its only concordance also with this Munich collection, on the latter's preceding folio 13 (Table 3).

Other anonymous *rondeaux*, which in our analysis have evidenced Binchois's authorship, possess equally interesting relationships within the family of Burgundian manuscript collections that suggest a possible validation of attributions made

TABLE 3. *Family Relationships among MS Sources (i)*

| Concordant mss | fo. | EscA | |
		Anon., attr. to Binchois	Binchois
MüEm	5^r		26
	87^r	27	
	45^v		28
Tr 87	135^r		9
Mü	13^r	10	
	13^v–14^r		11

upon grounds of craft. 'De ceste joieuse advenue' (*EscA* 38, *CMM* 77/18) lies between two of Binchois's most popular songs: 'Dueil angoisseus' and 'De plus en plus'. In Trent Codex 92 it is recorded on the same folio (fo. 111^v) as 'Adieu, mes tresbelles amours', Binchois's *EscA* 26 (unascribed); on fo. 112^r is *EscA* 27, 'Adieu, ma tresbelle maistresse'. 'Dueil angoisseus' is concordant with *EscB*, fos. 15^v–17^r; on *EscB*, fo. 14^r is recorded 'Adieu, ma tresbelle maistresse', the anonymous 'Binchois' *EscA* 27. 'De plus en plus' is paired with 'Soyés loyal à vo povoir' (*EscA* 56, *CMM* 77/30), possibly by Dufay, in the Bodleian Library Can. misc. 213 (*Ö*), fo. 67^v. 'Bien viengnant, ma tresredoubtée' (*EscA* 34, *CMM* 77/16) is recorded in *EscB*, fos. 8^v–9^r, and on fo. 62^r of Paris, Bibl. nat., nouv. acq. fr., 4379 (*PC*); the only other concordance with the latter manuscript is on its fo. 64^v, Binchois's 'Adieu, adieu, mon joieulx souvenir' (*EscA* 28, *Rehm* 1), and that song was notated on a folio just preceding *EscA* 34, 'Bien viengnant', in *EscB*, fo. 7^r.

What we find is a connection, on the one hand between the placement of anonymous *rondeaux* that we attribute to Binchois and those already known to be his, and on the other between the concordances of these anonymous *chansons* in their manuscript order with other pertinent Escorial Manuscript pieces. From Table 4 may be derived the series *EscA* 26–8, 34, 37–9, 56. The *contrafacta* pertaining to *EscA* 26–8 have not been included.

TABLE 4. *Family Relationships among MS Sources (ii)*

| Concordant mss | fo. | EscA | |
		Anon., attr. to Binchois	Binchois
Tr 92	111^v	38	26
	112^r	27	
EscB	7^r		28
	8^v–9^r	34	
	14^r	27	
	15^v–17^r		37
PC	62^r	34	
	64^v		28
O	64^r	56	39

The anonymous *chansons* were found to be imbued with the influences of English music, but seven could be set apart for being especially related to the style:

EscA 40, 56, 62 presence of Hamm's 'English figure';
      10, 29, 34 other melodic idioms;
      52 kinship with the carol.

Of these, four go to Binchois, three to Dufay.

EscA 40, 'En bonne foy vous estez belle' (*CMM* 77/19), was assigned to the 'school of Dufay' in Ch. 4. The tonal architecture of *EscA* 56, 'Soyés loyal à vo povoir' (*CMM* 77/30), ultimately persuades us to place it within Dufay's sphere. Also qualifying is *EscA* 62, 'Jugiés se je doy joye avoir' (*CMM* 77/34), because of its melodic drive and 'English figure'.

Within a 'school of Binchois' may be gathered five songs. These reflect the early meeting of English and French practices and also certain traits which Binchois's style had in common with this *entente*. The carol-like *EscA* 52, 'Loez soit Dieu' (*CMM* 77/27), heads the list, a Continental example being the slightly dissonant *EscA* 33, 'Belle, esse dont vostre plaisir' (*CMM* 77/15). Related to them in melodic patterns of pitch and rhythm are *EscA* 36, 'Cuid'on que je poille castaingnes' (*CMM* 77/17) and 49, 'Je cuidoye estre conforté' (*CMM* 77/26). To these we add the lone Cantus of *EscA* 46, 'Je n'ay quelque cause de joye' (*CMM* 77/24), because of the concern therein for musical rhyme.

It must be remarked at this point that 'Je cuidoye estre conforté', *EscA* 49, was included in Rehm's edition of Binchois's songs among the 'Chansons mit zweifelhafter Autorschaft' (*Rehm* 60). Our system may authenticate one other of those five songs. *Rehm* 59, 'Va tost mon amoureux desir' (*EscB*, fos. 73ᵛ–74ʳ), was offered by Rehm, noting that, like 'Mon cuer chante' (*Rehm* 29), it is a setting of a poem by Charles d'Orléans, and also that Marix had previously published it as being by Binchois. One of the mid-cadences (m. 22) sports the ♫♩ with lower auxiliary note, and so the attribution may be founded on musical as well as on poetical grounds.

Fourteen *chansons* now may be added to the list of works attributable to Binchois. The criteria we established may be codified:

(*a*) Contratenor final iambic rhythm ♩ ♩ on a repeated pitch;
(*b*) rhythmic pattern ♫♩ involving lower auxiliary note;
(*c*) Cantus structural rhythmic order ♩ ♩. ♪
(*d*) systematic imitation;
(*e*) 'English' triadic figure, and melodic rhyme;
(*f*) Cantus late-dropping third;
(*g*) MS rank and relationship with concordances.

The attributions are divided into two classes, the second comprising those attributed by only one trait (Table 5).

TABLE 5. *The Attributions to Binchois*

Class I		a	b	c	d	e	f	g
EscA	2	x	x	x				
	10		x		x	x		
	12		x				x	
	14	x	x	x				
	23		x	x				
	27	x						x
	34		x			x		x
	38	x	x					x
	54		x	x				
Class II								
	8				x			
	29				x			
	58			x				
	59		x					
	61		x					

In Table 6 is outlined the Binchois repertoire of the manuscript Escorial V.III.24, as it appears after our attributions have been made. In Column I are listed songs already ascribed to Binchois. Columns II and III are devoted to the two respective classes of attribution. In Column IV is the 'school of Binchois'.

Tables 4 and 6 show very clearly the serial ranking of related compositions within the manuscript. The ten unique anonymous songs with French text that could be attributed to no specific composer's style or national influence also are grouped into sets: *EscA* 1, 4, 18–20, 42–5, 48. It is a significant fact that examination of the unique anonymous songs in the chief concordant manuscripts with comprehensive repertoires—those preserved in Bologna, Oxford, and Paris—reveals that these pieces too did not possess the characteristics which enabled us to separate the Escorial *Chansonnier*'s anonymous songs into two lots: twenty-two with referential qualities, twelve without.

Until more can be discovered about the circumstances and means by which songs were chosen to be recorded in notation, these findings must remain suggestive witnesses to sequences of common repertoires both within individual sources and among the manuscript family of Burgundian *chansons*.

The Anonymous Chansons

TABLE 5. *The New Binchois Repertoire of* EscA

I	II	III	IV
	2		
3			
7			
		8	
9			
	10		
11			
	12		
	14		
15			
16			
17			
21			
	23		
26			
	27		
28			
		29	
30			
32			
			33
	34		
35			
			36
37			
	38		
39			
41			
			46
47			
			49
51			
			52
53			
	54		
		58	
		59	
		61	

PART TWO

The Chanson *in Burgundian Court Culture*

Introduction

IN order to accept the concept that the court songs of the Escorial MS V.III.24 were 'Burgundian' in a dynastic sense, it must be appreciated that Burgundy was a distinct state, a powerful combination of Valois traditions and Flemish enterprise. Its four successive dukes were consumers of artistic products dedicated expressly to championing that state. At the same time, as Toynbee has pointed out, Burgundy's unique geographical situation between an emerging France and the established Hapsburg empire caused its internationally fused state dynamic to initiate a series of political struggles that would lead to a fission of European powers extending over four hundred and fifty years. So, too, the international fusion of musical styles in Burgundian court and cathedral created a new sound which eventually accelerated the proliferation of personal styles in Tonal composition. Philip the Good, the third Burgundian duke, fashioned a court culture in a dream, a pseudo-medievalism: Chivalric Humanism. The *chanson* coloured the atmosphere of that dream, and in turn the charade of a past-tense *courtoisie* relied upon the reiteration of its formulary verse to sustain the fantasy. It was possible for a confident musical individualist, as Binchois would appear to have been, to identify a Self through the vestigiary style of his composition. The unknown poet, however, hid feeling behind the mask of Style, a style of pathos in which a universal Model restrained an aspiring Humanism.

What was 'Burgundian' Music?

THE adjective 'Burgundian', applied to the songs that pleased the courts of the four *grands ducs d'Occident*, 1364–1477, must be understood as dynastic.

It took some time for musicologists to attach a valid label to the polyphony composed during the initial decades of the fifteenth century.[1] The oversimplification 'age of Dufay' used by Kiesewetter was succeeded by the only slightly less confined title of the Stainers' *Dufay and his Contemporaries*. This 'great man' tradition continued in currency in such publications as Reese's *Music in the Renaissance* (ch. 2, 'Composers, mainly of Northern France, in the Period of Dufay'), and *The New Oxford History of Music*, iii (Charles Van den Borren on 'Dufay and his school').[2] It has long been recognized that the term 'Netherlands School' was a misnomer, imposed by Romanticists such as Kiesewetter and Fétis upon a music written by French-speaking composers for courts founded in French culture.[3] An equally misleading invention was a 'Burgundian School' with varying emphases on 'French' and 'Flemish' characteristics; Paul Henry Lang referred to the French-texted songs of the 'Burgundians': 'the light and winged Gallic national traits are unmistakable in the simple yet cleverly composed songs of the musicians who gathered at the court of Dijon'.[4] Even in the *New Grove Dictionary* 'Burgundy' not only has its own article but also figures in the entries on 'France' and on the 'Low Countries'; Fallows names Binchois a 'Franco-Flemish' composer.

'Burgundian' and 'Netherlands' tend to imply racial traits that did not exist.[5] The decision by Henry Leland Clarke, that 'Franco-Flemish' is a cultural delimitation which 'fits the chief Northern Renaissance musicians with a snugness that is out of the question for either "Netherlandish" or "Burgundian" ',[6] is another example of what Reese knowingly referred to as 'all the hairsplitting to which

---

[1] See Clarke, 'Musicians of the Northern Renaissance', in LaRue, *Aspects of Medieval and Renaissance Music: A Birthday Offering to Gustave Reese*, 67–81. Of the previous publications dealt with in that paper, the most pertinent to our commentary are Lang, 'The So-Called Netherlands Schools', *MQ* 25 (1939), 48–59, and Van der Mueren, 'École bourguignonne, école néerlandaise au début de la Renaissance', *RBM* 12 (1958), 53–65 (esp. 56–7); material from Lang's article was taken over verbatim into his *Music in Western Civilization*, 175 ff.

[2] See especially Van den Borren's development of the statement 'Renowned for the greatness of his genius, Dufay's name was known to all' (*The New Oxford History of Music*, iii. 214).

[3] Lang, 'Netherlands Schools', 48–59; see the summary introduction to the article 'Low Countries', *New Grove*, xi. 261.

[4] Lang, 'Netherlands Schools', 51; and *Music in Western Civilization*, 178.

[5] As in Besseler, *Die Musik des Mittelalters und der Renaissance*, 184–227.

[6] Clarke, 'Musicians of the Northern Renaissance', 72; Brown, in his *Music in the Renaissance*, uses 'Franco-Netherlandish'.

historians' use of national names for the successive generations has given rise'.[7] At least the solution 'Franco-Flemish' reflects the fact that the first Valois Duke of Burgundy built his musical household upon Flemish musicianship, and names properly the political-geographical milieu for the recorded encounters of Dufay and Binchois after Chambéry, 1434: Brussels and Mons, 1444 and 1449.[8]

The historian, however, with his 'great men' and periodization by national adjectives like 'Franco-Flemish', muddles that very cultural phenomenon which he is trying to label: a tapestry woven not only of the dominant stylistic threads of French and Flemish composers but also of the interacting artistry of English, Swiss, German, Italian, Spanish, and Portuguese musicians that flavoured the song repertoires of the itinerant court of the third *grand duc*, Philip the Good (reigned 1419–67)—statesman, commander, and Maecenas.[9] Thanks to the archival research carried out by Craig Wright, it is established that Dufay spent twenty-eight of his last thirty-five years at Cambrai, whither he returned in 1439.[10] Dufay's service at Cambrai Cathedral balances the court career of Binchois, reaffirming that 'Burgundian' music pertains to the ecclesiastical and aristocratic centres within the domains of the Dukes and should not be confused with a particular reference to those centres specifically within the constituent duchy of Bourgogne and Franche-Comté. If this were accepted, there would be no longer any need to complain that the expression 'Burgundian' on the one hand 'fails to suggest French culture as a whole, and on the other it fails to suggest the North, where this culture was enhanced and carried with life'.[11]

Burgundy was a conspicuously distinct power, whose cultural expression was rooted in fourteenth-century Valois idioms but supported by the up-to-date commercial enterprise of its Flemish territories. The first Duke, Philip the Bold, had put together a political entity built upon French financial resources, administered by French personnel through institutions modelled upon those of France.[12] His son, John the Fearless, had recognized it as expedient to pursue the fortunes of his

---

[7] Reese, *Music in the Renaissance*, 9; Clarke himself approved of this statement: 'Musicians of the Northern Renaissance', 67.

[8] Wright, 'Dufay at Cambrai: Discoveries and Revisions', *JAMS* 28 (1974), 175–229, esp. 185, 203–4, 190; Fallows, *Dufay*, 64–6, whose opinion it is (p. 66) that even though Dufay's name does not appear in the court accounts book it is 'difficult to avoid the conclusion that he had official standing at the Burgundian court ...'.

[9] Payments to foreign minstrels and other musicians for service before the Burgundian household are recorded in Laborde, *Les Ducs de Bourgogne ... Seconde partie ... Preuves*, i. 170, 250 (England), 238–9, 470 (Portugal), 248, 260 (Cologne), 357 (Sicily); musicians of England, Burgundy, and Lombardy played for the Orleans court at Blois (ibid. iii. 341, 345). Among the seventy-two carts that transported the court from Dijon to Arras in April 1435, one was for the gear of the trumpets and minstrels (Vaughan, *Philip the Good*, 142). After an initial prolonged stay in St. Omer, 1439, and a stay in Dijon 1442–3, Philip moved between Bruges, Brussels, Lille, and The Hague, finally settling on Brussels only in 1459 until his death in 1467 (ibid. 135–6).

[10] Wright, 'Dufay at Cambrai', 192; 1439 also was the year in which Pope Eugenius IV allowed Philip's bastard brother Jehan de Bourgogne to assume the Bishopric of Cambrai (Vaughan, *Philip the Good*, 213).

[11] Clarke, 'Musicians of the Northern Renaissance', 69–70.

[12] Vaughan, *Philip the Bold*, 149. Philip habitually began his documents with the words 'Philippe, filz de roy de France' (ibid. 111).

duchy by dominating French affairs; he ruled from Paris through the agency of his wife in Burgundy and of his heir in Flanders.[13] The last Duke, Charles the Bold, would seek to complete the growing Franco-Burgundian estrangement, reopen the Hundred Years War and build a restored Lotharingian house upon a destroyed French monarchy.[14] It was Philip the Good who began to draw away from a Burgundian policy pursued in France and to create a Low Countries policy. The Treaty of Arras (1435), which united Armagnacs and Burgundians once more as Frenchmen, also prevented Philip from intervening in the subsequent affairs of the French monarchy, thus liberating his attention to dwell upon the Low Countries so successfully as to be hailed by a sixteenth-century historian *Conditor imperii belgici*.[15] Although a fief of the French crown, and ruled by a Duke steadfastly declaring loyalty as a French prince of the blood, the Burgundy of Philip the Good could regard itself as neutral in the Anglo-French hostilities after Arras.[16]

A description of the Burgundian Duchy based upon a Franco-Flemish bisection would deny the independent position on the European scene that was the achieved policy of its rulers. A definition of the Duchy's music following a similar principle would effect the same denial. The meeting of English, French, Dutch, and Italian repertoires and styles as collected in such a *chansonnier* as Escorial MS V.III.24 was brought about by those same personal policies of the cadet Valois household in whose service they were sung which had formed the political and territorial buffer state called Burgundy. Concerning the Burgundian economic prosperity that had its source in the variety of its rulers' territorial acquisitions, Calmette wrote that the 'multifarious products and activities of the mosaic of provinces . . . were complementary to each other . . .';[17] concerning Burgundian music, Lang considered it an artistic manifestation of a culture group of which the components were many and varied.[18] Although Chancellor Rolin and other of its administrative officials acknowledged that it was 'a somewhat uneasy alliance of widely divergent lands and peoples, where sectional interests were never dormant',[19] Burgundy was a 'state' in that it was a political entity 'under a single ruler and capable of acting in its own interests and of having its own relations with its neighbours . . .'.[20]

Richard Vaughan has listed the unifying elements of the Burgundian state as:

[13] Vaughan, *John the Fearless*, chs. 6, 7, 9.

[14] Calmette, *Les Grands Ducs de Bourgogne*, 234, 255–6; English translation in Weightman, *The Golden Age of Burgundy*, 172, 191.

[15] ibid. 190, 207, 220, 228; Eng. trans. 138, 150, 161, 167.

[16] ibid. 221; Eng. trans. 162. After 1422 Philip had 'emerged as a sort of *tertius gaudens*' (Vaughan, *Philip the Good*, 8).

[17] Calmette, *Les Grands Ducs de Bourgogne*, 343–4; Eng. trans. 255.

[18] Lang, 'Netherlands Schools', 53.

[19] Dickinson, *The Congress of Arras, 1435*, 55; some historians prefer to stress regional federalism as the Burgundian reality (Vale, Review of Vaughan's *Valois Burgundy*, TLS, 5 Sept. 1975, 1005).

[20] Vaughan, *Philip the Bold*, 238. For a critical discussion of Vaughan's interpretation of Burgundy as a state see the review of his books on the first two dukes by Brown, *Speculum*, 43 (1968), 544–50. On the building and maintaining of the Burgundian state see four articles by Armstrong collected in *England, France and Burgundy in the Fifteenth Century*: 'The Language Question in the Low Countries', 'Had the Burgundian Government a Policy for the Nobility?'; 'La politique matrimoniale des ducs de Bourgogne . . .', and 'La double monarchie France–Angleterre et la maison de Valois'.

(a) the combination of smaller units into larger ones, by dynastic marriage; (b) in 'French' Burgundy, a central government with regional administration of the French model, a single Order of Chivalry, and the Church; (c) in 'Flemish' Burgundy, a single currency, a States General of the Burgundian Netherlands, a policy of war, and a cultivation of the concept of the Duke as ruler over a populace of loyal subjects.[21] Burgundy existed as the product of a policy of 'self-aggrandizement',[22] the four generations of dukes presiding over its growing cosmopolitan spirit.[23] The music its courts consumed for entertainment likewise was 'Burgundian' in this dynastic sense.

Vaughan's statement suffices both for the second Burgundian Valois duke and for the music adorning the dynasty's courts and places of worship: 'There ought to be no controversy as to whether John the Fearless was a French or a Low Countries prince. He was both, and yet neither: he was Burgundian.'[24]

Burgundy as a state power, founded in a late medieval French hegemony but charting policies against its founding house, marked the dawn of a new era in Western civilization: the era of national encounters.

The outstanding political phenomenon in what Toynbee has called the 'Modern and post-Modern chapters' of our history was 'the epiphany of a Balance of Power between parochial states and the progressive inclusion of an ever widening circle of states within the field of force governed by this unitary system of inter-state power politics'.[25] The first round in the cyclic pattern of alternating phases of war and peace exhibited by this Modern Balance of Power was the Royal French Valois duel with the Burgundian Ducal French Valois, the latter 'thinly disguised under a Hapsburg Imperial mask'.[26] It was in this conflict that 'the original constellation of Modern Western Great Powers had crystallized out of a Late Medieval nebula surrounding the city-state cosmos in Northern Italy, Southern and Western Germany, and the Netherlands' and thus had become 'the overture to the rhythmic fluctuations of a Balance of Power in the subsequent course of Western political history'.[27]

Burgundy was an initial force in the gradual fissions of powers up to 1914, one result of which was 'a capacity to obtain for a society a maximum ... degree of cultural diversity . . .'.[28] The musical encounters experienced in Burgundy that made it an initial force in the gradual fission of distinct idioms within European composition were not so much those of contemporary collisions as of the welding together of the collective achievements of various national styles and a rediscovered expressive power of ecclesiastical chant. 'A great stylistic reconciliation took place: French, English, and Italian elements united and found new relationship to the

[21] Vaughan, *Valois Burgundy*, 27–31.
[22] Vaughan, *John the Fearless*, 287.
[23] Calmette, *Les Grands Ducs de Bourgogne*, 111; Eng. trans. 110.
[24] Vaughan, *John the Fearless*, 288.
[25] Toynbee, *A Study of History*, ix. 234.
[26] ibid. 237, 238.
[27] ibid. 237.
[28] ibid. 238.

Gregorian melodies, thereby opening a new chapter in the history of sacred music. The resulting spiritual art was of such profundity and sincerity as church music has seldom known.'[29] This 'reconciliation' of a nascent international culture with its dormant medieval ecclesiastical tradition is a prime example of that type of encounter, evocation, or *revenant* that Toynbee called a 'renaissance' by a 'feat of cultural necromancy'.[30]

The evocation of a dead culture by the living representatives of a civilization that is still a going concern proves to be a species of historical event for which the proper label is ... 'renaissances' ... The raising of a ghost by a necromancer produces an encounter between the medium and his oracle; and such encounters between the living and the dead are one species of a generic phenomenon which presents itself in a different specific form in encounters in which both parties are alive at the time when they collide with one another.[31]

The contribution made by its composers of sacred polyphony was a manifestation of Burgundy in a 'renaissance' dynamic.

The court *chanson* repertoire, however, was maintained consciously in direct continuity with the forms, sonority, and tone of Machaut's work.[32] The retention of what Lang terms 'late Gothic' structures and flavour, although softened and simplified by the reconciliatory influences of those national styles to which allusion has already been made, indicates on the part of both ducal consumer and song-maker a deliberate encounter that was at once a *revenant* and an archaism.

In the case of Archaism the *a priori* necessity of a corresponding difference between the respective psychological situations of the necromancer and the ghost of his own past self is still more obvious; for the very fact that the necromancer is recalling a past phase of his own life carries the implication that this resuscitated past and the living present represent different stages in the formation of a single cumulatively growing experience.[33]

Philip the Good adopted a 'resuscitated' Romantic pose in public pageantry, in tourney and banquet, in private cultural taste: fertile soil for a correlative musical 'experience'. 'It was in Burgundy that the forces of medieval culture converged to stage a final great manifestation of their heritage. ... the medieval spirit was so strongly embedded in the art of music that it would not develop organically outside the Gothic territory where it first grew to adulthood'.[34] *Chansons* such as those of the Escorial collection were the accompaniment and the tonal atmosphere in which were made the last gestures of International Court Culture.[35]

---

[29] Lang, 'Netherlands Schools', 51, and *Music in Western Civilization*, 178. See map of the dissemination of this international polyphony, ibid., 234–5; also map 9 of Collaer and Van der Linden, *Atlas historique de la musique*. See two articles in International Society for Musical Research, *Report of the Fifth Congress (Utrecht, 1952)*: Anglès, 'Les musiciens flamands en Espagne et leur influence sur la polyphonie espagnole', 47–54, and Moser, 'Die Niederlande in der Musikgeographie Europas', 296–302.

[30] Toynbee, *A Study of History*, ix. 2, 6.

[31] ibid. 4.

[32] Lang, 'Netherlands Schools', 178.

[33] Toynbee, *A Study of History*, ix. 5.

[34] Lang, 'Netherlands Schools', 176.

[35] The International Court Culture has been sketched in the opening chapters of Mathew, *The Court of Richard II*.

That the same group of composers could both participate in developing a vitally progressive 'reborn' art of sacred polyphony and perpetuate for ducal pleasure a music of an essentially medieval text, tone, and function was not only a paradox in the Arts but also a counterpart to the pattern of paradoxes that was Philip the Good and his Burgundy. One may draw a parallel with Burgundian social history. In economic policy the dukes 'took steps which imply the inspiration of pre-mercantilist notions . . . and the enterprise shown by Philip the Good in exploiting the mineral resources of his lands makes him a ruler far more "modern" than "medieval" '.[36] Yet, pseudo-feudal behaviour was an expected part of victory—as in 1453, when 2,000 Ghent burghers 'came and knelt in their shirts before duke Philip and begged for mercy. They undertook to pay an indemnity of 350,000 gold *ridders* and, in token of submission, to wall up one of the town gates and to keep another shut every Thursday.'[37]

In music history, as in any other historical discipline, it is impossible to apply a clearly defined periodization to years whose composers' creativity displayed renaissances both progressive and archaic.[38] The term Renaissance, as customarily associated with Classical Humanism, education, and antiquities, does not apply to Burgundy and its *chansons*. The two chief intellectual currents of Humanism cannot be found there: humanism *per se*, championed in the treatises reviving earlier styles and doctrines of practice, and Platonism, expounded in music by Ficino a century before Vincenzo Galilei and the Florentine Camerata.[39] It would be unwise, however, to hide the connotations of 'rebirth' in too generalized a terminology. A blanket of periodization such as the sequence Ancient, Medieval, Modern—in which scheme of time 'the Renaissance is the moment when Medieval moved into Modern'[40]—smothers the individuality of the constituent repertoires, and is as much an escape exit as the notion 'Age of Ambiguity', in which the shifts of emphasis that one is to consider the phenomena in all aspects of human activity do not conform to a single pattern.[41] The preference for placing the Burgundian composers in an Early Renaissance has stylistic justifications, to be summarized in

[36] Van Werveke in Postan, Rich, and Miller (eds.), *Economic Organization and Policies in the Middle Ages*, 343–4.

[37] Pirenne, *Early Democracies in the Low Countries*, 193; for a more detailed translation from a contemporary source see Vaughan, *Philip the Good*, 331–2.

[38] Of the many discussions on the historical 'Renaissance', several are particularly helpful: Ferguson, *The Renaissance in Historical Thought*; Ferguson, 'The Interpretation of the Renaissance: Suggestions for a Synthesis', in *Renaissance Studies* (originally published in *Journal of the History of Ideas*, 12 (1951) 483–95; Ferguson, 'The Reinterpretation of the Renaissance', in Werkmeister (ed.), *Facets of the Renaissance*, 1–18; Chabod, *Machiavelli and the Renaissance*, Part IV; Jacob, *Essays in the Conciliar Epoch*, ch. 10; Jacob, 'An Approach to the Renaissance', in *Italian Renaissance Studies: A Tribute to the late Cecilia M. Ady*, 15–47.

[39] Kristeller, in 'Music and Learning in the Early Italian Renaissance', in *Renaissance Thought*, ii, *Papers on Humanism and the Arts*, esp. 153–6, 157–60 (orig. pub. in *Journal of Renaissance and Baroque Music*, 1 (1947), 255–74, and reprinted in *Studies in Renaissance Thought and Letters* (Rome, Edizioni di Storia e Letteratura, 1956), 451–69).

[40] Hay, *The Renaissance*, 13.

[41] Morrall, *Political Thought in Medieval Times*, 119.

the Conclusion to this book.[42] And yet the paradoxical duality of 'Renaissance' is not sufficiently suggested for this to be a completely satisfactory term in justice to the *chanson* repertoire.

The court *chansons* of Valois France, and the resuscitation in Valois Burgundy of this genre that is our particular study, belonged to the opening years of transition in Western Civilization: an age 'containing much that was still medieval, much that was recognizably modern, and also, much that, because of the mixture of medieval and modern elements, was peculiar to itself and was responsible for its contradictions and contrasts and its amazing vitality'.[43] In the fourteenth and fifteenth centuries 'we must be prepared for the coexistence of the reactionary and the progressive, the obstinate remnants of the feudal world and the hopeful efficiencies of the new'.[44]

In this light it must be considered a most worthwhile analogy that the Burgundian *chanson* was the musical representative of Chivalric Humanism.

---

[42] 'Early Renaissance' is favoured by Clarke, 'Musicians of the Northern Renaissance', 80. Tilley, in *The Dawn of the French Renaissance*, 56–65, 72–3, saw 'premonitions' of the Renaissance in the activities of fourteenth-century Valois rulers; but this nascent Renaissance was the victim of the assassination of Louis of Orleans (1407), and Tilley is rather hard on the Burgundian Valois for ruining France's culture up to the return of Charles d'Orléans. Writers have tended to smell 'Renaissance' in every late fourteenth-century tapestry flower (e.g. Calmette, *Les Grands Ducs de Bourgogne*, 95; Eng. trans. 67).

[43] Ferguson, 'The Reinterpretation of the Renaissance', 16.

[44] Jacob, *Essays in the Conciliar Epoch*, 170; see the conclusion of Vaughan's *Valois Burgundy*, 227, for a succinct summation of the 'medieval' and 'progressive' character of the Valois Duchy.

Chivalric Humanism and the Chanson

THE term 'chivalric humanist' was employed by Alfred von Martin when referring to Burgundian chroniclers who wrote up their ducal masters as classical heroes reincarnated.[1] In the Prologue to *Gérard de Roussillon*, the best example of a traditional epic Burgundianized at the behest of Philip the Good, the 'prosifier' Waucquelin states the purpose of this genre: 'öir, dire, lire et recorder les beaulx dis et les bienfais des preudhommes, c'est la chose au monde qui plus fait toutes bonnes gens resjouyr; car les bons en deviennent meilleurs et les mauvais en amendent, et moult de biens en viennent'.[2] A man 'de tout bon sens et de toutes bonnes vertus plain' whose valour had conquered the French twelve times, Gérard had to be re-created as the ideal hero of the Burgundian chivalric age so that, by adopting his glory, this new age might be celebrated for generations to come. In Chivalric Humanism the aura of bygone greatness merged with renascent *superbia* and its desire for memorial in perpetuity. The heroes of courtly literature, such as those created by Marie de France, were distinguished both by their allegiance to an ennobling ethic of love and by 'the attribution to them of positive qualities conveyed to us by the use of a restricted number of epithets covering their military and their social lives: *proz, hardi, fier, bel, fort, vaillant, franc* and *curteis*'.[3] Likewise, the very surnames imposed upon the Valois Burgundian dukes—*Hardi, Sans Peur*—were 'inventions calculated to place the prince in a nimbus of chivalrous romance'.[4]

Medieval man had not been characteristically a dreamer. He had formalized ambition and its wars into rules of chivalry, its sexual instincts into a code of love. He had been what C. S. Lewis in his study *The Discarded Image* had called him: 'a builder of systems'. In these structures, however, was the fresh, genuine voice of their own epoch; the efflorescent love songs of the troubadours and minstrels and the free associations of knightly orders 'had sprung naturally from the necessities of

---

[1] Martin, *Sociology of the Renaissance*, 53.

[2] *Le Roman en prose de Gérard de Roussillon*, ed. Montille, 23. For the original epic hero see Meyer, *Girart de Roussillon* and Vaudin, *Gérard de Roussillon: Histoire et légende*; this 'legendary first duke of Burgundy' and twelfth-century 'hero of literature . . . had the merit, from the modern Burgundian point of view, of having quarrelled with the king of France' (Vaughan, *Valois Burgundy*, 163). An adverse criticism of the Burgundian prose romance, hence a criticism of the prime literary basis of chivalric humanism, was made by Gautier in his study *Les Epopées françaises*, i. 494–505, esp. 498–9.

[3] Burgess, 'Social Status in the *Lais* of Marie de France', in Burgess & Taylor (eds.), *The Spirit of the Court*, 73; q.v. 76.

[4] Huizinga, *The Waning of the Middle Ages*, 95.

medieval conditions'.[5] Burgundian chivalry, on the other hand, was a preservation
of a memory, a conscious medieval*ism*. For the chivalric spirit the Burgundian court
'avait assumé la tâche d'en être le refuge suprême, le dernier asile'.[6] It was to be a
tool of personal and dynastic power, employing the forms and symbols of the old
order 'to integrate the nobility of many far-flung provinces into the new State and
provide new outlets in the princely service for the ambitions of noblemen';[7] it could
'disguise well-adjusted calculations under the appearance of generous aspirations'.[8]

Descriptions of the effect produced by the spirit of chivalry upon the court of
Philip the Good and upon his own character and deeds have been published so
sufficiently as to require little restatement here.[9] Certain aspects of Philip's medieval
posture were of particular worth to the minstrels and chaplains who produced the
musical atmosphere for Burgundian chivalry. It was said of a true knight that he
was 'cortois et saige, et larges pour doner', and this phrase describing Raoul de
Cambrai was multiplied and garnished through subsequent centuries of romance
literature.[10] *Largesse* possessed its own niche in the System: in a thirteenth-century
manual on chivalry, *Les Ailes de prouesse* by Raoul de Houdenc, it was recorded
that *Prouesse* had two wings—*Largesse* on the right, *Courtoisie* on the left.[11] In the
Roman de la Rose (ll. 1173–5) Dame Largesse is of Alexander's lineage and linked
with King Arthur, both models for Philip the Good's chivalry:

> Largeice la vaillant, la sage,
> tint un chevalier dou lignage
> le bon roi Artu de Bretaigne

In the tradition of Arthurian romance *largesse* 'increases five hundred fold the value
of other good traits which it finds in the man who acquits himself well'.[12]

As a chivalric ideal, co-equal with good manners in deed and conversation,
largesse demanded from its late fourteenth- and fifteenth-century emulators a
prodigal generosity, without regard for personal wealth.[13] It may be suspected that
the minstrels of the twelfth and thirteenth centuries celebrated the legendary

[5] Baron, 'Fifteenth-Century Civilisations and the Renaissance', in Potter (ed.), The *New Cambridge
Modern History*, i, *The Renaissance, 1493–1520*, 58. The concepts of *amour courtois* and *Fin amours*
are surveyed by Topsfield, *Troubadours and Love*, 59–60, 87–9, 105–6, and 122–3.

[6] Doutrepont, *La Littérature française à la cour des ducs de Bourgogne*, 194.

[7] Baron, 'Fifteenth-Century Civilisations', 59.

[8] Huizinga, *The Waning of the Middle Ages*, 92. There was an immediate practical point in Philip
the Good's reviving the glorification of nobility. He had to replace the policy of justified tyrannicide
espoused by his father, who had been supported by the *Cabochiens*, with an ideal renewing the strength
of his aristocratic support (Cartellieri, *The Court of Burgundy*, 53).

[9] A survey of Burgundian court life has been offered by Vaughan in ch. 5 of his *Philip the Good*,
which, however, touches only briefly on its constituent activities.

[10] Gautier, *La Chevalerie*, 84.

[11] Quoted in Cohen, *Histoire de la chevalerie en France au moyen âge*, 147.

[12] '. . . la ou largesce avient, | Desor totez vertuz se tient, | Et les bontez que ele trueve | An prodome
qui bien se prueve | Fet a .V^c. dobles monter.'; Chrétien de Troyes, *Cligés*, ed. Micha, 7 (ll. 207–11);
trans. Comfort, *Arthurian Romances*, 93. A copy of *Cligés* was in the library of Philip the Good
(Doutrepont, *La Littérature française*, 66), possibly inherited from his grandfather (see Vaughan, *Philip
the Bold*, 194).

[13] Mathew, 'Ideals of Knighthood in late fourteenth-century England', in Hunt, Pantin, and Southern
(eds.), *Studies in Medieval History presented to F. M. Powicke*, 360. The major feasts of the Christian

liberality of ancient heroes in order to extract an enhanced *largesse* from their own *chevaliers*.[14] There are the lines from the poem *Echecs Amoureux* (*c*.1370–80) which declared the interacting doctrines of chivalry and musical *ethos*:

> musique a tel puissance . . .
> que'elle ramaine
> le cuer d'avarisce a larguesce[15]

The minstrels who entertained Philip the Good knew that they would be rewarded by the constraint upon him to fulfil the dictates of a fictionally inspired chivalry, in which he wore the halo as 'la perle des vaillans et l'estoile de chevalerie . . . large et libéral en dons . . . en toutes nations fit ses largesses . . .'.[16]

Aux menestrelz de révérend père en Dieu mons[r] l'evesque de Liège et pluseurs autres cy apres nommez la somme de quarante deux livres dix-sept solz du pris de XL gros monnoie de Flandres la livre laquelle du commandement et ordonnance de MdS leur a esté paiée, baillée et delivrée comptant particulièrement que icelui S par manière de largesse et courtoisie leur a donné à pluseurs fois et en divers lieux, ainsi et en la manière qui s'ensuit. C'est assavoir: ausdits menestrelz de mons[r] de Liège qui, par aucuns jours, ont esté devers MdS VII l. X s. Aux menestrelz de madame la duchesse de Bavière, tante de MdS qui icelui MS, estant à La Haye, ont par pluseurs fois joué devant lui de leurs instrumens VII l. X s. Aux trompetes et poursuivans du duc de Ghelres qui estoient venuz veoir MdS VII l X s.[17]

A second aspect of Duke Philip's chivalric stance that affected certain of his artistic retainers was the informality of his relationships with his *valets de chambre*. Jacques Vide, composer of 'Il m'est si grief vostre depart' (*EscA* 6), was numbered among this household.[18] Michault Taillevent, disciple of Alain Chartier and literary father of the *rhétoriqueurs* Chastellain and La Marche (who also were *valets de*

---

year, national feasts, and New Year were times that members of the court *familia* would have expected those bonuses which in England were called 'generall giftes' (Green, *Poets and Princepleasers: Literature and the English Court in the Late Middle Ages*, 23–5). Christine de Pisan cited John of Salisbury as her authority in advising the wise princess to be liberal in *largesse*, which should include comforting words (*The Treasure of the City of Ladies*, trans. Lawson, i. 19, 78).

[14] Gautier, *Le Chevalerie*, 85. Doubtless a similar motive lay behind Eustache Deschamps's complaints about the degenerate state of chivalry; instead of covetousness, generosity should return with a renewal of the old codes, for where *largesse* flourished no misadventure befell: Les bons chevaliers anciens | Eurent en leur compaignie | *Largesse* toute leur vie: | Si ne leur mesadvint riens. (Eustache Deschamps, *Œuvres complètes*, ed. Marquis de Queux de Saint-Hilaire, ii. 309); see Kilgour, *The Decline of Chivalry as shown in the French Literature of the Late Middle Ages*, 93. For examples of twelfth- and thirteenth-century imitators of the fabled *largesse* of Alexander see Whitney, 'Queen of Mediaeval Virtues: Largesse', in Fiske (ed.), *Vassar Mediaeval Studies*, 181–5.

[15] Abert, 'Die Musikästhetik der Echecs Amoureux', *Romanische Forschungen*, 15 (1903–4), 912.

[16] Chastellain, *Œuvres*, ed. Baron Kervyn de Lettenhove, vii. 222; the quotation is from the *Déclaration de tous les hauts faits et glorieuses adventures du duc Philippe de Bourgogne*. A critical view of Philip's generosity: 'Lui-même thésaurisa, mais princièrement, ignorant ce que contenaient ses coffres lourds; et nul n'a dépensé plus largement, à une époque où les pièces bourguignonnes étaient à peu près seules à circuler' (Champion, *Histoire poétique du quinzième siècle*, ii. 290).

[17] Laborde, *Les Ducs de Bourgogne . . . Seconde partie . . . Preuves*, i. 237–8; the entry is for 1425–6.

[18] Marix, *Histoire de la musique et des musiciens de la cour de Bourgogne sous le règne de Philippe le Bon, 1420–1467*, 161–2; Wright points out that although Vide was a talented composer, he was never listed as a member of the ducal chapel ('Vide', *New Grove*, xi. 712).

chambre), was listed in their company as *joueur de farces*;[19] a favourite poet of Philip, his small pay (6 *sous* per day)[20] should be suggested as a remuneration for 'piece-work', not a set salary. In addition to writers, painters, and musicians, the *valets de chambre* held a diversity of occupations: a *garde de joyaux, tapissier, cordonnier, chasublier, brodeur, chirurgien, marchant, garde-robe, fourreur de robes, tailleur, enlumineur*.[21] It was the pride of Chastellain that as *valet de chambre* he had the privilege of ducal intimacy denied to the court and visiting noblemen, which latter could be escaped by Philip for an evening passed in company with his valets.

Avoit de condition encore, qu'en chambre se tenoit clos souvent avec valets, et s'en indignoient nobles hommes. Le parement de cecy est honneste et juste; car luy, le plus honneste du monde, le fit, ce maintiens-je, par honnesteté de courage: il avoit aucunes fois des accidens pour lesquels il s'esseuloit, et desquels aux valets, non aux nobles gens, il appartenoit le congnoistre; se fust esvergondé devant les nobles, ce qui'il ne faisoit de sa privauté en basse main, car oncques de nobles hommes ne se souffrit oster soulier. Aussy en sa solitude valets ne l'eussont osé travailler, mais aux nobles il luy eust fallu complaire; car les honoroit de singulier honneur et amour.[22]

By sponsoring the child of his *valet de chambre* Jan Van Eyck at the baptismal font, Philip was personifying a paternalism that lay at the root of his relationships with these men.[23] Seen here is a residue, or revival, of the opportunity for personal contact enjoyed by selected vassals during the formative period of their feudal service, to live as a *nourri* of the lord—a word dating from Frankish Gaul but still occurring in the writings of Commynes.[24] Like the lovers in his *chansons*, the Burgundian court musician sacrificed personal will to service. As Cartellieri wrote, the court household 'was a State within a State ... not based like the Flanders communes, proud of their freedom, on the idea of opposition to the Prince. It was founded on the principle of unconditional and unqualified submission.'[25]

It is true that the centralized administration of the Burgundian territories wrought a unified culture quite dissimilar to the diversified Italian situation.[26] Also it is true that the Burgundian retention of chivalric systems delayed the emancipation of those middle-class economic and social forms based upon patriotism and civic loyalty which aided the promotion of the Italian Renaissance.[27] Nevertheless, when

---

[19] Champion, *Histoire poétique*, i. 287.

[20] ibid. 289.

[21] Laborde, *Les Ducs*, vol. i, p. xl.

[22] Chastellain, *Œuvres*, vii. 224–5.

[23] Laborde, *Les Ducs*, i. 342; the same honour was accorded a minstrel, or fool (ibid. xl). On the genuine feelings of responsibility demonstrated by the ruler in his role as paterfamilias see Green, *Poets and Princepleasers*, 29–32.

[24] See Bloch, *Feudal Society*, i. 224–7, esp. 226.

[25] Cartellieri, *The Court of Burgundy*, 73. In England the king's chamber operated not as an administrative but as a social nucleus within which the members of the *camera* formed an élite inner family in close relationship with their lord; see Green, *Poets and Princepleasers*, 33–7.

[26] Jacob, 'An Approach to the Renaissance', in *Italian Renaissance Studies: A tribute to the late Cecilia M. Ady*, 45.

[27] For this pattern as relating to the history of styles see Hauser, *The Social History of Art*, ii. 9–13.

Olivier de la Marche praised Philip the Good 'non pas comme prince ou personnage de prix ou d'estime, tel qu'il estoit, mais comme un homme chevalereux, tout plain de hardement et de prouesses',[28] he was participating in the chivalric humanist's endeavour to paint honour and glory in a blend partly classical, essentially feudal: Burgundy's peculiar 'antique garb'. The concern for *largesse* and imitation of vassalage as substitute for kinship are but two instances of the return to antiquity and its hero-worship that made Burgundian chivalry a 'naïve prelude' to the Renaissance.[29] Maurice Keen has found in the ceremonials of both medieval chivalry and what is referred to here as Chivalric Humanism a demonstration that 'the debate about the nature of nobility and the verdict which gave priority to virtue over lineage in the definition of its ultimate essence . . . were directly related and relevant to a complicated system designed to provide for the social recognition of virtue, in practice'.[30] Duke Philip entertained a genuine sense of honour, within his code; honour was a principal force in his diplomacy, notable in the Arras negotiations.[31] Apparently he was interested in the Italian humanist debate on the true nature of nobility, since in his library he possessed the *De Nobilitate* of Bonaccursius de Montemagno among several Italian humanist texts prepared for him in French translations.[32] The pursuit of ancestral virtue, the external pomp of *superbia*, the involvement of chivalric humanism with the dynastic goals of these cadet Valois, the cloud of tyrannicide that had hung over the scene since the assassination of John the Fearless: here was a Northern version of that despotism that marked the Burckhardtian interpretation of the Renaissance.[33]

Thus the age of feudalism is linked to the Renaissance. 'In cloaking itself in the fanciful brilliance of the heroism and probity of a past age, the life of the nobles elevated itself towards the sublime', and thus attempted 'to act the vision of a dream'.[34] Medieval man built systems. Renaissance man aspired to antiquarian splendour, and in Burgundy he rooted this aspiration in the fancy of a chivalrous ideal.[35]

While the position of Keen may be valid, that late medieval chivalry was not only a

[28] Quoted in Calmette, *Les Grands Ducs de Bourgogne*, 180; Eng. trans. Weightman, *The Golden Age of Burgundy*, 130.

[29] Huizinga, *The Waning of the Middle Ages*, 70.

[30] Keen, *Chivalry*, 177.

[31] Dickinson, *The Congress of Arras, 1435*, 75–7.

[32] Willard, ' "Nobility" as a Humanistic Problem in Burgundy', *Studies in the Renaissance*, 14 (1967), 33–48. This article serves to broaden the perspective of Kristeller's stress upon the diffusion of humanism through vernacular translations ('The European Diffusion of Italian Humanism', in *Renaissance Thought*, ii. 84–5, reprinted from *Italica*, 39 (1962), 1–20).

The library of Philip the Bold was mainly devotional and religious, with didactic works, standard medieval French literature, and a few romances based upon classical antiquity see Vaughan, *Philip the Bold*, 192–5); Philip the Good, who himself *did* read (Doutrepont, *La Littérature française*, 17, 467), caused the significant increase in his library to be in the collection and commission of prose romances (ibid. 18 ff., 45–7; see list in Tilley, 'The Prose Romances of Chivalry', in his *Studies in the French Renaissance*, 19–25).

[33] See Ferguson, *The Renaissance in Historical Thought*, 188–92, 202.

[34] Huizinga, *The Waning of the Middle Ages*, 40.

[35] ibid. 71.

cultural phenomenon but also had a social significance and so 'retained its vigour because it remained relevant to the social and political realities of the time',[36] nevertheless the 'reasoned and reasonably coherent social ideology' of the chivalric system had acquired 'a full measure of articulate literary expression'.[37] The *chanson* was the musical voice of literary chivalric humanism.

From the excessive glare of a rational civilization the romantic humanist retired into the twilight of a purely literary and imaginary world; he sought a distant dream world in the remote past in which he could give free rein to his wish-dreams. Because he was dissatisfied with his own times, as Petrarca explicitly admitted, he sought refuge in an idealized past, access to which was denied to the mass of the people. That was his way of cutting himself off from his day; unlike the revolutionary intellectual who seeks refuge in a Utopia of the future, he was the reactionary type, a *laudator temporis acti* cut off from reality and from life. Humanism was the ideal framework for such inclinations.[38]

Chivalric humanism was not fertile soil for originality or greatness in lyric poetry. Eustache Deschamps and Christine de Pisan had passed through the court of Philip's father and grandfather at a formative period in Burgundy's territorial development when these poets could have left no intellectual imprint; others, like the Savoyard Martin Le Franc, were institutional poets; the finest blossoms of fifteenth-century courtly lyric—the poetry of Charles d'Orléans—were written outside the Burgundian dominions. Of the court as a literary fount Doutrepont wrote: 'Elle n'enfante pas des génies; elle n'infuse pas à ses hommes des dons littéraires, mais elle agit sur leurs aspirations intellectuelles'.[39] If there was a truly 'Burgundian' literature, it was the product of the historians employed to recreate the prose romance, the narrative style of a former era redesigned for a new *toilette* in a language of dynastic flattery;[40] 'romanticism in action was replaced by romanticism in the intellectual field ...'.[41] For several centuries sexual relationships had possessed media of literary intellectualization through the doctrines of *l'amour courtois* expressed in theoretical treatise (the *De Arte Honeste Amandi* of Andreas Capellanus), allegory (*Le Roman de la Rose*) and lyric verse. The *chanson* at the Burgundian court was first of all an expected conducement to the perpetuated chivalric aura. The poem was aptly expressive of the adopted chivalric ideal, in that its stylized passion, now ossified into clichés of form and phrase, preserved sentiments and attitudes 'little accessible to the corrections of experience'.[42] Secondly, the *chanson* was functional in those extravagances of what Huizinga called 'applied literature': the banquets and shows, when Alexander, Jason and Gideon took on the physiognomy of the courts of Philip and Charles the Bold.[43] To

[36] Keen, *Chivalry*, 219.
[37] ibid. 177.
[38] Martin, *Sociology of the Renaissance*, 54–5.
[39] Doutrepont, *La Littérature française*, 502.
[40] ibid. 17, 27, 45–7, 72 ff.
[41] Martin, *Sociology of the Renaissance*, 57.
[42] Huizinga, *The Waning of the Middle Ages*, 131.
[43] The phrase is from Doutrepont, *La Littérature française*, 145 ff. A Parisian chronicler recorded (1461) that Philip 'stayed up at night almost till dawn, turning night into day to watch dances, entertainments and other amusements all night long.' (Vaughan, *Philip the Good*, 128). On 'applied literature' see Huizinga, *The Waning of the Middle Ages*, 253.

be present at a banquet of the Order of the Golden Fleece was to transcend the pettiness of a household in which Malebouche 'fait maint dommage'.[44] One was willingly manipulated into a surrender of the self, to be transported to a fantasy castle which Taillevent described as rivalling the fabulous palaces of Constantinople and of the age of Clovis: paved with silver, decorated with gold of Arabia, set with fine wood, ivory, crystal, beryl, diamonds, and other precious stones; the poet conjures a New Jerusalem.[45] It was music that triggered the desired affective response in this carefully orchestrated environment:

> Et depuis ne demoura guaires
> Que j'öy moult grant melodie
> De trompettes et de naquaires:
> Ne scay se c'estoit fantasie,
> Art magique ou nigromancie
> De si doulz accors entonner
> Mais puis la feste commenchie
> On n'eust point oÿ Dieu tonner.[46]

The medieval order had placed adventure within chivalry; its sphere of action was the Crusade. In chivalric humanism where true venture was impossible[47]—as witness the two disasters of Nicopolis and Agincourt, and the Crusade against the Turks that never materialized[48]—its sphere of action was the decorative tourney. The fifteenth-century tourney highlighted the mimetic element, certainly present in medieval jousts; instead of training for war in a mêlée there was polite tilting with blunted spear, as an escape from actual martial participation; team war-games, once a powerful force of political cohesion, were replaced by 'futile but highly stylized and ornamental pageants'.[49] The springtime of lyricism for *l'amour courtois* had been distinguished by a personal engagement in the affair at hand, a personal pride in the craft of its text and melody, whether the maker was a knight or a minstrel. But even as adventure became intellectualized, so the *chanson* progressively lost the personal mark of its creator.

When a fifteenth-century author did confess the desirability of making *chansons* it was an obvious literary pose, a declaration that he too was a poet within the tenets of *l'amour courtois*. So when Charles d'Orléans wrote, from prison, that to

---

[44] Jean Meschinot, cited in Champion, *Histoire poétique*, ii. 219, and Cartellieri, *The Court of Burgundy*, 74.

[45] Michault Taillevent, *Le Songe de la Thoison d'Or*, xii–xix (ed. Deschaux, *Un Poète bourguignon au XVᵉ siècle: Michault Taillevent*, 62–4).

[46] *Le Songe . . .* , xx (ed. Deschaux, *Un Poète bourguignon*, 64–5).

[47] Martin, *Sociology of the Renaissance*, 56.

[48] On the anachronism of crusading ambitions in Burgundy see Atiya, *The Crusade in the Later Middle Ages*, 170, 204, 438, 459–61, 481; for a résumé of Philip the Good and the Constantinople crisis see Calmette, *Les Grands Ducs de Bourgogne*, 222–4, Eng. trans. 162–4; Runciman, *The Fall of Constantinople, 1453*, 166–8; and Vaughan, *Philip the Good*, 358–72. Possibly it was the recognition of the impossibility of the vaunted task that led to what Keen suggested were 'high spirits overlaying a real chivalrous "intention" in the cynicism of at least one vow made at the Feast of the Pheasant' (*Chivalry*, 107).

[49] Denholm-Young, 'The Tournament in the Thirteenth Century', in Hunt, Pantin, and Southern (eds.), *Studies in Mediaeval History presented to F. M. Powicke*, 241.

obey the commandments of Love one had to be a diligent scholar, learning with all his power the feats of grace (*les gracieux tours*):

> C'est assavoir a chanter et dansser,
> Faire chançons et balades rimer
> Et tous autres joyeux esbatemens . . .[50]

he was merely restating 'authority':

> Chascuns doit fere en totes places
> ce qu'i set qui mieuz li avient,
> car los et pris et grace en vient.
>
> .   .   .   .   .
>
> Se tu as la voiz clere et saine,
> tu ne doiz mie querre essoine
> de chanter, se l'en t'en semont,
> car biaus chanter abelist mont;
> si avient bien a bacheler
> que il sache de vïeler,
> de citoler et de dancier:
> par ce se puet mout avancier.[51]

Chaucer interpolated his own lines for good measure:

> Among eek, for thy lady sake,
> Songes and complayntes that thou make;
> For that wol meve [hem] in hir herte,
> Whan they reden of thy smerte.[52]

The courtier had abandoned the field of song composition to his poets and chapel singers trained in musical crafts. It was sufficient that his courtesy encompass a willingness to hear the songs of love, to listen to the sounds of the minstrels:

> Qu'à Chevalier est cortoisie
> Qu'il oïe volentiers chançon,
> Notes et vieles et sons
> Et deduit de menestreus.[53]

Sir Degrevant could sing sweetly and play the lute, but in the tale it was not

---

[50] Charles d'Orléans, *La Retenue d'amours*, ll. 375–7 (*Poésies*, ed. Champion, i. 13).

[51] Guillaume de Lorris and Jean de Meun, *Le Roman de la Rose*, ll. 2180–2, 2191–8 (ed. Lecoy, i. 67–8). The passage is from the rules given to the lover by Amors.

[52] Chaucer, *The Romaunt of the Rose*, ll. 2325–8 (*The Complete Works*, ed. Skeat, i. 174).

[53] Raoul de Houdenc, *Les Ailes de prouesse*, quoted in Cohen, *Histoire de la chevalerie en France au moyen âge*, 148. In late fourteenth-century documents the song-maker was listed as a 'faiseur', some of these also named as 'menstrel de bouche': 'while little is known of them today, these musical bards, variously called "faiseurs des diz", "faiseur des ballades", and "faiseur des rondeaux", were an integral part of the late-medieval court scene. They composed their own text and music, and then performed their works before the lord and the princes of any of the other courts they happened to visit' (Wright, *Music at the Court of Burgundy, 1364–1419: A Documentary History*, 20).

recorded that he possessed the talent for composing songs or music.[54] The musicianship of the Burgundian dukes also would seem to have been digital; only Charles the Bold is known to have composed.[55]

The increased number of women present in the courts was another factor suffering the melodic love-message to decline into impersonality. Love's birth, progress, and engendered emotional experiences had been represented in troubadour poetry with stress upon the relation and attitude of the lover to the lady sought, and the effect on the lover's behaviour of this personal passion. Even the most ill-bred becomes courteous upon speaking with the lady, for he must appear worthy to become her vassal.[56] This vassalage, *domnei*, was intensely personal in its feudal origins, albeit a conception 'strengthened by the Latin love-elegists, who all call their mistresses *dominae*, and practise or advise complete subjection to the will of the beloved'.[57] He who enjoys love's pleasures must also expect love's servitude:

> quam iuvat inmites ventos audire cubantem
> et dominam tenero continuisse sinu

> Hic mihi servitium video dominamque paratam:
> iam mihi, libertas illa paterna, vale.[58]

A *vida* could declare: 'Raimbauz d'Aurenga si fo lo seingner d'Aurenga e de Corteson e de gran ren d'autrez castels. E fo adreich e eseingnaz e bons cavalliers d'armas e gen parlans, e mout se deleitet en domnas onradas e en domnei onrat; e fo bons trobaires de vers e de chansons, mas mout s'entendeit en far caras rimas e clusas.'[59]

As courtly literature became progressively more involved with the psychopathology of the lover, so grew the convention that, unable to be eloquent in the lady's presence, the male must withdraw to his private chamber in order to sing her praise to himself. So the knight in Chaucer's *Book of the Duchess*, having declared '. . . I durste noght | For al this worlde telle hir my thoght',[60] enters into his own privacy:

> But, for to kepe me fro ydelnesse,
> Trewly I did my besinesse

[54] *Sir Degrevant*, ll. 37 ff., ed. Casson (EETS 1949), 221; this reference is in Mathew, *The Court of Richard II*, 125. At the English court the king's henchmen received musical training, while at the French courts some secretaries were singers, others poets (Green, *Poets and Princepleasers*, 58, 69, 81–5); Binchois was made an Honorary Secretary by Philip the Good (Fallows, 'Binchois', 710).

[55] Charles the Bold received a harp at the age of 7–8 years: 'A Jehan de la Court, harpeur de madame la comtesse de Charollais pour une harpe que ma dite dame a fait prendre et achetter de luy et donner à MS le comte de Charrolois pour soy jouer et prendre son esbatement' (Laborde, *Les Ducs*, 380; entry for 1440–1). For Charles the Bold as composer see Fallows, *Dufay*, 73–4.

[56] See passages from Bernart de Ventadorn *inter alia* as quoted in Dodd, *Courtly Love in Chaucer and Gower*, 8 ff.

[57] Highet, *The Classical Tradition*, 578.

[58] Tibullus, I. i. 45–6 and II. iv. 1–2, cited after Cornish, Postgate, and MacKail (eds.), *Catullus, Tibullus and Pervigilium Veneris*, 194, 266.

[59] Hill and Bergin (eds.) *Anthology of the Provençal Troubadours*, 2nd rev. edn., i. 58.

[60] Chaucer, *Book of the Duchess*, ll. 1149–50 (*The Complete Works*, ed. Skeat, i. 316).

> To make songes, as I best coude,
> And ofte tyme I song hem loude;
> And made songes a gret del . . .[61]

In the superlative worth of the lady was quantified the self-eminence of the lover, his heart and mind bared 'with all the intimacy of the confessional',[62] the narcissism of this poetry is implicit in the lyric's egocentric intimacies:

> Algates songes thus I made
> Of my feelings, myn herte to glade;[63]

It would continue a romantic fiction to agree that *l'amour courtois* brought about 'an evident progress in feminine destiny—progress closely interwoven with that of general civilization'.[64] The status of women in the Burgundian dynasty remained bound by the feudal custom of political child betrothals; there is, too, the contemporary testimony that Philip the Good had thirty mistresses (not permitted to be at court) and seventeen acknowledged bastards.[65] However, the elaborate dances, tourneys, Mayings, and love-courts of the late Middle Ages did flourish because of the lady's exposure to society. In *Le Livre des faits du bon chevalier Messire Jacques de Lalaing* we read that jousts were introduced into the French court at Nancy in imitation of the Burgundians (1444); the conversation between the counts of Maine and Saint Pol doubtless was prompted by a fear of personal shame, once the ladies had heard of Burgundian glories:

Vous avez oy raconter devant les dames comment, un chacun jour, toutes festes, joustes, tournois, danses et carolles se font en la cour du duc de Bourgongne, et vous voyez que nous, qui sommes en grand nombre en la cour du roy, ne faisons que dormir, boire et manger, sans nous exercer au mestier d'armes, qui n'est pas bien seant à nous tous d'ainsi passer notre temps en huiseuse.[66]

The Monk of Saint Denis seemed overwhelmed by the beauty and dress of the ladies assembled for a three-day tourney given by Charles VI. He recorded that the knights, who had been chosen by the King to enter the lists, giving the event as much *éclat* as possible, awaited the ladies and conducted them to the lists to imitate the gallantry of ancient worthies: 'ut in priscorum dissolucionis lasciviam lacius evagerent'.[67]

The presence of large groups of ladies not only restimulated the shows of

---

[61] ibid., ll. 1155–9.

[62] Valency, *In Praise of Love*, 37; q.v. 26–7.

[63] *Book of the Duchess*, ll. 1171–2 (*The Complete Works*, ed. Skeat, i. 317).

[64] Luchaire, *Social France at the Time of Philip Augustus*, 350.

[65] Reiffenberg, *Enfants naturels de Philippe le Bon*, 172, is the source for the references more customarily cited: Calmette, *Les Grands Ducs de Bourgogne*, 179, Eng. trans. 129, and Cartellieri, *The Court of Burgundy*, 55; Vaughan would suspect that the numbers be reduced to twenty mistresses and fifteen bastards (*Philip the Good*, 133). Acknowledgement and public appointment of 'natural' males was a Valois policy; see Harsgor, 'L'Essor des bâtards nobles au XVᵉ siècle', *Revuew historique*, 253 (1975), 319–54.

[66] Chastellain, *Œuvres*, viii. 41.

[67] *Chronique du religieux de Saint-Denys, contenant le règne de Charles VI, de 1380 à 1422*, Bellagnet, i, 594–9.

chivalric humanism but also encouraged the formation of literary clubs, *cours amoureuses*.[68] In the charter were sworn 'humilité et leauté, a l'onneur, loenge, recommendacion et service de toutes dames et damoisselles'.[69] The association of lords and poets reputedly was founded on St Valentine's Day, 1400, at the Paris *hôtel* of Philip the Bold, who was chief *conservateur* together with Charles VI and Louis de Bourbon; among others, the dukes of Berry and Orleans, William IV of Bavaria, John the Fearless (then Conte de Nevers), and his son Philip (the Good), not yet ten years old. Although initiated to counter the gloom of a plague, this Burgundian-inspired exercise in fictional chivalry was part of a feminist trend at the turn of the century, in reaction to the prevalent clerical denigration of *courtoisie*. The *Prince d'Amour*, a Burgundian retainer, was described as having with him 'musiciens et galans, qui toutes manieres de chancons, balades, rondeaux, virelais et autres dictiés amoureux savoient faire et chanter, et jouer en instrumens melodieusement'.[70] There is little proof with which to validate Doutrepont's opinion that these evenings must have continued over into Philip the Good's court.[71] At the least, the atmosphere was engendered within which the *chanson* could function, part of the new International Court Culture of feminine presence.[72]

Music in Valois chivalric humanism was clearly adumbrative of its role in sixteenth-century England and Italy as society's 'food of love'.[73] The pristine personality, the personal sentiments and values in the courtly phrases, already blunted by several centuries of doctrinal codification and allegorical symbolism, became more stilted and vacuous in a game of applied literature. Addressed to no particular member of the company, the *chanson* was to help constitute the sensual air enveloping the new group-eroticism to which chivalric humanism had given birth, a sensuality and eroticism so well captured by Christine de Pisan as she depicted the Duke of Orleans's Banquet of the Rose (14 February 1401):

> La ot moult bons menestrelz plus d'un paire
> Qui haultement faisoient le repaire
> Tout retentir.
>
> .   .   .   .   .   .

---

[68] See Piaget, 'La *Cour amoureuse* dite de Charles VI', *Romania*, 20 (1891), 417–54, and 31 (1902), 597–603; also Poirion, *Le Poète et le Prince*, 37–43, esp. 40; Green, *Poets and Princepleasers*, 120–4; and Wright, *Music at the Court of Burgundy*, 134–7.

[69] Piaget, 'La *Cour amoureuse*', *Romania*, 31 (1902), 599.

[70] Leroux de Lincy and Tisserand, *Paris et ses historiens aux XIVᵉ et XVᵉ siècles*, 234, as reprinted in Piaget, 'La *Cour amoureuse*', *Romania*, 20 (1891) 449, Marix, *Histoire*, 98–9, and Pirro, *La Musique à Paris sous le régne de Charles VI, 1380–1422*, 24. The Prince of Love was Pierre de Hauteville, *écuyer d'écurie* to the first two dukes, then councilor and *maître d'hôtel* to Philip the Good (Marix, *Histoire*, 98–9). Two composers whose *chansons* were collected in the Oxford Canonici MS (O) probably were of this company: Briquet and Charité (Pirro, *La Musique à Paris*, 24–5).

[71] Doutrepont, *La Littérature française*, 366–9. Marix, *Histoire*, 98–9, mentions one: at the ducal *hôtel* at Brussels, 1460.

[72] Mathew, 'Ideals of Knighthood', 28–9.

[73] On music and eroticism as implied in Castiglione's *Libro del Cortegiano* (1528) see Leichtentritt, *Music, History and Ideas*, 81–2, and Kemp, 'Some Notes on Music in Castiglione's *Il Libro del Cortegiano*', 357.

> Et en dançant leurs cuers entrelaçoient
> Par les regars que ils s'entrelançoient.
>   Qui veist jolies
> Femmes dancier a contenances lies
> Si gayement de manieres polies,
>
>   .   .   .   .   .
>
>   Les contenances
> De ces amans a chascun tour des dances,
> Muer coulour, faire maintes semblances,
> Moult en prisast les doulces ordenances.
>   Et puis après
> Les menestrelz, qui bien jouoient très
> Parmi chambres et parmi ces retrès,
> Oist en chanter hault et cler a beaulz trèz
>   Bien mesurez.[74]

In another work, however, she warned the ladies at court that it was 'established custom' for all men to attempt seduction, to give the impression of being captivated with love, and to say that they will serve when in reality they are self-serving.[75] Venus, music, and the courtier were sufficiently interwoven by 1405 to necessitate this rebuke:

in tua curia domina Venus solium occupans, ipsi eciam obsequntur ebrietas et commessacio, que noctes vertunt in diem, continuantes choreas dissolutas. Hec maledicte et infernales pedissece, curiam assidue ambientes, mores viresque enervant plurium, et impediunt sepius ne milites vel scutiferi delicati adeant expediciones bellicas, ne in aliqua parte corporis deformentur.[76]

Missing in the Burgundian *chanson* are allusions to classical heroes, such as are found in fourteenth-century repertoires.[77] Apparently in chivalric humanism it was preferred to realize 'humanistic' personalities in more tangible media: visual art and applied literature. Philip the Good, heir to his grandfather's tapestries depicting Jason, Hector, Alexander, Semiramis, *et al.*,[78] was engaged in a medieval task when he traced his ancestry back to Hercules and conjured the ideal into flesh through the necromantic *Ordre de la Toison d'Or*.[79]

Missing is the author's licence for explicit sexual encounter, which spiced a distinct vein of late medieval literature and which was occasionally traceable within the court song:

---

[74] Christine de Pisan, *Œuvres poètiques*, ii. 52–3 (*Le Debat de deux amans*, ll. 101–3, 122–6, 132–40).

[75] Christine de Pisan, *The Treasure of the City of Ladies*, trans. Lawson, 75, 90, 102.

[76] *Chronique du religieux de Saint-Denys*, iv. 268; extract from a sermon preached by an Augustinian monk, Jacques Legrand, before Queen Isabella of France and her ladies.

[77] e.g. two *ballades* by Trebor, 'Se Alixandre et Hector' and 'Se July Cesar', dedicated to Gaston Phoebus, Comte de Foix (1331–91), *CMM* 53. i/112, 113, and Greene, *Polyphonic Music of the Fourteenth Century*, xviii/38, xix/66.

[78] Calmette, *Les Grands Ducs de Bourgogne*, 94, Eng., trans. 66, and Vaughan, *Philip the Bold*, 191.

[79] Seznac, *The Survival of the Pagan Gods*, 25–6.

> Joieux de cuer en seumellant estoye
> Quant je sentoie vostre tresdoulce alayne
> Et vo gent corps, ma dame soveraine,
> Qu'entre mes bras si doucement tenoye.[80]

Missing, too, is the lusty naturalism of the next generation:

> Le joly tetin de ma dame
> A touché nu a nu le myen,
> De quoy trop heureulx je me tien
> Quant il m'en souvient, par mon âme.[81]

Not yet the gay brunette, *joie de vivre* and overall simplification of the later *chanson*'s model and content, the *rapprochement* between 'learned' and 'popular' audiences to which Dufay and Binchois only rarely conceded (respectively, in 'La Belle se siet' and 'Files a marier').[82] In the repertoire of the manuscript Escorial V.III.24 the Lady's eyes are her only physical feature explicitly praised, this being a weak residue of earlier imagery pertaining to the doctrine that it is those *rians yeux* that wound the Lover ('Je vous salue, ma maistresse', *EscA* 2 (*CMM* 77/2)).[83] The *chansons* in the courts of John the Fearless and Philip the Good still had their part in *courtoisie*, whose literature, fashion, and conversation 'formed the means to regulate and refine erotic life': to formalize love being even more 'a social necessity' the more vehement the emotions and passion of the situation.[84] A young courtier, ambitious for social profile, aspired to sing a lover's song because it would elevate him in esteem above his fellows.

> Joenne et moult enfant estoye
> Quant ja grant peine mettoye
> A amoureux devenir.
> Pour ce qu' ouoye tenir
> Les amans plus qu'autres gens
> Et gracïeux entre gens
> Et mieux duis, si desiroie
> A l'estre; . . .[85]

A man more conscious of the grosser realities of his 'courtly' setting recognized that

[80] *Virelai* 'Joieux de cuer' by Solage, *CMM* 53. i/101 and Greene, *Polyphonic Music*, xix/97; the physical encounter separated two degrees from reality: first, by its setting in a love-dream, and second by the floral imagery employed.

[81] Jeppesen (ed.), *Der Kopenhagener Chansonnier: Das Manuscript Thott 291 der königlichen Bibliothek Kopenhagen*, 32–3.

[82] *CMM* I. vi/12 and *Rehm* 55; see Lesure, *Musicians and Poets of the French Renaissance*, 13–15. Note, in passing, the pseudo-rustic charm of the opening of *EscA* 36: 'Cuid'on que je poille castaingnes | Entreus que je pense à amours' (*CMM* 77/36).

[83] See also Binchois's 'Vostre tres doulx regart plaisant' (*EscA* 7, *Rehm* 47), Dufay's 'Estrinez moy' (*EscA* 60, *CMM* I. vi/58) and the anonymous 'Va t'en, mon désir gracieux' (*EscA* 61, *CMM* 77/33). Characteristically it is the Netherlandish song *EscA* 55 (*CMM* 77/29) that discusses the kiss.

[84] Huizinga, *The Waning of the Middle Ages*, 109; q.v. 108–13. It should be noted that troubadour/trouvère imagery was far from free of allusions to physical sexual activity: see, for example, Lazar, *Amour Courtois et 'Fin Amours'*, 118–34.

[85] Christine de Pisan, *Le Livre du Duc des vrais amans*, in *Œuvres poétiques*, iii. 60–1.

music, like apparel, tapesteries, tourneys, and imaginary crusading, could be a sanitizing agent; as Deschamps called it, 'la medecine des .VII. ars'.[86] The lady, then, although the idealized subject of address, was not the *persona* most crucial to the self-interested lover at play in the game of love.[87]

Disenchanted contemporaries wrote of the prevalence of lust at those courts in which was maintained the charade of chivalry—a chivalry in decay wherein the princes and married nobles vied with each other in amatory conquest—'Lors le péchié de luxure regnoit moult fort et par especial ès princes et gens marriés, et estoit le plus gentil compaignon qui plus de femmes scavoit tromper et avoir au moment, qui plus luxurieux estoit.'[88] And certainly Philip the Good preferred the fleece of Jason to the fleece of Gideon:[89]

le duc Phelipe de Bourgoinge estoit pour ce temps moult resmeu, et estoit de sa personne très abille en toutes choses donc il se vouloit mesler, et par espécial de dancer et de bien jouster, passoit tous ceulx de son hostel. Et avec ce estoit fort amoureux sur les dames, et mesmes à ceste feste fut amoureux de la contesse de Salesbri . . .[90]

As a man, Duke Philip was characterized by Chastellain as being possessed with 'le vice de la chair . . . Ce qu'il en vouloit, luy venoit, et ce qu'il en désiroit, s'offroit';[91] as principal actor in the theatrical world of chivalric humanism he was known by his circle as 'le plus loyal serviteur d'amours et des dames qui au siècle vive'.[92]

> Je Phelippes de Bourgongne, tel est mon nom tenu,
> Qui en aymer me suis tout mon temps maintenu
> Ou le dieu d'Amours m'a doulcement soustenu.[93]

In the prose romance *Paris et Vienne*, Paris, conscious of his untitled status (although born of a noble family), decides to serenade Vienne incognito. He and his friend Edward place themselves by night under her window 'faisant oubades de leurs chansons, quar ilz chantoient souveraynement bien, et puys jouoyent de leur instrumens chanssons mellodyoses, comme ceulx qui de celluy mestier estoient les

---

[86] Page, 'Machaut's "Pupil" Deschamps on the Performance of Music', *Early Music*, 5 (1977), 488; see Olson, 'Deschamps' *Art de Dictier* and Chaucer's Literary Environment', *Speculum*, 48 (1973), 714–23.

[87] On the game of love see Green, *Poets and Princepleasers*, ch. 4.

[88] Jacques du Clercq, *Mémoire*, ed. Michaud and Poujoulet (Paris, 1836–40), ii. 204, as quoted in Kilgour, *The Decline of Chivalry*, 268.

[89] Kilgour, *The Decline of Chivalry*, 252–3.

[90] Pierre de Fenin, *Mémoires, comprenant le récit des événements qui se sont passés en France et en Bourgogne sons les règnes de Charles VI et Charles VII (1407–1427)*, ed. Dupont, 225. The occasion recorded was the wedding of Jehan de la Trimoulle, grand *maître d'hôtel* and chamberlain to John the Fearless and Philip, 17 July 1424; Salisbury, Bedford, and 'le conte de Suffort' (Suffolk) attended.

[91] Chastellain, *Œuvres*, vii. 224; that this character assessment was made by a leading Burgundian chivalric humanist supports the veracity of Pierre de Fenin's reporting (in the previous quotation), which otherwise might be questionable on the grounds of anti-Burgundian bias.

[92] As quoted in Cartellieri, *The Court of Burgundy*, 86; on the theatricality of decadent chivalry ('a literary mask hiding a sordid reality') see Kilgour, *The Decline of Chivalry*, 195–6, 227–8, 242, 257.

[93] Motto in René, duc d'Anjou, *Livre du Cuer d'Amours Espris*, ed. Smital and Winkler, ii. 103; see also Cartellieri, *The Court of Burgundy*, 87.

maistres'.[94] Desiring to learn the identities of the mysterious serenaders, Vienne's father, the dauphin, mounts several *fêtes* to which all the nobles of the land should come and demonstrate their musical skill, for those who could make such sweet music must be *gens joyeuses et notables*. Of course, Paris and Edward do not show their hand, being *gentilz hommes et saiges*. It is only after the failure of her father's song festivals that Vienne realizes that *her* singers had meant something more than the vicarious entertainment of minstrels' professional services or courtiers' chivalric poses. As she remarks to her confidante: 'certeynly they come not hyther for nought, for they love outher you or me'.[95]

Vienne was surprised that personal sincerity would be intended in a love-song, where sincerity customarily lay in the fidelity of its emotion to the poetic images of *courtoisie*.[96] The lover's song was still incorporated within the literature of True Love, 'a rhetorical fiction set to music'.[97] The lover as an individual was as yet half awake beneath that veil, 'woven of faith, illusion, and childish prepossession,' the melting of which Burckhardt hailed as the dawn of the true Renaissance.[98]

---

[94] Robert Kultenbacher, 'Der altfranzösiche Roman Paris et Vienne', in *Romanische Forschungen*, 15 (1904), 321–688; the episode of the serenade, 396–9.

[95] Leach (ed.), *Paris and Vienne: Translated from the French and printed by William Caxton*, EETS 234, p. 4. Caxton's translation, dated 1485, afforded local realism: e.g. his Paris and Edward play recorders. In Caxton the dauphin seeks the serenaders amongst the minstrels of the land: again, a touch of contemporary realism indicating that a serenading *nobleman* was unexpected. Literary evidence indicates that the story was well known by 1400 (Leach, pp. xxi–xxii); for dates of fifteenth-century manuscripts and printed sources see ibid., pp. xvii ff., and Kultenbacher, 'Der altfranzösische Roman Paris et Vienne', 362.

[96] Valency, *In Praise of Love*, 115.

[97] ibid. 117.

[98] Burckhardt, *The Civilization of the Renaissance in Italy*, 100. For discussion of this 'veil' image see Jacob, 'An Approach to the Renaissance', 18 ff., and Ferguson, *The Renaissance in Historical Thought*, 189 ff.

8

The Chanson *and* la Courtoisie

CHIVALRIC Humanism perpetuated the allegorical characters of *Le Roman de la Rose*. They peopled its heraldic display:

> Cottes d'armes avoit de Joye
> Ou figuree estoit Liesse;
> De gens y avoit grant monjoye
> Ou furent Bel Acueil, Proesse,
> Deport, Melodie et Noblesse,
> De parvenche habilliés tous vers
> Et de marjolaine a largesse
> Estoient leurs chapiaulx couvers.[1]

In the songs of the manuscript Escorial V.III.24 the cast of characters included Dangier (six appearances), Bel Acueil (three), Liesse, Envie, and Male Bouche (one each).

Dangier and Bel Acueil retained their salient characteristics, but mainly expressed through stock patterns which had become conventionalities of convenience for the song-maker. No longer active in a developed allegory, these *personae* in fifteenth-century court song were referential or reminiscent symbols. In their most unremarkable employment they were tags for a customary state in the play of courtly wooing, as may be seen in the role of this pair in Binchois's 'C'est assez pour morir de dueil' (*EscA* 35, *Rehm* 11):

> Quant nulle foys je ne la voy
> Que dangiers n'y ayt tousjours l'ueil
>
> Jamais il n'eslonge le seul
> Du lieu où remaint bel acuel

And likewise that of Bel Acueil in 'Je vous salue, ma maistresse' (*EscA* 2, *CMM* 77/2):

> Je vous salue, ma maistresse,
> Et mon cuer devers vous s'en va.
> Pour raconter la distresse
> Dont vo bel acuel le priva.

The use of Dangier in 'Je cuidoye estre conforté' (*EscA* 49, *CMM* 77/26) is more

---

[1] Michault Taillevent, *Le Débat du cœur et de l'œil*, lxii (ed. Deschaux, *Un Poète bourguignon au XV⁰ siècle: Michault Taillevent*, 213).

developed, as this song deals with the power of Dangier to cause suffering not only
by effecting separation between the wooer and his goal but also by inflicting actual
physical harm ('Maulgre dangier qui tant me blesse' (*EscA* 24, *CMM* I. vi/60)):

> Dangier ma'a bien d'un hault osté
> Et d'esperance debouté
> Pour ce que de moy l'estoit donnée

By such lines would be recalled the fear and recriminations of the Lover when first
threatened with Dangier's attack:

> N'osai ilec plus remenoir
> por le vilain hideus et noir
> qui me menace a asaillir.
> La haie me fet tressaillir
> a grant pooor et a grant heste.
> et li vilain crolle la teste
> et dit, se ja mas i retor,
> il me fera prendre un mal tor.
>
> .   .   .   .   .
>
> De ma folie me recors,
> si voi que livrez est mes cors
> a duel, a poine et a martire;
>
> .   .   .   .   .
>
> Nus n'a mal qui Amors n'essaie;
> ne cuidez pas que nus conoisse,
> s'il n'a amé, qu'est grant angoisse.
> Amors vers moi mout bien s'aquite
> de la poine qu'il m'avoit dite.[2]

and again, after he had kissed the Rose, when Dangier pursued him in earnest,
driving away Bel Acueil:

> Lors s'est Dangier en piez dreciez
> semblant fet d'estre corociez,
> en sa main a un baton pris
> et vet cerchant par le porpris
> s'il trovera sentier ne trace
> ne pertuis qui a bouchier face.
> Des or est changiez mout li vers,
> quar Dangier devient plus divers
> et plus fel qu'il ne souloit estre.
> Mort m'a qui si l'a fet irestre,
> car je n'avré ja mes loisir
> de veoir ce que je desir.
> Mout ai le cuer du ventre irié
> dont j'ai Bel Acueil adirié[3]

[2] Guillaume de Lorris and Jean de Meun, *Le Roman de la Rose*, ed. Lecoy, ll. 2927–41, 2944–8.
[3] ibid., ll. 3737–50.

Bel Acueil and Dangier personified facets of the Lady's personality with which the aspiring Lover must contend successfully before acquiring his desire. *Bel acueil*, in general courtesy, was the art of welcome, the ideal friendliness 'based on the recognition of the essential connaturality of all men'.[4] In the narrower amatory system it represented a 'fair welcome', in which the Lady opened herself to pleasant conversation:

> Mi dons, per son bel aculhir
> E per son belh plazent esguar;[5]

> Hé, bel acueil, ou je prens noureture,
> Vo cuer vueilliez de m'amor alumer[6]

Whither the Lady's 'fair welcome' led was greatly dependent upon the reaction of her 'danger': the 'real enemy who cannot be flattered or overcome, who must be kept asleep because, if he wakes, your only course is to take to your heels, the everpresent dread of lovers and the stoutest defence of virgins'.[7] Guillaume de Lorris gave Dangier the physical attributes common to a *vilain*, still traceable in the unchivalrous terminology subsequently reserved for him: 'Faulx Dangier', (Merques, 'Las! comment porraye', *EscA* 22), 'Dangier le rebelle' ('Helas! Je n'ose descouvrir', *EscA* 44, *CMM* 77/22), and 'Dangier le dissolut' (Binchois, 'Liesse m'a mandé salut', *EscA* 16, *Rehm* 25).[8] Gower confessed that he could find no ruse to slip around 'Daunger . . . mi ladi consailer', thus pointing up the legalism rooted in the source word of 'danger', the judicial term *dominiarium*.[9] Dangier may have represented the area in which the Lady herself must decide, her own will and integrity. An uncourtly attempt to violate her 'danger' would arouse fear, shame, and slander, and thus stir up its retaliation with an equally uncourtly weapon, the cudgel of a churl.[10]

---

[4] Mathew, 'Ideals of Friendship', in Lawlor (ed.), *Patterns of Love and Courtesy: Essays in Memory of C. S. Lewis*, 51. Hence this welcome in Chrétien de Troyes's *Yvain*, which is a prelude to acts of courtesy: 'All those who were in the garden leaped to their feet when they saw him come, and cried out: "This way, fair sire. May you and all you love be blessed with all that God can do or say"'('Or ça, biax sire, | de quan que Dex puet feire et dire | soiez vos beneoiz clamez, | et vos et quan que vos avez!') (Chrétien de Troyes, *Le Chevalier au Lion (Yvain)*, ed. Roques, 164 (ll. 5397–400); trans. Comfort, *Arthurian Romances*, 250–1). See also Mathew, 'Ideals of Knighthood in Late Fourteenth-Century England', in Hunt, Pantin and Southern (eds.), *Studies in Medieval History*, 354–62, for further literary references to 'welcome' as 'son of courtesy'.

[5] *Les Chansons de Guillaume IX, Duc d'Aquitaine (1071–1127)*, ed. Jeanroy, 23; another version is quoted in Lewis, *The Allegory of Love*, 122.

[6] Verse 2, ll. 1–2, of *ballade* by Philipoctus de Caserta 'En remirant' (*CMM* 53 i/79, text p. lxiv).

[7] Lewis, *The Allegory of Love*, 123.

[8] Compare Guillaume de Lorris's *Dangier* (*Le Roman de la Rose*, ll. 2927 ff.) with that of the peasant in *Aucassin et Nicollete* (see Luchaire, *Social France at the time of Philip Augustus*, 384–7, for the 'villainous' serf, complete with cudgel); Dangier is so portrayed in an illumination in a manuscript of *Le Roman de la Rose* probably prepared for a Valois court *c.*1415 (Pierpont Morgan 245, fo. 22ᵛ), reproduced in Guillaume de Lorris and Jean de Meun, *The Romance of the Rose*, trans. Robbins, 62, q.v. xxviii.

[9] John Gower, *Confessio Amantis*, Book 3, l. 1538; ed. Macaulay, (EETS e.s. 81–2), i. 267.

[10] This interpretation is at variance with Lewis, *The Allegory of Love*, 364–6; it is derived from several generous and helpful conversations on the subject with Mrs D. R. Sutherland, Lady Margaret Hall, Oxford.

If he gained the Lady's 'fair welcome' and cajoled her integrity to sleep, the Lover would be well away toward the Rose. No wonder, then, that Dangier and Bel Acueil should have topped the poll of allegorical characters in the Burgundian *chanson*. Of the fifty-five secular works Rehm authenticated as being by Binchois, seven included a reference to Dangier. Two of these were in the Escorial collection, 'Liesse m'a mandé salut' (*EscA* 16) and 'C'est assez pour morir de dueil' (*EscA* 35);[11] he prevents the Lover from holding the Lady in his arms (*Rehm* 9), from receiving *le don* (*Rehm* 26), and he is 'sur moy envieux' (*Rehm* 45). Of the seventy-four secular works (in French) Besseler authenticated as being by Dufay, five included a reference to Dangier, of which *EscA* 24, 'Or pleust à Dieu', was one:[12] 'Las, que feray, se dangier m'est actif' (*CMM* I. vi/34), 'Dangier me tient en tel soussi | Qu'eschever ne puis sa rudesse' (*CMM* I. vi/14). Bel Acueil received three references in Binchois, of which 'C'est assez pour morir de dueil' (*EscA* 35) and 'La merchi, ma dame et amours!' (*EscA* 51) were two;[13] there was only one in the songs of Dufay.[14] The function was explicit: 'Je loe amours et ma dame mercye | Du bel acueil qui par eulx deux me vient' (*Rehm* 52).

In their exploitation of allegorical characters Burgundian song-makers were in the mainstream of that contemporary neo-courtly poetic expression whose master, Charles d'Orléans, made forty-five references to Dangier in his writings (as against seven to Bel Acueil). Dangier is 'faulx' (*Ballade* XXII l. 28, *Chanson* XIV l. 3) and 'le rebelle' (*Ballade* XXXI l. 9), threatens with 'sa rudesse' (*Ballade* XXIX l. 7), has the power to wound (*Ballade* XXIX l. 20), yet is defied by the Lover who will persist 'maugré Dangier' (*Ballade* XX l. 27, XXII ll. 17–20, XXXVIII l. 31, LXVIII *in toto*, *Chanson* XXV l. 12).[15]

Seldom in the Burgundian *chansons*, however, was an allegorical character treated as the theme of the lyric. Dangier was the subject of two refrains, neither in the Escorial repertoire: 'Quoy que dangier' by Binchois and 'Belle, vueilliés moy vangier' by Dufay.[16]

Indeed, in this collection there are two indications that the courtly traditions are weakening, even in the treatment of these diminished *personae*. The first case involves Bel Acueil, of whom Binchois's *rondeau* 'La merchi, ma dame et amours!' (*EscA* 51, *Rehm* 22), sings:

[11] *Rehm* 9, 11, 25, 26, 37, 38, 45.

[12] *CMM* I. vi/14, 34, 52, 60, 78.

[13] *Rehm* 11, 22, 52.

[14] *CMM* I. vi/22.

[15] Charles d'Orléans may have employed a personal interpretation of *Dangier*, to represent the English captors who prevented him from seeing his Lady France (Fox, *The Lyric Poetry of Charles d'Orleans*, 81–2). For an index to the poet's references to *Dangier* see Charles d'Orléans, *Poésies*, ed. Champion, ii. 617. Planche, in her extensive analysis *Charles d'Orléans ou la recherche d'un langage*, describes Bel Acueil as 'l'incarnation prometteuse' of the thing represented, like a modern public relations 'welcome hostess' who assumes the manner of the institution or place she symbolizes (p. 429); Planche reviews the various facets of *Dangier* (pp. 443–99), concluding however that in her opinion this image is not defined in a moral perspective (p. 449).

[16] *Rehm* 37 and *CMM* I. vi/78 respectively; cf. references to 'bel acueil' (*CMM* 53. i/67) and 'faus dangier' (*CMM* 53. ii/142) in earlier courtly song.

> Mais Bel Acueil la grand meslée
> Desfit, et y vient au secours.

It was Venus, not Bel Acueil, who carried the day in the battle described by Jean de Meun; only then did Fair Welcome receive release from captivity and, urged by his father Courtesy, offer the Lover access to the Rose—whereupon the Lover was cared for by Dame Nature. The maker of this song confuses his inherited formulae. A second confusion appears in another Binchois *rondeau*, 'Liesse m'a mandé salut' (*EscA* 16, *Rehm* 25), involving three personality traits personified in *Le Roman de la Rose*. Liesse, the sweet singer, was the feminine partner of Deduiz ('Sir Mirth' in the Robbins translation):

> Leesce, qui nou haoit mie,
> l'envoisie, la bien chantanz,
> que, des qu'el n'avait que VII anz,
> de s'amor li dona l'otroi.
> Deduiz la tint par mi le doi
> a la querole, et ele lui.[17]

In verse 2 of 'Liesse m'a mandé salut', 'disreputable Danger' is paired with Envy *la doleureuse*: a description preserving her nature as one 'Qui ne rist onques en sa vie'.[18] According to Guillaume de Lorris, those unpleasant people such as Envy who were opposed to a realm of Love belonged to the realities of daily life outside the garden. In a song celebrating courtly Gladness, a permanent inhabitant of the *hortus conclusus*, to put Envy who dwelt in 'reality' outside the wall together with Dangier, one of the leading players in the garden's drama, is definitely symptomatic of the reduction to empty husks suffered by these once-meaningful literary creatures.[19]

> Fuiés, Dangier le dissolut,
> Et envie la doloreuse.

The courtly sense of place has been lost; instead of an invocation of the *locus amoenus*, the Burgundian *chanson* is the embroidery on the decor within the enclosed scene.[20]

Male Bouche, *le losengier*,[21] was the tale-bearer, the gossiping scandalmonger. Alone, he was named in two *rondeaux* by Binchois, of which 'Margarite, fleur de valeur' (*EscA* 53, *Rehm* 27) was one:[22]

---

[17] Guillaume de Lorris and Jean de Meun, *Le Roman de la Rose*, 11. 830–5, q.v. 839–47.

[18] ibid., l. 236.

[19] The *rondeau* 'Rendre me vieng' by Binchois (*Rehm* 38) also pairs two figures on the outside of the garden, Hate and Envy, with two *personae* of the drama—Gladness being unpersonified: 'Haine, dangier, malebouche et envie | Ont de tous poins ma liesse ravie'.

[20] See Pearsall and Salter, *Landscapes and Seasons of the Medieval World*, 83–9, 172, 199; Robertson, 'The Doctrine of Charity in Medieval Literary Gardens', reprinted in *Essays in Medieval Culture*, 43–6; Fleming, *The Roman de la Rose: A study in Allegory and Iconography*, 33–4.

[21] Guillaume de Lorris and Jean de Meun, *Le Roman de la Rose*, l. 3551.

[22] The other is *Rehm* 33, with the refrain: 'Nous vous verens bien malebouche | N'il env[i]eux tenir plais.'

Et vous garde de deshonneur
Et de male bouche vilaine.

He could be a partner of Dangier and Jealousy,[23] and on occasion share their characteristics.[24] Hence he is at work in Binchois's 'Liesse m'a mandé salut' (*EscA* 16) ('Maulgré jaloux en est songneuse | Qui tant parler en ont volut') and is warned against in 'Soyés loyal à vo pouvoir' (*EscA* 56, *CMM* 77/30). There may be traced in the poems of these two *chansons* a vein within the tradition that had stimulated erotic imagination by the proposal to seize pleasure in defiance of scandal:

Oriolant li dist: 'Amis,
Malgré losengeors chaitis,
Estes vos or de moi saisiz.
Or parleront à leur devis,
Et nos ferons tout nos plaisirs.'[25]

The risk of gossip and disclosure had bred the matter of love's secrecy, a topos which had served satirical amatory doctrine,[26] had exposed the impossibility of *amour courtois* in real life,[27] and had provided both urgency and distance to the affairs celebrated by the troubadours and trouvères.[28] In Burgundian Chivalric Humanism Male Bouche and the *losengiers* are pale stereotypes compared to their former literary selves, although remaining appropriate figures for the defeatist strain in the personality of courtly love, a defeatism written of by Marcabru who, in introducing the *lauzengier* into the tradition, knew no security in relationships nor a love free from inherent decay:

---

[23] See n. 19 and Binchois's *rondeau* 'Quoy que dangier, malebouche et leur gent' (*Rehm* 37). Guillaume de Lorris had the Rose guarded by Danger, aided by Evil Tongue, Shame, and Fear, Shame bringing Jealousy with her (*Le Roman de la Rose*, ll. 2809–49); hence Charles d'Orléans, in *La Retenue d'Amours*, (ll. 425–8) (*Poésies*, ed. Champion, i. 15): 'Le soustenant, sans y espargnier riens, | Contre Dangier avecques tous les siens: | Malle Bouche, plaine de faulx maintiens, | Et Jalousie'; also Grenon's 'Je ne requier' (*CMM* II. vii/4), verse 3: 'Et se Dangier en riens me contrarie | que me vueylle mes biens d'amours tolir, | et mesdisans se pour leur faulse envie, | ou envieulx me vullient assaylir | pour moy grever ou fayre desplaysir'.

[24] Dufay's 'Belle, vueilles moy vangier' (*CMM* I. vi/78): 'Ne me souffres ou dangier | De ce cruel lozangier.'

[25] Anonymous *Chanson de toile*, 'Oriolant en haut solier', as printed in Woledge (ed.), *The Penguin Book of French Verse*, i. 87.

[26] Ovid, *Ars Amatoria*, in *The Art of Love and Other Poems*, ed. and trans. Mozley, 62–5: 'Nomen amicitia est, nomen inane fides. | Ei mihi, non tutum est, quod ames, laudare sodali; | . . . | Cognatum fratremque cave carumque sodalem: | Praebebit veros haec tibi turba metus' (i. 740–1, 753–4); Andreas Capellanus, *The Art of Courtly Love*, trans. Parry, 81, 185; 'Thou shalt not have many who know of thy love affair'; 'When made public love rarely endures.'

[27] Anon., *La Chastelaine de Vergi*; see Introduction to edition by Whitehead.

[28] See Scheludko, 'Ovid und die Trobadors', *Zeitschrift für romanische Philologie*, 54 (1934), 149; Scheludko quotes the following from Bernart de Ventadorn, which we quote from the more recent edition of Bernart's poems by Lazar (*Bernard de Ventadour: Troubadour du XIIe siècle. Chansons d'Amour*, 132): 'El mon tan bon amic non ai, | fraire ni cozi ni paren, | Que, si'm vai mo joi enqueren, | qu'ins e mo cor no'l n'azire. | E s'eu m'en volh escondire, | no s'en tenha oer traït. | No volh lauzengers me tolha | S'amor ni'm leve tal crit | per qu'eu me lais morir de dol.' For further discussion see Valency, *In Praise of Love*, 171–5.

So per qu'amor segurana
Non truep ses ruylha.[29]

Fortune, also, loses the symbolic properties that had been her literary value. In the medieval system Fortune had been discovered as being the circulating force, earth's Intelligence.[30] Binchois's reputed patron, the Duke of Suffolk, invokes her:

O Thou, ffortune, whyche hast the gouernaunce,
Of alle thynges kyndly mevyng to and fro,
Thaym to demene aftyr thyn ordynaunce,
Rhyght as thou lyst to graunt hem wele or wo;[31]

The second verse of his poem is a typical complaint against the duress imposed by her, and reads like a translation from a Burgundian *chanson*:[32]

Me-thynk thou art vnkynd, as in this case,
To suffre me so long a while endure
So gret a payn wyth-out mersy or grace,
Which greuyd me right sore, I the ensure;

For Fortune, in the songs of Valois chivalric humanism, no longer is considered as a cosmic phenomenon. She is deprived even of her wheel,

qui torne
et, quant ele veut, ele met
le plus bas amont ou somet,
et celui qui est sor la roe
reverse a un tor en la boue.[33]

Only the action of her instrument of mutability would be suggested, as by Christine de Pisan:

Ha! Fortune très douloureuse,
Que tu m'as mis du hault au bas![34]

It is hinted at by Fortune's one appearance (by name) in the Escorial collection, 'Puis que Fortune m'est si dure' (*EscA* 18, *CMM* 77/8):

c'est trop fort
Quant soudanement me desnie.

and in both 'Cuid'on que je poille castaingnes' (*EscA* 36, *CMM* 77/17: 'Tous mes biens vienent à rebours'), and 'Je cuidoye estre conforté' (*EscA* 49, *CMM* 77/26):

---

[29] As cited in Topsfield, *Troubadours and Love*, 78.

[30] Lewis, *The Discarded Image*, 139–40. See Green, *Poets and Princepleasers*, 145–9.

[31] Robbins (ed.), *Secular Lyrics of the XIVth and XVth Centuries*, no. 187, pp. 185–6; source: Oxford, Bodleian Library, MS Fairfax 16 (Summary Catalogue 3896), fo. 321ʳ⁻ᵛ.

[32] Which it was not; see Robbins, *Secular Lyrics*, 285 (with reference to Crow, *Speculum*, 17 and McCracken, *PMLA* 26).

[33] Guillaume de Lorris and Jean de Meun, *Le Roman de la Rose*, ll. 3958–62.

[34] Christine de Pisan, *Œuvres poétiques*, ed. Roy, i. 8 (*Cent Ballades*, vii, ll.1–2).

Je cuidoye estre conforté
D'amours et de joieuseté
A ce premier jour de l'année
Mais la chose en est retournée
Au rebours de ma volenté.

She is a convenient target for complaint, because of the grief that is in her power to bring (*EscA* 18):

Puisque fortune m'est si dure,
Plaine de mortel disconfort,
Et que tant longement me dure
Je ne desire que la mort.

and Charles d'Orléans:

il me couvient souffrir
Tant de douleur et de dure destresse
Par Fortune, qui me vient assaillir
De tous costez, qui de maulx est princesse![35]

In such lines as these Fortune becomes, as an obstructive power, the female equivalent of rude Dangier and his cohorts. Fortune and Dangier were twice teamed by Charles d'Orléans, the same poet describing her as *la felle* and as a *losengiere*;[36] in Dufay's *ballade* 'Je me complains piteusement' they were partners:

Dangier me tient en tel soussi
Qu' eschever ne puis sa rudesse,
Et fortune le veult aussi[37]

Thus Fortune, like her allegorical associates in the world of the Lover's suffering, was declining into a cliché of abuse.

Songs for special occasions in the Valois chivalric charade were included in the Escorial manuscript. Among them were four welcome songs, all anonymous (but now attributed to Binchois in Part 1 of this book). They were the musical gestures that accompanied a stylized court ritual, within which conduct was appropriate to rank and circumstance. Thus Isabel of Portugal used gesture to raise the worth of Margaret of Scotland in the eyes of her husband: 'he appeared to study the behaviour of my lady the Dauphiness, how she would prevent my lady the Duchess from kneeling right down to the ground; but my said lady would do so—as my

[35] Charles d'Orléans, *Poésies*, ed. Champion, i. 63 (*Ballade* XLII, ll. 12–15); see also Fox, *The Lyric Poetry of Charles d'Orléans*, 72.

[36] *Ballades* LVIII and CV, XLI and XXV respectively; he made a total of twenty-six references to Fortune (*Poésies*, ii. 620). For more on Charles d'Orléans and 'Les jeux de Fortune' see Planche, *Charles d'Orléans ou la recherche d'un langage*, 375–85.

[37] *CMM* I. vi/14. There was only one other reference to Fortune in a Dufay song, *CMM* I. vi/62; there were none in the Binchois canon. Charles d'Orléans made Fortune an aid of *Soussy* (*Poésies*, i. 144, *Ballade* XC). Fortune, 'mere de douleurs', is coupled with 'faulx Dangier' in a *rondeau* preserved in the Chansonnier Cordiforme, *CMM* 42/37. For a brief list of other appearances of allegorical characters in *chansons* see Cazeaux, *French Music in the Fifteenth and Sixteenth Centuries*, 156.

mother told me, who had witnessed these things';[38] Louis the Dauphin, in temporary exile at the Burgundian court (1456), was so eager to honour his protector that he insisted on being part of the family welcome-home party:

When my lord Duke Philip returned from the war of Utrecht he came to Brussels; there my lady the Duchess [Isabel of Portugal], his wife, and my lady of Charolais, his daughter-in-law, went down into the middle of the courtyard to give him *bien veigner*: and when the Dauphin learned of it he came out of his chamber where he had been, advanced toward my lady, and, standing there quietly, awaited my lord Duke Philip. All this time my lady spoke to him and prayed him retire to his room, for it was not his duty to come so before my said Seigneur, the Duke; but no power of my lady could make him go back.[39]

A specific noblewoman appears to have been welcomed to the sounds of 'Bien viengnant, ma tresredoubtée' (*EscA* 34, *CMM* 77/16), 'De ceste joieuse advenue' (*EscA* 38, *CMM* 77/18), and 'L'onneur de vous, dame sans per' (*EscA* 58, *CMM* 77/31). The sentiments expressed in these songs are similar to those of an anonymous chronicler who described the disembarkation of Philip the Good's bride, Isabella of Portugal, 1430: 'Grant foison y ot aussi de trompetes, menestrelz et joueurs de pluiseurs instrumens de musique, et tous s'efforçoient d'en faire le mieulx qu'ilz savoient, pour la feste et joye de la venue de madite dame tant desirée ...'[40] The singers of 'Bien viegnés vous, mon prinche gracieux' (*EscA* 59, *CMM* 77/32) seem to have been in attendance at the arrival of a particular prince and his company, possibly a *Prince d'Amour* judging by its conviviality:

> Je sui à vous comme amant à s'amie,
> Obeissant à tout vous playsans veux.

Conviviality among the minstrels themselves might be suggested by the unusual

---

[38] '... il sembloit à veoir la manière de Madame la Dauphine, qu'elle eust voulu garder que Madame la Duchesse ne se fust pas agenouillée jusques à terre: mais maditte Dame le vouloit faire, comme m'a dit Madame ma mere, laquelle a veu toutes ces choses' (Aliénor de Poitiers, *Les Anciens Honneurs de la Cour de Bourgogne*, published in La Curne de Saint-Palaye, *Mémoires sur l'ancienne chevalerie*, ii. 198 (my trans.).

[39] 'Quand Monsieur le Ducq Philippe retourna de la guerre d'Utrecht, il vint à Bruxelles où Madame la Duchesse, sa femme, et Madame de Charrolais, sa belle-fille, allerent en bas environ le milieu de la cour pour le *bien veigner*: et quand le Dauphin le sceut, il vint de sa chambre là où il estoit, jusques devers Madame, et là de *pied coy* il attendit Monsieur le Ducq Philippe. Touttes fois Madame luy dit et prie qu'il se retire en chambre et qu'il n'appartenoit qu'il vint ainsi au devant de mondit Seigneur le Ducq; mais il ne fut au pourvoir de Madame de le faire retourner.' (ibid. ii. 212). For the duke's exaggerated courtesy to Louis see Vaughan, *Philip the Good*, 353–4.

[40] Gachard, *Collection de documents inédits concernant la Belgique*, ii. 65 ff.; also quoted therefrom by Marix, *Histoire*, 27. In 1389 another Isabella—Queen of Charles VI—had made her ceremonial entry into Paris; at the second St. Denis Gate two choir-boys as angels crowned her singing: 'Lady with the lilied gown, | Queen you are of Paris town, | Of France and all this fair countrie: | Now back to paradise go we.' (Froissart, *Chronicles*, ed. Brereton, 353.) In 1409 John the Fearless entered Paris, preceded by twelve trumpeters and many musicians, to be greeted by flowers and 'Noels' from the populace; the next day Isabella 'made as splendid an entry as anyone had ever seen her do since the very first time she came to Paris' (Shirley, *A Parisian Journal, 1405–1449*, 49–50; q.v. 153–4, 268–70, 319 for subsequent joyous entries); see also Poirion, *Le Poète et le prince*, 87–9. Burgundian Chivalric Humanism must have relished the frequent civic welcomes for Philip the Good, welcomes so enthusiastic 'que le mistère en seroit ou trop long pour escrire ou trop tirant à vanité d'en faire le contée (Chastellain, *Chronique des ducs de Bourgogne*, iii. 6, as quoted in Marix, *Histoire*, 74).

text of 'Loez soit Dieu des biens de ly' (*EscA* 52, *CMM* 77/27), perhaps a moment in a Feast of Fools mocking the customary service of dinner music: 'pour élever les grossières satisfactions de la table jusqu'á la dignité du plaisir esthétique'.[41]

> Le corps en est tresbien garny,
> Loez soit Dieux et l'oste ossy
> Qui nous si bonne chiere fache:—
> Ainsy conclud chi nostre grace.

A song-maker was not normally expected to celebrate people or incidents relating to his own station; the honour paid to Fontaine by his colleagues is an exception: 'Fontaine, à vous dire le voir' (*EscA* 42, *CMM* 77/20).[42]

> Vray est qu'à la fois bon voloir
> Vous fera en pensant douloir
> Et regreter ces doulx ymages;
> Mais neantement [*sic* = neantmains] devenir sages
> Vous convient, pour mieulx en valoir.

There are five New Year songs: Binchois's 'La merchi, ma dame et amours!' (*EscA* 51, *Rehm* 22), Dufay's 'Porray je avoir vostre merchi' (*EscA* 25, *CMM* I. vi/ 33) and 'Estrinez moy, je vous estrineray' (*EscA* 60, *CMM* I. vi/58), and the anonymous 'Bon jour, bon mois' (*EscA* 19, *CMM* 77/9) and 'Je cuidoye estre conforté' (*EscA* 49, *CMM* 77/26). 'Bon jour, bon mois' could have been directed to a particular individual; the other four songs (of which 'Estrinez moy' is in dialogue) deal with the general notion of an exchange, not of tangible objects, but of Lady's *merchi* for Lover's service.[43] These are typical of the *estrenne* lyric formulae, from 'Porray je avoir vostre merchi':

> Et supposé qu'il soit ainsy
> Que cuer, corps, et tous biens aussy
> A l'estraine je vous presente

compared with lines from Christine de Pisan and Charles d'Orléans respectively:

> Ce jour de l'an que l'en doit estrener,
> Trés chiere dame, entierement vous donne
> Mon cuer, mon corps, quanque je puis finer;
> A vo vouloir de tous poins abandonne
> Moy, et mes biens vous ottroy, belle et bonne;
>
> Ad ce premier jour de l'année
> De cueur, de corps et quanque j'ay,

---

[41] Poirion, *Le Poète et le prince*, 76. Philip the Good encouraged his chaplains and minstrels to enjoy their *fête des fous*: Fontaine was the *abbé de joieuse folye* in 1433 (Marix, *Histoire*, 53, 166). For extracts from contemporary chronicles describing banquet music see Marix, 35–7.

[42] 'L'écriture musicale de la pièce s'accorde fort bien avec le style contemporain de la vieillesse du musicien', an old age in which his *sagesse* was commended (Marix, *Histoire*, 167).

[43] Poirion (*Le Poète et le prince*, 117–18) draws attention to *Le Jour de l'an* as the time for renewal of a minstrel's service, hence the songs are pledges of personal loyalty in a feudal relationship.

> Privéement estreneray
> Ce qui me gist en ma pensée.[44]

Eustache Deschamps employed this idea coupled with the patterns of 'Bon jour, bon mois, bonne sepmaine' (*EscA* 19, *CMM* 77/9, q.v.):

> De mon cuer et corps vous estraine,
> Tout vous doing a ceste journée
> Et pour estre mieulx estrenée
> Bon an, bon jour et bonne estraine,
> Ma dame, vous soit hui donnée
> Au commencement de l' année.[45]

Baude Cordier's 'Ce jour de l'an' had been an earlier musical setting of the same theme:

> Ce jour de l'an que maint doist estrenier
> joyeusement sa belle et doulche amie,
> quant est de moy, je veul de ma partie
> mon cuer, mon corps, entierement donner
> a ma dame qui tant fait a loer,[46]

Deschamps evoked the season of nature's and lovers' reaffirmation:

> A ce bon jour que temps se renouvelle,
> Que moys et ans et la lune est nouvelle,
> Vous doing mon cuer, mon corps et quanque j'ay
> Comme cellui qui tous vostres seray
> A tous jours maiz, ma dame bonne et belle.[47]

Thus the anonymous 'Lune tresbelle, clere lune' (*EscA* 23, *CMM* 77/11) is not unusual in having as its motif the moon and her mutability in love's service:

> Lune tresbelle, clere lune,
> Qui servez d'un esmay en may:
> A quoy proufite cest esmay
> L'autre dez fois trop plus que l'une?
>
> Vous ne vestés que robbe brune;
> N'avez vous vert [ne] brun ne gay?
> Lune tresbelle, clere lune,
> Qui servez d'un esmay en may.
>
> Garde qu'on ne crye commune
> Sur vous, comme on fist que bien sçay;
> Sur celle d'avril qui pour vray
> S'enfuy muchier so[u]bs la dune.

---

[44] Christine de Pisan, *Œuvres poétiques*, ed. Roy, i. 81; Charles d'Orléans, *Poésies*, ed. Champion, ii. 323.

[45] Eustache Deschamps, *Œuvres complètes*, ed. Marquis de Queux de Saint-Hilaire and Raynaud, iv. 40.

[46] Ed. Reaney, *CMM* 11. i, 1–2; for songs by Dufay on this subject see *CMM* 1. vi/38, 39, 59, 63.

[47] Deschamps, *Œuvres complètes*, iv. 52.

The light of Ovid's goddess in progress of snowy white (*Ut solet, in niveis Luna vehetur equis*)[48] inspired lovers early in Western secular expression, as in Walafrid Strabo:

> Cum splendor lunae fulgescat ab aethere purae,
> tu sta sub divo cernens speculamine miro,
> qualiter ex luna splendescat lampade pura
> et splendore suo caros amplecitur uno
> corpore divisos, sed mentis amore ligatos.[49]

The inheritors of the courtly poetic traditions sought to bathe in a wishful reflection of that literary moon-magic and madness once invoked by Theocritus;[50] so Chaucer's Troilus every night

> as was his wone to done,
> He stood the brighte mone to beholde,
> And al his sorwe he to the mone told;[51]

and Lydgate's lover, standing alone on New Year's night, prayed:

> vnto the frosty moone, with hir pale light,
> To go and recomaunde me vnto my lady dere.[52]

The moon of the anonymous Escorial *rondeau* is not simply the object of the singer's address; it is the boundary of our sublunary world of contingence and mutable fortune.[53] Hence it, too, becomes the cause and object of complaint— complaint being never far away in any courtly pattern:

> Hé lune! trop luis longuement,
> Par toy pers les biens doulcereux
> Qu'Amours donne aux vrais amoureux.
>
> Ta clarté nuit trop durement
> A mon cuer qui est desireux,
> Hé lune! trop luis longuement.[54]

The classical habit of Luna was preserved in Humanist manuals of iconography: a very thin veil dress of different colours, now white, now yellow, now red; she also wore one entirely black, yet bright and shining as it was almost covered with glittering stars.[55] Not a classical but a chivalric tradition of colour symbolism

---

[48] Ovid, *Remedia Amoris*, l. 258, in *The Art of Love, and Other Poems*, ed. and trans. Mozley, 194.

[49] Waddell, *Mediaeval Latin Lyrics*, 116–17.

[50] Theocritus, *Idyll* II, in *Works*, ed. Gow, i. 16–29, wherein 'the car of night' is charged: 'shine bright, O Moon, for to thee, goddess, will I softly chant' (ll. 10–11).

[51] Chaucer, *Troilus and Criseyde*, v, ll. 647–9, q.v. verses 91–8 for complete song (*The Complete Works*, ed. Skeat, ii. 377).

[52] John Lydgate, 'A Lover's New Year's Gift', ll. 12–14, ed. MacCracken, *The Minor Poems of John Lydgate*, ii, *Secular Poems* (EETS 192), 425–7.

[53] Lewis, *The Allegory of Love*, 108–9.

[54] Christine de Pisan, *Œuvres poétiques*, ed. Roy, i. 171.

[55] See the *Ragionamenti* of Vasari (1558) and the *Imagini degli dei antichi* of Cartari (1571), printed and discussed in Seznec, *The Survival of the Pagan Gods*, 288–95, esp. 292–3.

would have been suggested by the second verse of the Escorial collection's moon-plaint:

> Vous ne vestés que robbe brune;
> N'avez vous vert ne brun [*sic* = bleu?] ne gay?

Brown customarily symbolized sadness, green was recognized as the symbol of love's passion—to be clad in green was to wear *la livrée aux amoureux*.[56] The text of 'Lune tresbelle' might have had a veiled political allusion, for Philip the Good had exchanged his father's Burgundian green for sombre hues.[57]

In 'Lune tresbelle, clere lune' were combined the shadows of patterns: seasonal reaffirmation, invocation to Luna, the lover in 'lunacy', his complaint in this mutable realm, and chivalric humanism's colour symbolism. Another combination of patterns makes up Binchois's 'Margarite, fleur de valeur' (*EscA* 53, *Rehm* 27):

> Margarite, fleur de valeur,
> Sur toutes aultres souverayne:
> Dieux vous doinst hui en bonne estraine
> Tout le desir de vostre coeur,
>
> Et vous garde de deshonneur
> Et de male bouche vilaine,
> Margarite, fleur de valeur,
> Sur toutes aultres souverayne.
>
> Estrinez soit il de douleur
> Qui ne mettera toute sa paine
> A louer vo doulceur haultaine,
> Car vo loz n'a per ne meilleur.

The daisy of this song is a flower 'de valeur', 'sur toutes aultres souverayne'; to be admired for her 'doulceur haultaine'. These phrases were common in the stock of floral tributes paid by Machaut, Froissart, and Deschamps, and found their antecedents in the classical Pearl symbolism preserved in medieval lapidaries:[58]

---

[56] Huizinga, *The Waning of the Middle Ages*, 272–4, q.v. for further examples from 14th- and 15th-century French poetry; also Cartellieri, *The Court of Burgundy*, 127. Upon her engagement to Louis III of Anjou in 1434, Margaret, daughter of Amadeus VIII of Savoy, was entitled to wear the green that was the privilege of queens; this livery for herself and her household took three months to prepare (José, *La Maison de Savoie: Amédée VIII*, i. 69). Charles VII was pictured during the 1450s wearing one of his favourite short green tunics (Vale, *Charles VII*, 223). Giovanna Cenami is clad in green in the *Arnolfini Betrothal* by Van Eyck. Green satin was added to the traditional red of the minstrels' dress at the wedding of John the Fearless and Margaret of Bavaria, 1385 (Wright, *Music at the Court of Burgundy*, 37); green for gaiety was contrasted with grey for hope (Thibault, 'Le Chansonnier Nivelle de la Chausée', *Annales Musicologiques*, 7 (1964–77), 12); 'vert perdu' was a symbol for sadness (Planche, *Charles d'Orléans*, 186, q.v. 190–2).

[57] Calmette, *Les Grands Ducs de Bourgogne*, 312; Eng. trans., Weightman, *The Golden Age of Burgundy*, 233. Political colour changes well described the situation in the Paris of John the Fearless, with the mutable fortunes of Burgundian green, Armagnac violet, and Cabochian white (ibid. 145–57; Eng. trans. 105–7); see Shirley, *A Parisian Journal*, 80.

[58] See the thorough treatment of the Marguerite's floral imagery by Lowes, 'The Prologue to the *Legend of Good Women* as related to the French Marguerite Poems and to the *Filostrato*', *PMLA* 19 (1904), 593–683; for a briefer treatment see Skeat's introduction in the third volume of his edition of

Principium ergo columenque omnium
rerum preti margaritae tenent.[59]

Tresdoulce fleur . . .
Qui au monde n'avez pas vo pareille
.   .   .   .   .   .
Mon cuer pour vous amer pert,
Qui a tousjours a vo douceur s'ahert;
Car au jour d'uy n'est fleur de tel merite
Com vous estes; pour ce tous biens dessert:
Vostre nom est precieux, Marguerite.[60]

Combined with the daisy/pearl idioms in 'Margarite, fleur de valeur' are those of the *étrenne*, suggesting a more personalized tone: 'God grant you *en bonne estraine* all that your heart desires', and '*Estrinez soit il de douleur*' who does not spend himself in your praise. Like the aforementioned welcome songs in this collection (*EscA* 34, 38, 58) this *rondeau* would seem to have been addressed to a particular lady of rank. The minstrel is the voice of the poet as political *louangeur*. This suggestion is strengthened by the third idiom in the text selected from the courtly patterns: the wish that the lady, and her reputation (*loz*), be guarded from dishonour and from *Male Bouche vilaine*.

One only can speculate on the identity of the lady addressed in 'Margarite, fleur de valeur'. If the ascription to Binchois be presumed correct, then certain candidates could be singled out from among the many noble Marguerites of that era.[61] Lacking

Chaucer's *Complete Works*, pp. xxix–xxxiii. For the symbolism of the Marguerite as gem see Pannier, *Les Lapidaires françaises du moyen âge*, 182; Evans, *Magical Jewels*, 91–4, 231; Studer and Evans, *Anglo-Norman Lapidaries*, 64; Evans and Serjeantson, *English Mediaeval Lapidaries* (EETS 190), 107–8; the source for the Latin and vernacular lapidaries of the Middle Ages, Marbode's *De Gemnis*, is available in Migne, *Patrologiae cursus completus . . . Series Latina*, clxxi cols. 1735–80, esp. item 1673–4 (col. 1766), 'de Margaritis', see also Gordon's introduction to his edition of *Pearl*, and Schofield, 'Symbolism, Allegory, and Autobiography in *The Pearl*', PMLA 24 (1909), 585–675. There was little reference in later medieval poetry to the Marguerite as gem; a fairly isolated example occurred in the poem *Annot and Johon* from MS Harley 2253 (ed. Brown, *English Lyrics of the Thirteenth Century*, no. 76, pp. 136–7), where the mistress is praised by a series of comparisons grouped into specific branches of knowledge, the line in question being included in stanza i (the gems), rather than that pertaining to flowers: 'The myht of the margarite haveth this mai mere' [adj. 'beautiful', 'noble']'; by the fifteenth century the symbols were conflated, hence 'A delectable daysye ye be to beholde, | yow be more rycher vnto me syght | then oder precyouse stoune or golde' (Robbins (ed.), *Secular Lyrics*, no. 200, p. 205). Thomas Usk's *Testament of Love* has the acrostic 'Marguerete of virtu': see Chaucer, *The Complete Works*, ed. Skeat, vii. 1–145, as cited and discussed in Lewis, *Allegory of Love*, 222–31.

[59] Pliny, *Naturalis Historia*, IX. liv. 106 ff.

[60] Eustache Deschamps, 'Eloge d'une dame du nom de marguerite' (*Œuvres complètes*, ed. Marquis de Queux de Saint-Hilaire and Raynaud, iii. 379).

[61] The name appeared frequently in court families, from Margaret of Bavaria (d. 1422), wife of John the Fearless, who proved an able administrator on behalf of her husband (Vaughan, *John the Fearless*, 15–17, ch. 7), to Margaret 'la bastarde de Bourgongne', whose mother, *damoiselle* Ysabeau de la Vigne, according to the accounts of 1448–9, received money for her living in Louvain (Laborde, *Les Ducs de Bourgogne: . . . Seconde partie . . . Preuves*, i. 398). The Valois of Burgundy were avid in the collection of pearls, lavish in their gifts. Margaret (d. 1405), wife of Philip the Bold, possessed a treasure in which were enumerated over 4,000 pearls; she evidently delighted 'to honor the precious gem to which she owed her name, and fully recognized its poetical significance' (Kunz and Stevenson, *The Book of the Pearl*, 425 ff.); see Calmette, *Les Grands Ducs de Bourgogne*, 95, Eng. trans. 67; Vaughan, *Philip the Bold*, 43; and Beaulieu and Baylé, *Le Costume en Bourgogne de Philippe le Hardi à la mort de Charles le Téméraire*, 101–4.

much detailed knowledge of Binchois's biography, selection must be made by seeking congruencies of time, political events, and geography. For example, his service to the Duke of Suffolk in the 1420s cannot be advanced as supporting Margaret of Anjou as the lady concerned. Suffolk was not to meet her until 1444; by then Henry VI and Philip the Good had fallen out, and Binchois was firmly in Burgundian employ. Unless the song was connected with the unsuccessful negotiations for her proposed marriage with the future Charles the Bold or with the Count of Nevers, we must look for another daisy girl.[62]

Margaret of Burgundy, daughter of Philip the Bold, married William IV of Hainault in 1385; the daughter of this marriage was Jacqueline of Bavaria. Binchois, born *c*.1400, was the son of Jean de Binche, bourgeois of Mons; a person of this name, who is presumed to have been his father, was councillor to William IV and later (1417) to Jacqueline of Bavaria.[63] Jacqueline surrounded herself with chaplains and minstrels, in imitation of the Parisian tastes brought to the court of Hainault by her mother Margaret. In 1417 her four minstrels and a trumpet received 75 *livres tournois* to defray expenses on a trip to their *escolles*, and Philip the Good rewarded some other of her musicians at The Hague (1428) and at Brussels (1431). Binchois, therefore, grew up in the sound of secular music performed both in the circle of his father's allegiance and before the puissant Burgundian duke. Margaret was frequently involved in the political activities of her brother John the Fearless, and subsequently had to intervene in the troubled affairs of her daughter—acting as regent when Jacqueline was in England (1421–4); Binchois apparently served the cause of the English regency and the Burgundians against Jacqueline's husband, Humphrey of Gloucester.[64] After the acquisition of the family's territories by Burgundy (Treaty of Delft, 1428),[65] Margaret lived quietly at Le Quesnoy; in June and July 1434, at Mons, she reached a financial settlement with Philip and continued to live at Le Quesnoy, Binche, and Baudour. At her death on 8 March 1441, she was esteemed as a pious woman, generous in endowments.[66]

In Philip the Good's campaigns, opportunities were never infrequent for musicians of opposing sides to play in each other's presence, and during the struggle leading to the 1428 treaty 'Dutch' minstrels played for the Burgundian duke (who at that time was accompanied by his chaplain Fontaine).[67] Jacqueline of Bavaria knew a 'Binchois', as revealed in a letter written by her from Valenciennes, dated 23 November 1428.[68] We would suggest that it was in the later stages of the Hainault story—when Margaret was less an open opponent than a respected

[62] See Jacob, *The Fifteenth Century, 1399–1485*, 475–7; for Suffolk and Margaret see Wolffe, *Henry VI*, ch. 10. Suffolk's poem in service to the flower is available in Robbins, *Secular Lyrics*, no. 188, pp. 186–9.

[63] For the relevant biographical items on Binchois see Fallows, 'Binchois', *New Grove*, 709, updating Marix, *Histoire*, 176–7.

[64] Marix, *Histoire*, ii. 178–9.

[65] Details in Vaughan, *Philip the Good*, ch. 2; also Armstrong, *England, France and Burgundy in the Fifteenth Century*, 363–6.

[66] *Biographie nationale* (Brussels, 1894–5), xiii.

[67] Marix, *Histoire*, 80–1.

[68] Hence after the Treaty of Delft (dated 3 July); ibid. 179.

dowager—that 'Margarite, fleur de valeur' could have been sung. In October 1428, after touring Holland, Zealand, and Friesland as a demonstration of the new Burgundian hegemony, Philip, with Jacqueline, returned to Mons. On the 24th the nobles of Hainault offered them a spectacle of jousts 'à le joyeuse revenue de noditte très redoubtée damme et princhesse hiretière, donnet de courtoisie . . .' at which Margaret also was in attendance: the 'très haulte et puissante princhesse, no très redoubtée dame la dowagière, venue à Mons asdites joustes'.[69]

The contemporary evidence is suggestive of the honour in which this Margaret was held, although her support of her daughter had left her open to criticism by political *Males Bouches* in the new Burgundian administration. Binchois's activities just before his entry into Philip the Good's chapel are unknown, but as a musician employed either by Hainault or by Burgundy he could well have had occasion to celebrate Margaret of Burgundy in the *louange* in question.[70]

Margaret of Burgundy inspired the political hyperbole of chivalric humanism. Margaret of Scotland exemplified, to an extreme, aristocracy wrapped in its lyrical dream.

Margaret of Scotland (*c.*1425–45), the elder child of James I of Scotland and Joan Beaufort, embarked for France, 27 March 1436, to become the bride of the French Dauphin (later Louis XI).[71] Ceremonial welcomes at La Rochelle (by chancellor Regnault de Chartres) and Tours (by the Queen and Dauphin) preceded the wedding ceremony at Tours Cathedral, 25 June, following which was a feast with Moorish dancers and chorus-singing provided by the city. The marriage was a disaster; Louis hated his young bride. She buried herself in the consolations of poetry, considering herself a disciple of Alain Chartier.[72] She did not take the

[69] Leopold Devillers, *Cartulaire des comtes de Hainault, de l'avènement de Guillaume II à la mort de Jacqueline de Bavière (1337–1436)*, (Brussels, 1892), v. 22.

[70] Two points can be made here that support the case advanced on behalf of Jacqueline of Bavaria's mother as being the 'Margarite' of *EscA* 53, and also put into focus a particular aspect of the Escorial manuscript's repertoire. Philip the Good was so preoccupied with affairs in Holland that from Sept. 1425 until Apr. 1428 he did not visit France (Vaughan, *Philip the Good*, 40); the Middle Dutch song 'Ope es in minnen groot ghenuecht' (*EscA* 55, *CMM* 77/29) would appear to be flavoured with Frisian dialect (Kemp, 'The Manuscript Escorial V.III.24', *MD* 30 (1976), 106). What is highly interesting in this regard is the nature and order of Scribe A's contribution of Dutch and Welcome songs to the collection: *EscA* 31 'Al eebaerheit' (Middle Dutch), 34 'Bien viengnant, ma tresredoubtèe (in which 'La plus gratieuse of Franche' is welcomed 'En ceste amoureuse contrée'), 38 ('De ceste joyeuse advenue | Doit bien chascun estre esjouy | C'est la meilleur c'onques je ouy, | Elle soit la tres-bien venue' . . . 'Elle est à present revenue | Je vous fais asçavoir que ouy'), and subsequently 53 and 55; near the head of Scribe A's last contribution (*EscA* 41–55) is *EscA* 42 in praise of Fontaine, who was with Duke Philip when the Dutch minstrels played for him (see n. 67). In keeping with the mood and subject of *EscA* 38, *EscA* 40 was interpolated into Scribe A's work by Scribe B (verse 2: 'En Franche n'en a point de telle | Ne plus digne d'estre amoureuse.'); Scribe B placed two more Welcome songs near the head of his final group of pieces also: 58 ('L'onneur de vous, dame sans per') and 59 ('Bien viegnés vous, mon prinche gracieux').

[71] This material drawn from *The Dictionary of National Biography*, xii, 1021–3, and Du Fresne de Beaucourt, *Histoire de Charles VII*, iv. 89–109.

[72] Chartier had been part of the original embassy to Scotland to seek her hand (Beaucourt, *Histoire de Charles VII*, ii. 396). Binchois set his 'Triste plaisir' (*Rehm* 45), a poem which had brought comfort to the poet Regnier, imprisoned while on a secret mission for Burgundy (Champion, *Histoire poétique du quinzième siècle*, 253, and Piaget, 'La complainte du prisonnier d'Amours', *Mélanges Picot*, ii. 155–62 (esp. pp. 157–8). Thus Binchois's literary taste was paralleled by men of letters who had a taste for his own art (see Marix, *Histoire*, 182–6).

counsel offered by Christine de Pisan, that the envious are an expected part of a noble lady's life, and hence should be ignored and forgiven; no matter how virtuous she may be, they will speak slander.[73] Although she lived in a feminine circle of literary connoisseurs, and was reported to pass away the night composing lyrics, she was the subject of rumour and abuse. It was said that she had been caught in a compromising situation of infidelity to Louis—one too many of those nocturnal *rondeau* sessions? In spite of her enjoyment of the courtly games—Maying in 1444, dancing the *basse danse de Bourgogne* in 1445—her unhappy marriage and reputed scandalous behaviour worked their effects in debilitated health and melancholia. She died 16 August 1445, unforgiving of her *losengier*: 'Si je meurs, c'est pour vous et vos bonnes paroles que vous avez dites de moi, sans cause ne sans raison'. The Duchess of Burgundy, Isabella of Portugal, had come to the French court at Châlons after attending negotiations at Rheims. She must have stayed two months, dining and passing the time with Margaret, who revered her; she berated the Dauphin for the treatment given his wife. It is recorded that Isabella brought a numerous suite with her, suitable to a court which was attempting to resurrect French Valois chivalric pomp in imitation of the Burgundian scene. The text of 'Margarite, fleur de valeur' would have been particularly applicable to the lot of the Dauphiness, and in keeping with the considerate feelings of the Duchess of Burgundy.

A third name may be proposed: Margaret (d. 1441), daughter of John the Fearless, widowed Duchess of Guienne, who could be advanced as an alternative candidate on the basis of certain political movements of her second husband, Arthur of Brittany, Conte de Richemont.[74]

Arthur, brother of Duke John V of Brittany, had lived a prisoner in England after Agincourt; freed on parole at the end of September 1422, he passed his time in Normandy under the surveillance of Suffolk, and eventually became a useful ally of the English. After the death of Henry V, Philip the Good sought to bring Brittany into an alliance between himself and England; as part of this plan de Richemont was to wed his widowed sister Margaret. Awaiting his marriage, de Richemont lived with Philip at Arras and Ghent. The wedding took place on 10 October 1423, in the chapel of the Burgundian *hôtel* at Dijon. The espousal had been made with great magnificence, with the added distinction of a secret Breton–Burgundian alliance. After this de Richemont travelled a Paris–Brittany circuit on behalf of Burgundy; he clashed with Bedford (1424), was present at Dijon for the entry of Philip's new duchess, Isabella, and—as Constable of France—aided in reconciling Franco-Burgundian views, leading to the Congress of Arras.

De Richemont was in Brittany at the time of an alleged plot to assassinate Philip (1424), but could have had a hand in directing the forged letters copied by his wife's treasurer which implicated Suffolk, Gloucester, and Bedford.[75] It is of interest to

[73] *The Treasure of the City of Ladies*, trans. Lawson, 75, 90, 102.

[74] The following paragraph draws on Cosneau, *Le Connétable de Richemont*, 47–88.

[75] See Desplanque, *Projet d'assassinat de Philippe le Bon par les Anglais (1424–1426)*, 70; also Beaucourt, *Histoire de Charles VII*, ii. 658–60, Marix, *Histoire*, 177–8, and Rutherford, 'The Forgeries of Guillaume Benoit', *English Historical Review*, 30 (1915), 216–33.

remember that the connection established between Suffolk and Binchois at this time rests upon the testimony (evidently questionable) given at a legal inquiry of 1427 by Guillaume Benoit, a servant of Suffolk,[76] and that the request that Binchois make a song to assuage Suffolk's misery implied an appreciation of Binchois's talents on the part of Breton and English already by 1424 and of Burgundian at least by 1427. From the previous relationship of de Richemont and Suffolk and from this subsequent estrangement there could be suggested a convenient Anglo-Breton experience for Binchois's unknown youth and an opportunity for him to pass over into Burgundian employ. It is of particular interest, then, to record that in the household accounts of John V's treasurer was contained an entry for February 1419, on the occasion of a journey to Rouen on which John V and Henry V conferred. Singing before them 'plusieurs fois, de jour et de nuit' were four minstrels, who received 15 *livres*. One of these was 'Gillequin'.[77]

It must remain conjectural whether these political events or noble Margarets were connected with any one of the *chansons* in the Escorial collection. On the evidence of the music itself 'Margarite, fleur de valeur' cannot be said with certainty to belong to the late 1420s or to the years 1436–45, because unlike those of Dufay the secular songs of Binchois did not go through obvious periods of stylistic change. The makers of ceremonial songs kept them in the tradition of the courtly lyric by not naming the person addressed. There are no clues afforded by reference to heraldry.[78]

What is certain is that these occasional pieces are brief patches of sunshine in a prevailing mood of melancholy, of which the *chansons* were the musical mirror.

---

[76] . . . je lui [Suffolk] fey venir Binchois qui, par son command, fist ce rondel: *ainsi que à la foiz my souvient*' (Desplanque, *Project d'assassinat*, 70).

[77] Laurencie, 'La Musique à la cour des ducs de Bretagne aux XIVe et XVe siècles', *Revue de Musicologie*, 14 (1933), 2. This would be before the first recorded evidence of Binchois's professional life, which was playing the organ at Ste. Waudru, Dec. 1419 (Fallows, 'Binchois', *New Grove*, ii. 709).

[78] As in 'En la saison' by de Salinis, *CMM* 11. vii, 67.

9

The Musical Mirror of Burgundian Melancholy

THE song-maker knew that he was a toy of Fortune who must live in expectation of change. Centuries of schooling in the philosophy of Boethius had entrenched in his world the view that insecurity was Nature's way: 'Hi semper eius mores sunt, ista natura. Seuauit circa te propriam potius in ipsa sui mutabilitate constantiam . . .'.[1] He accepted the fact that unlike the limner and the mason he practiced a craft whose products would have no lasting purpose or effect; he did not speak fondly about the making of his song as the troubadour had done, and he knew that, although his music was necessary to the sustaining of a courtly atmosphere, in the actual conduct of inter-sexual relations his song was useless. Little had altered since Ovid—a song might have its intrinsic value, but it is money that talks, even in the mouth of the uncourtly: 'Carmina laudantur, sed munera magna petuntur; | Dummodo sit dives, barbarus ipse placet.'[2] From the minstrels' gallery and the chaplain's stall he could watch the uncourtliness that festered within the confines of his daily experience, courts 'never disgarnyshed of peple deceyvyng by fayr langage or ferying by menaces | or stryving by envye | . . . the good wyl of true men'.[3] Fortune's servant, his ultimate expectation from Nature's mutability was a hastened death: 'Mais entre nous curiaulx qui sommes serfz a fortune, vivons desordonneement et vieillissons plus par force de cures que par nombre d'ans, et par faulte de bien vivre sommes frustrez de la souefveté de nostre vie que tant desirons et nous hastons d'aler a la mort que tant redoubtons.'[4]

The musicians and the poets were in subjection to the vicissitudes of violent times. They made their songs in days haunted by the ghosts of assassinated rulers—Richard II, Louis of Orleans, John the Fearless—in courts obsessed with the Turkish menace, in a Europe which for a while was in divided allegiance to three popes, in an unconditional service to lords dominated by quarrels and motives of passion.[5] Man to a certain extent still behaved in a manner similar to the way Philip Ziegler so vividly described the generation that survived the Plague: it 'could not

---

[1] Boethius, *Philosophiae Consolatio*, ed. Bieler, ii. 18; for the influence of the *Consolatio* on French and English aristocracy and letters see Green, *Poets and Princepleasers: Literature and the English Court in the Late Middle Ages*, 144–8.
[2] Ovid, *Ars Amatoria*, ii. 275–6, in *The Art of Love, and Other Poems*, ed. and trans. Mozley, 84.
[3] William Caxton's translation (1484) of *The Curial made by maystre Alain Charretier*, 3–4.
[4] Alain Chartier, *Le Curial*, ed. Heuckenkamp, 27; Caxton trans. 16.
[5] Huizinga, *The Waning of the Middle Ages*, 17–18.

believe but did not dare deny' as it groped 'myopically towards the future, with one nervous eye always peering over its shoulder towards the past'.[6]

Contemporary writers lamented that those who had been nourished by a glorious Late Gothic Valois France now slew the source of their power, stabbing it to the womb: 'Filios enutrivi et exaltavi, ipsi autem spreverunt me. Nam utrinque non ad protectionem nostram, sed ad eorum mutuam necem arma movent hostilia ... milicia degenerans Gallicana sic in viscera Francie dulcissime genitricis seviebat ...'.[7] By 1444, even though France was on the road to recovery, 'not a man, of whatever estate, whether monk, priest, one of the religious orders, whether nun, minstrel, herald, woman, or young child of any age, but was in great danger of death if he set foot outside Paris'.[8] Evidently times were lean for the church musician, for in 1441 the Paris confraternities had only one sung low Mass, instead of celebrating with their customary two with music and two low.[9] Willingly or compulsorily, the entertainer followed the draining of cultural resources into Burgundy where he became confined and absorbed. Poets and musicians found a haven of *dons* in the midst of a world of brutal, mortal anguish, as into the courts of Burgundy was gathered the inheritance of four centuries of courtly love-grief. A woeful world-view was sublimated in the lyrical, stylized sorrow whose threads were woven into the tapestry of Chivalric Humanism. Sorrow joined and coloured what Huizinga called that 'complex of ... fine forms' whose apparent harmony veiled cruel reality and 'made life an art'.[10]

Burgundy was not an oasis of perfect peace. In the realm of Philip the Good there was intense suffering. For example, Dijon, which could count 2,353 taxable *feux* in 1376 (11,765 inhabitants), had but 771 *feux* (3,355 inhabitants) in 1431; with the reduction of brigandage in the early 1440s the population again grew, to number 2,614 *feux* (13,070 inhabitants). In 1431 a new category had been introduced, to admit three classes on the rolls: *les solvables*, *les misérables*, and the new group— *les mendians et quérans leur pain*.[11] A Burgundian minstrel could echo the justification for his art uttered by the troubadour Raimbaut d'Aurenga: 'I do not know how long I have to live, and so I surrender myself to my heart' ('No sai qant m'ai a viure, | Per qe mon cors al cor liure').[12] The tragedies and pessimism of the

---

[6] Ziegler, *The Black Death*, 288.

[7] *Chronique du religieux de Saint-Denys contenant le règne de Charles VI, de 1380 à 1422*, ed. Bellagnet, vi. 168–71, 288. See Shirley, *A Parisian Journal, 1405–1449*, 145–6, 189, 252 for contemporary lamentations on the state of France; also Champion, *Histoire poétique du quinzième siècle* i. 227–8; Mother France destroyed by her children was a theme for Chartier's *Le Quadrilogue invectif* (*c*.1422).

[8] Shirley, *A Parisian Journal*, 355. Matters were no better than twenty years before, when it was recorded that Vincent Grec, king's minstrel, was recompensed in January of 1420 'pour pertes subies en allant de Paris à Troyes où il a été détroussé par les ennemis du roi' ('Comptes de Pierre Gorremont, Receveur general du royaume, Dons du Roi', 1.230, in Pocquet du Haut-Jussé, *La France gouvernée par Jean sans Peur: les dépenses du receveur général du royaume*, 298.

[9] Shirley, *A Parisian Journal*, 344. Between 1418 and the 1440s even the yield and purchase of wine suffered; see Jehanno, 'Boire à Paris au XVᵉ siècle: le vin à l'Hotel-Dieu', *Revue Historique* 276 (1986), 3–28.

[10] Huizinga, *The Waning of the Middle Ages*, 54.

[11] Garnier, *La Recherche des feux en Bourgogne aux XIVᵉ et XVᵉ siècles*, 5–6.

[12] Topsfield, *Troubadours and Love*, 139.

age had become part of the fabric of Burgundian neo-chivalry. The Chartreuse de Champmol, the 'gigantic sepulchral monument' conceived by Philip the Bold, was a manifestation of the Burgundian pageantry of death.[13] By dramatizing the effects of grief, mourning became poetic and literary: 'The cultural value of mourning is that it gives grief its form and rhythm. It transfers actual life to the sphere of the drama. It shoes it with the cothurnus.'[14]

In the first half of the fifteenth century, the thoughtful poet regarded his own era no more pessimistically than his immediate predecessors had viewed their own.[15] For him, however, the ceremony of sorrow was troubled by the sounds of misery in the real world, sounds which the fourteenth century generally had ignored for the gratification of the ceremony itself. Although to imagine him an artist of tragic personality would posit anachronistically a Romantic type, we may see the Burgundian poet's mark of tragedy as the more authentic because it not only was donned in the spirit of a style but also represented the sum of daily details, accidents in an adverse existence.[16] The pathos in songs of separation and of farewell was made stronger by the awareness of the personal hazards of a life which might very easily end in confinement and death.[17] In the experience of contemporary afflictions and loneliness lay the true poet's sources of creation:

Ou sont les ménestrels de jadis, les tisseurs de haute lice, les orfèvres, les bons poètes courtois, les disciples de Machaut, de Froissart, de Christine? Ils ont disparu, n'ayant plus rien à dire ni à faire dans un monde sans joie. En fait, c'est la douleur, c'est l'ennui de la prison qui vont inspirer les deux poètes de cette première moitié du XVᵉ siècle: Charles d'Orléans et Jean Régnier.[18]

Once, in that growth of self-consciousness that had marked the second feudal era after AD 1200,[19] the lyric expression of self in the flowering of courtly song had been deepened in its awareness of love and of the ego. In the joy of that awareness Arnaut Daniel had declared that Love delighted him and harmonized his words and music, 'and do not imagine that in my grief I hope to compose a fine song' ('e no.us cugetz que de mon dol | esper a far bona chanson'): 'the feelings he has in love and the feelings he has for artistic perfection are inseparable'.[20] For the Burgundian

---

[13] See Vaughan, *Philip the Bold*, 202 ff.; for bizarre funereal pomp see ibid. 31–2. For fine photographic studies of Burgundian mourning statuary see Quarré, *La Sculpture en Bourgogne à la fin du moyen âge*, where an idea can be gained of the variety of sweetness and sorrow in that artistic idiom.

[14] Huizinga, *The Waning of the Middle Ages*, 52.

[15] For examples of the pessimism of Deschamps, *et al.*, see ibid. 32 ff.

[16] Poirion, *Le Poète et le prince*, 96–7. Schrade wrote of a possible tragic nature for the artist of late medieval melancholy, a Romantic exposure of the Artist as Tragic Figure which he himself admitted breaks down because the conventions of the vogue were so in unison with the pessimism and darkness of reality (Schrade, *Tragedy in the Art of Music*, 111).

[17] Poirion, *Le Poète et le prince*, 550, where *EscA* 27 is quoted (from *Jard*). See the texts of 'Adieu, mes tresbelles amours' (*EscA* 26, *Rehm* 5), 'Adieu, ma tresbelle maistresse' (*EscA* 27, *CMM* 77/12), 'Adieu, adieu' (*EscA* 28, *Rehm* 1), 'Adieu, jusques je vous revoye' (*EscA* 30, *Rehm* 2), and 'Adieu, mon amoureuse joye' *EscA* 32, *Rehm* 48).

[18] Champion, *Histoire poétique*, i. 228.

[19] See Bloch, *Feudal Society*, i. 106, 108.

[20] Paterson, *Troubadours and Eloquence*, 188–9. Cf. 'Pel joi qu'ai d'els e del tems | Chant, mas amors mi assauta, | Qui ls motz ab lo son acorda' (Lavaud, *Les Poésies d'Arnaut Daniel*, 42).

lyricist the poetry of desire and of the analysis of desire was altered into a frieze—an ornamented introspective study.

The courtier and the artist, equals in that they lived in sworn service to a neo-feudal duke of monarchical aspirations, were engaged in a quest for personal values. Their absorption in the community of the ducal household put self-worth in tension with their place within that community. Helpless to alter their condition, they found in the inherited conventions of the courtly lyric a private religion of renunciation in which to solve what the Canadian literary critic Louis Dudek has called 'the dichotomy of the self and the not-self, the I-myself and mankind-to-which-I-belong'.[21] They continued the literary pretence of waiting for the Lady without mentioning the desired physical reward: a poetry that 'has the air of being, like Oxford, the home of lost causes'.[22] The physical conquest did not need a song, and the time was long past when the anonymous author of the verses was of the suitable social status to have a hope of winning the lady. Through the repetition of *chanson* repertoire the Burgundian courtier and the poet/minstrel sought continual reaffirmation and reinforcement of his acceptance as an individual. The 'Lover' and the 'Lady' were one person, in despair at the pool of Narcissus.[23]

Le poème est donc comme un miroir flatteur que le prince ou le chevalier consulte avec anxiété ou complaisance pour y retrouver l'image de ses amours . . . la tradition courtoise a enfermé la littérature dans un univers essentiellement masculin: la dame que l'on consulte est imaginée par ou pour l'amant. Objet d'un culte ou jouet des désirs, l'idole féminine ne pouvait réellement parler: son oracle n'était qu'un écho déguisé.[24]

If one subscribes to the theory that literature 'moves from impersonality to personality, from universality to the completely private experience',[25] the morbid defeatism in many of the Burgundian *chansons* was a reflection of the poet's awareness that he was unable to be anyone but a prisoner of literary convention. The poet's 'abdication of originality', as C. S. Lewis referred to it,[26] was accompanied by neither the insight nor the detailed realism of a Deschamps or a Charles d'Orléans. In a Burgundian *chanson* the novelty that must invigorate the stereotype was rarely present. The felicity of the following two passages is enhanced only by their relative uniqueness:

> Je suis comme entre deux montaignes
> En faisant criz plaintes et plours.
> ('Cuid'on que je poille castaingnes', *EscA* 36, CMM 77/17)

---

[21] Dudek, *The First Person in Literature*, 57.

[22] Morris, *The Discovery of the Individual, 1050–1200*, 113.

[23] The narcissistic element in courtly poetry has been much discussed; see *inter alia* Valency, *In Praise of Love*, 26 ff; in *Le Roman de la Rose*, the fountain in which the Dreamer sees the Rose is the Well of Love, where the fair Narcissus wept himself to death (Guillaume de Lorris and Jean de Meun, *Le Roman de la Rose*, ed. Lecoy, l. 1438).

[24] Poirion, *Le Poète et le prince*, 131.

[25] Dudek, *The First Person in Literature*, 6.

[26] Lewis, *The Discarded Image*, 211.

> Esclave puist yl devenir
> En une galée sur mer,
> Qui monstrera samblant d'amor
> S'il ne le veult parmaintenir.
>   ('Esclave puist yl devenir', *EscA* 41, Rehm 15)

Also weak are the instances of that courtly fondness for amplifying and embellishing the formulae of parting, of elegy and of panegyric—'un cortège de mots réunis en un mouvement hyperbolique'.[27] Such attempts as in 'Adieu, ma tresbelle maistresse' (*EscA* 27, *CMM* 77/12), 'Je n'atens plus de resconfort' (*EscA* 29, *CMM* 77/13) and 'En bonne foy vous estez belle' (*EscA* 40, *CMM* 77/19) do not measure up to the rhetorical power of cumulative grief in the craft of Christine de Pisan's decasyllables in her *ballade* 'Dueil angoisseus' (*EscA* 37):

> Dueil angoisseus, rage demeseurée,
> Grief desespoir plain de forcenement,
> Langor sans fin et vie maleurée
> Plaine de plour, d'angoisse et de torment;
> Coeur doloreux qui vit obscurement,
> Tenebreux corps sur le point de partir
> Ay, sans cesser, continuellement;
> Et si ne puis ne garir ne morir.

In only eight songs did the anonymous poets represented in the Escorial *Chansonnier* employ one of the principal stylistic traits of the medieval first-person love lyric: praise of the Lady in superlative words.[28] Three of these are within a Lover's soliloquy (*EscA* 1, l. 5, 'Celle qui d'onneur a le pris'; *EscA* 4, l. 3, 'De ma dame tres doucée; *EscA* 33, l. 2, 'Devers la tresbelle aux biaulx yeulx'); two are in direct address to the Lady (*EscA* 5, l. 2, 'De vous, ma toute bonne et belle'; *EscA* 12, l. 1, 'Adieu, ma tresbelle maistresse'); and three are also direct but are in what appear to be occasional songs (*EscA* 16, 19, 31). Eight other complete poems in the first person which do not use superlatives in reference to the Lady comprise four soliloquies by the Lover in isolation (*EscA* 17, 23, 25, 26) and four direct addresses to the Lady (*EscA* 21, 22, 24, 28). Five of these sixteen pieces find the Lover so sunk in his lack of Fortune that he is hopeless, a combination of two other principal characteristics of this type of poetry: the monologue of complaint, in which the Lover expresses his state of being in quantitative terms (*EscA* 17, l. 6, 'Tous mes biens viennent à rebours'). The quantitative element emphasising the completeness of the Lover's misery is in contrast to the superlative references when present, the cure for the misery which is ascribed to the source of the highest good, the Lady. This balance affords a vertical dimension, present in *EscA* 1, 4, 5, 12, and 33. Another type of dimension is given to those poems where there is an expressed hope in, or at least the plea for, future bliss: the aspiration to rise onto the plane of

---

[27] Poirion, *Le Poète et le prince*, 462; q.v. 449 (where *EscA* 37 is quoted), 462–5.

[28] On the three stylistic traits of medieval poetry listed in the above paragraph see Taylor, 'The Terms of Love: a Study of Troilus's style', *Speculum* 51 (1976), 69–71.

the Lady's favour and to gain the psychological benefit which would result. Here was not only a contrast through a vertical hierarchy in the present state of the Lover–Lady relationship but also through the implied comparison between the miserable present and a blissful future, the wished-for progress of the relationship toward happiness giving to the poem the longitudinal dimension of time (*EscA* 1, 5, 33, 21–5).[29]

Primarily, however, the lyricists continued to repeat the desire of the Lover to be in feudal service to the Lady (*EscA* 1, 3, 5, 7, 12, 21, 24, 33, 39, 44), and to crave her *merchi* (*EscA* 25, 43, 51, 62).[30] Failing to receive it, or being separated from it, could bring only thoughts of dolour and death (*EscA* 1, 5, 8, 9, 10, 17, 18, 21, 22, 33, 35, 36, 39, 40, 46, 47, 48, 54, 57).

The *thoughts* of dolour and death—not the suicidal energies of early nineteenth-century Romantic youth, but a melancholy worn in the chivalric charade as a costume suitable to its sentimentality: the desire for gravity in the self-conscious preservation of exhausted forms. In this sense the Burgundian song-makers themselves were practitioners of Death, 'servants of an expiring mode of thought'.[31] Like the courtiers of Southern France after the Albigensian Crusade they would seek in vain for lost Joy: 'Puois poiran dompnas e drut | Tornar el joi q'ant perdut.'[32] As individuals their personalities are hidden to us behind a mask of style. Sons of a declining, melancholy age, they sang an impersonal song of declining, melancholy *courtoisie*, merging translated reality and literary pose. 'Such are the powers of style, a safeguard of man and his life, that substance and appearance merge forever in a solid compact.'[33]

[29] For a systematic treatment of these dimensions see Zumthor, 'Style and Expressive Register in Medieval Poetry', in Chapman (ed.), *Literary Style: A Symposium*, 263–77, especially the diagram, p. 272.

[30] The Lady's avowal is declared in 'Jamais ne quiers avoir liesse' (*EscA* 45, CMM 77/23), 'J'ayme bien celui qui s'en va' (*EscA* 50, CMM I. vi/86), and 'Jugiés se je doy joye avoir' (*EscA* 62, CMM 77/34).

[31] Huizinga, *The Waning of the Middle Ages*, 276; q.v. 34, 276–7, 323. See the critical discussion of Huizinga's concept of a 'waning' medieval spirit in Ferguson, *The Renaissance in Historical Thought*, 372–6, and Jacob, 'Huizinga and the Autumn of the Middle Ages', in his *Essays in Later Medieval History*, ch. 7.

[32] Raimon de Miraval, as cited in Topsfield, *Troubadours and Love*, 237.

[33] Schrade, *Tragedy in the Art of Music*, 108.

Conclusion

STYLE can be deceptive. The listener, accustomed to a Romantic composer's pursuit of individuality, may be deceived by the Model in which the medieval work participated. One may accept the similarities within the structural and the constituent patterns, but may not recognize the significance of, let us say, rhythmic inflections, that were the individual creator's personal animation of the Model. Bukofzer's reference to the fifteenth-century carol, a style he had made correlative to the Burgundian *chanson*, shows how even for the musicologist the impact of style could have been a barrier to the more complete appreciation of subtleties inherent in late medieval art-music: 'The melodies sound fresh but at the same time very much alike, so that if one knows a dozen the rest sound somehow familiar.'[1]

To escape from that deception the listener must remember that '*Style is not an absolute . . .* A style emerges only from the restless activity of many temperaments . . . A style is only an aspect of the course of a larger history, and the critic must try to relate the emergence of different styles with the emergence of the human attitudes which represent themselves, in one direction, by the arts.'[2] Style in the Burgundian *chanson* meant a poetry of parched *courtoisie*, only rarely distinguished by what may be called an analysis of the self *vis-à-vis* the world's grief. It was the musical setting of this portion of the literary basis for the Archaism/ *revenant* Chivalric Humanism which was a sensuous inducement to escape from the grossness and violence of reality. Style in the Burgundian *chanson* also meant that fusion of linear, consonant, textural and formal techniques which because of their geographical origins—Italian, English, and French—were the musical realization of the economic and political cross-currents that gave the archaistic court the power to encourage and preside over future 'renaissances'. In the coming to terms with the accomplishments of several nations lay 'the restless activity of many temperaments' from which emerged a style that must be called Protean, not Procrustean.[3]

Burgundian style was a transition from the medieval conception of the musician as re-enactor of universal truths to that of the new role for the creative artist as seeker, dedicated to a personal, even a private expressive voice. As the post-Burgundian polyphonists responded to each successive step in the development of the art, as harmonic polyphony was exaggerated into chromaticism, as the

---

[1] Bukofzer, *Studies in Medieval and Renaissance Music*, 169.
[2] Sypher, *Four Stages of Renaissance Style: Transformations in Art and Literature, 1400–1700*, 7.
[3] ibid.

controlling factor of *basso continuo* was introduced, as Tonality was diversified into increasingly individual mannerisms and 'styles' until the cadential demarcations through which the system was sustained were altered through atonality, so the encounters of international crafts which fused to form Burgundian style became analogous to the fissions of political powers in Western Europe up to 1914, of which Toynbee declared Burgundy was the prime force.[4] There is no longer any need to postulate a musical Renaissance produced by the melting of Flemish intellectualism in the sunshine of an Italy upon whose soil the *ultramontani* would sacrifice the 'engineering approach of the Gothic Age to the enjoyment of sound'.[5] Burgundian style may be seen as a 'renaissance' of its own, triggering a chain of subsequent renaissances which is being concluded only in our own century.

By the fourth quarter of the fifteenth century there was an awareness that something of unusual significance had happened in Philip the Good's Burgundy, something which had the effect of increasing the possibilities of music so marvellously that there appeared to be what Tinctoris ventured to call a new art: 'Quo fit ut hac tempestate facultas nostrae musices tam mirabile susceperit incrementum quod ars nova esse videatur, cujus, ut ita dicam, novae artis fons et origo apud Anglicos quorum caput Dunstaple exstitit fuisse perhibetur, et huic contemporanei fuerunt in Gallia Dufay et Binchois . . .'.[6] Now, continued Tinctoris, the *moderni* (Ockeghem, Busnois, Regis, and Caron) 'contrive music in the newest manner for the new times' ('in dies novos cantus novissime inveniunt').[7] The Burgundians were responsible for the mastery of the 'moderns'; the 'moderns' are irreconcilably separated from the barbarian musicians of yesteryear. Tinctoris and his generation understood that they occupied a special discrete place in the chronological evolution of style. His words from the *Proportionale musices* possessed a 'sense of period, of mental and physical differences from the past . . . [which] is precisely what distinguishes the Renaissance from the Middle Ages'.[8] In recognition of its contribution to the development of the new late fifteenth-century composition, the Burgundian deservedly may be called an Early Renaissance style.

Renaissance tendencies are quite apparent in the repertoire of the Escorial MS V.III.24:

1. Lyricism is established through the refinement of fourteenth-century 'ballade style'. To create secular music the composer now is required to give first consideration to the soprano: 'qui vult condere baladam, rotundellum, viriledum, spalmodium fiat primo discantus'.[9] Grace, suavity, and fluidity become the desired

---

[4] See Ch. 6.

[5] Sachs, *Rhythm and Tempo*, 199.

[6] Johannes Tinctoris, foreword to *Proportionale musices* (*c*.1476), as cited in Blume, art. 'Renaissance', *MGG* xi. 232 (from Coussemaker, *Scriptorum de musica medii aevi*, iv. 154), trans. Herter Norton as *Renaissance and Baroque Music: A Comprehensive Survey*, 14–15. The complete foreword is translated in Strunk, *Source Readings in Music History*, 193–6.

[7] Blume, 'Renaissance', *MGG* xi, 231–2, 247–8; Eng. trans. 14–15, 37.

[8] Bennett, *The Humane Medievalist: An Inaugural Lecture*, 6.

[9] Cambridge, Corpus Christi College, MS 410, II, fos. 7ʳ–8; cited in Bukofzer, 'Fauxbourdon revisited', *MQ* 38 (1952), 38 n. 25; also see Gulielmus Monachus on the soprano as *cantus firmus* in English style in Part 1.

attributes of melody. Melody is desired. It has been described in technical
language—*die Melismatik im ruhigen Stromrhythmus*;[10] it has been painted in
rather fanciful Romantic terms—'divine things had lost their inexorability: God
was good, the Virgin smiled, and Dufay smiled back. With such felicity, melody
grew cantabile and "beautiful".'[11] In either case the Cantus itself is well described:
a series of tonally expressive triadic periods, a powerful, sweet, and expressive
melodic diatonicism of an era in which commenced 'the flowering of diatonic
music in Western European culture'.[12]

2. Unstable notational exactitude common to late medieval manuscripts to
some extent remained in Burgundian song collections, particularly in the various
Contratenors with which the Cantus–Tenor frame was provided. One of the
driving principles of the 'new' in Renaissance musical thought was the urge to
conceive a work as 'a completely unified musical organism', to abandon the
medieval structure of successive layers and to adopt techniques of 'simultaneous
conception'; the creator must think in terms of more systematic vertical consonance.[13] In the Escorial collection the Discant–Tenor frames of certain songs in
Texture Group Three, and those of Group Four, were a step forward in composing
harmonic units; the unstable factor, the Contratenor, must leap up and down to fill
in the triadic *concentus*: the whole procedure becomes primarily vertically oriented.
As the alternating senary patterns $\frac{6}{8}/\frac{3}{4}$ gave way to slower and smoother outer
movement in *tempus perfectum*,[14] so the performer of the Contratenor had more
time for action; his virtuoso displays in minims and semiminims betrayed his
desires for individualism and attention. This type of *chanson* already was advanced
in vertical conception, and was demonstrative of forceful personality.

3. Given, as Curt Sachs put it, that 'the most radical innovation in the process of
composition in the Renaissance is the transition from a successive to a simultaneous conception of parts', and hence the object of simultaneous polyphonic
conception would be 'the projection of each part in connection with every other
part',[15] the canonic compositions and fragmentary imitation by Dufay, the
systematic pervasive imitation of 'Vostre alée me desplait tant' (*EscA* 11, *Rehm* 46)
and other Binchois songs, and the anonymous pieces in Texture Group Two,
indicate that equal authority of the voices was indeed taking shape, 'at least in an
accessory sense'.[16]

4. Increased use of implied Tonality, number of voice parts (as in 'Dueil
angoisseus' (*EscA* 37, *Rehm* 37)), spaced texture, and depth of pan-consonant

---

[10] Besseler, 'Das Neue in der Music des 15. Jahrhunderts', *Acta Mus* 26 (1954), 82.

[11] Sachs, *The Commonwealth of Art: Style in the Fine Arts, Music and the Dance*, 105.

[12] Szabolcsi, *A History of Melody*, 59; q.v. for melodic relationships between Binchois's 'De plus en plus' (*EscA* 39) and a Mozart Divertimento.

[13] Lowinsky, 'Music in the Culture of the Renaissance', in Kristeller and Wiener (eds.) *Renaissance Essays from the Journal of the History of Ideas*, 358–9.

[14] See Sachs, *Rhythm and Tempo*, 200–1.

[15] ibid. 379.

[16] Blume, *Renaissance and Baroque Music*, 79.

sound: these Renaissance inheritances from Burgundian music were founded upon the increased range of the sounding score. The songs of the Escorial repertoire spanned the ambit of the new sonority, from the low D of the 'Contratenor trompette' in 'J'ayme bien' (*EscA* 50, *CMM* I. vi/86), to the *extra manus Fa fictum* of 'Jamais tant' (*EscA* 47, *Rehm* 17). It was a testament to the new space in which composers could subsequently work, the complete ranges constituting the vocal ensemble. This was the new *Klangraum*, as Blume has described it: 'Within this space equivalence, equipollency, equilibrium reign: humanity owes to the Renaissance a music in which each voice unrestrictedly, in equal freedom, value, authority, can weave at the whole fabric and each voice is an individuality intimately interwoven in the whole.'[17]

What was medieval in Burgundian musical culture was represented primarily by the *chanson*. The seeds of 'renaissance' still were encased in forms and functions nurtured in the deliberately fixed state required by Chivalric Humanism. Such a coexistence of the progressive and the static is not unnatural, and is an illustration of the behaviourial pattern described by Grout: 'In biological terms: older forms may continue to exist for a time after some individuals in the group have responded adaptively to changes in the environment. [Thus older forms] may continue to survive indefinitely because they find a niche in the environment where they are protected.'[18] This dependence upon environment is further support for the assertion made earlier in this book that the style under consideration is 'Burgundian' in a dynastic sense.

To return to our original problem: one must approach Burgundian secular music not only to contemplate the Model but also to penetrate the fresh forces at work within it. Perhaps, in defining *chanson* style, analysts placed too much emphasis upon the Model; in this definition by Charles van den Borren the elements of variety, of personality and of new matter were relegated to a parenthetical permissive nod: 'The *chanson* was an art of miniature, bound by the rules of formal rhetoric which, while permitting much variety in detail, would not allow the musician to break its laws and give his inspiration free rein.'[19] Yet by searching for the 'variety in detail', we were able to distinguish within the Model a distinct musical personality: Binchois. His contemporaries recognized his individuality.[20]

---

[17] ibid. 75. *Klangraum* is Blume's term (*MGG* xi. 276); Besseler ('Das Neue') refers to a setting's *Vollklang*, and in another musicologist's catalogue of Renaissance characteristics this is listed as *Berücksichtigung des Klangs und des Gehörs* (Wolff, 'Der Stillbegriff der "Renaissance" in der Musik der alten Niederländer', in International Society for Musical Research, *Report of the Fifth Congress (Utrecht, 1952)*, 453–4).

[18] Grout, '"Adaption" as a Hypothesis in the History of Music', in Finscher and Mahling (eds.), *Festschrift für Walter Wiora zum 30. Dezember 1966*, 75.

[19] Borren, 'Dufay and his School', *The New Oxford History of Music*, iii. 225.

[20] In Ockeghem's *Deploration sur la mort de Binchois* (Marix, *Histoire de la musique et des musiciens de la cour de Bourgogne sous le règne de Philippe le Bon, 1420–1467*, 176; pub. Marix, *Les Musiciens de la cour de Bourgogne au XVᵉ siècle (1420–1467)*, 83) he is lauded as 'Le pere de joyeuseté' and 'patron de bonté': 'En sa jonesse fut soudart | De honnorable mondanité, | Puis a esleu la milleur part, | Servant Dieu en humilité.' This is more information, scanty though it is, than customarily given in Renaissance laments.

The modern listener is able to recognize it through the idiomatic traits listed in Part 1 of this study. It is not necessary for us to know the private life of Binchois; it is sufficient that he engaged in making a love-music so successfully personalized as to be original. His relationship to the Romantic composers may be likened to that of the amatory poets from Sappho to Catullus and Tibullus: 'We are accustomed to Keats' private griefs, Andre Gide's confessions, William Carlos Williams' "old ecstasies"—the extreme developments of personal expression in modern times—so that these classical poems may seem distant, formal, and still generalized to some extent. But all the elements of personal self-indulgence are already there.'[21] The Escorial MS V.III.24 is the main source for Binchois's musical 'self-indulgences'; they cause it to rank among the chief *chansonniers*. We cannot agree with Rudolf von Ficker that the collection is deprived of a spirit of humanism because it lacks the comprehensive repertoire of the Trent Codices; although by comparison with them it may have a limited repertoire, 'dictated by local or personal considerations',[22] it is not the less humanistic. The Escorial repertoire is humanistic because it is pervaded by the originality of Binchois's musical personality. In this *chansonnier*, form was coloured by the medieval concept of the universal; content was coloured by the renascent humanism of the individual creative personality: a dichroism which is the key to a proper understanding of Style in the Burgundian *chanson* of Binchois's era.

This dichroic style is reminiscent of the Middle Ages' double vision of reality, presenting both the concrete fact and the conceptual form—'the changing existence of each human being who feels desire and pain and the sting of memory' within 'the ideal order of a universe expressing God's unchanging will'.[23] If this Gothic 'proto-humanism' was a sign that culture was becoming secularized,[24] the marks of personal style it contains are indications of the increased laicization of the creative arts that promoted fifteenth-century renascent humanism.[25] In this light Binchois, the protagonist of renascent humanism, may be accorded the accolade

---

The often-reproduced illuminated miniature of Dufay and Binchois (Paris, Bib. nat., fr. 12476, fo. 98) need not be symbolic of sacred and secular music, as is sometimes stated; the organ was as much a secular instrument as a sacred one, and Binchois too was recorded as being a church organist. It is the clothing that gives them personalities. Both composers wear floor-length one-piece *robes* open at the neck; Binchois has his red *robe* girded at the waist with a simple belt, Dufay's blue *robe* is worn loose in the manner of a cleric. The red round cap worn by Dufay also was common clerical/university apparel; Binchois has a court hat with what appears to be a short *volet* hanging down on the left. He is portrayed as altogether more 'secular' than 'Maistre' Dufay. The distribution of blue and red may have been a matter of invention or expediency on the part of the limner; however, red had been the colour traditional to Burgundian minstrels (Wright, *Music at the Court of Burgundy, 1364–1419: A Documentary History*, 35), blue being designated for chaplains (Beaulieu and Baylé, *Le Costume en Bourgogne de Philippe le Hardi à la mort de Charles le Téméraire, 1364–1477*, 126–7, q.v. 41–72).

[21] Dudek, *The First Person in Literature*, 4.

[22] Ficker, 'The Transition on the Continent', *The New Oxford History of Music*, iii. 151–2.

[23] Sypher, *Four Stages of Renaissance Style: Transformations in Art and Literature, 1400–1700*, 38; he is discussing Dante's *Commedia*.

[24] ibid. 42.

[25] Ferguson, 'The Interpretation of the Renaissance: Suggestions for a synthesis', in Kristeller and Wiener (eds.), *Renaissance Essays*, 68–9, 72; see also the introductory chapter, 'The Individual in Western Tradition', in Morris, *The Discovery of the Individual, 1050–1200*, 1–10.

bestowed upon his reported patron, William de la Pole, by Kingsford: 'one of the finest types of the old chivalry that was passing away, and also through his intellectual sympathies a forerunner of the new order'.[26]

Style in the Burgundian *chanson* means many matters—medieval, transitional, and 'renascent'. We have attempted to illustrate that style through the representative repertoire of the Escorial MS V.III.24. Of these songs it may be said, in the words Tinctoris wrote to honour his favourite composers, 'Eaquoque profecto nunquam audio, nunquam considero quin laetoir ac doctior evadam . . .'—'Indeed, I never hear them, I never examine them, without coming away happier and more enlightened . . .'.[27]

[26] Kingsford, *Prejudice and Promise in Fifteenth Century England*, 146.

[27] Tinctoris, foreword to *Liber de arte contrapuncti* [1477], from Strunk, *Source Readings*, 199; the passage is cited in Blume, 'Renaissance', *MGG* xi. 232 from Coussemaker, *Scriptorum*, iv. 77. Seay (Tinctoris, *Art of Counterpoint*, 15) translates it with equal effectiveness: 'Certainly I never listen to them or study them without coming away more refreshed and wiser.'

Appendix 1
Catalogue of Escorial MS V.III.24

No.	Folio	First Line	Voices	Form	Composer	Concordances
1	1ʳ	Se mon cuer à hault entrepris	3¹	R		*BLib* fos. 23ᵛ–24ʳ
2	1ᵛ–2ʳ	Je vous salue, ma maistresse	3¹	B		Text: *TrC* fo. 35ʳ
3	2ᵛ–3ʳ	Je ne fai tousjours que penser	3¹	R	(Binchois)	*EscB* fos. 25ᵛ–26ʳ (anon); *Mü* fo. 14ᵛ (C only) (Binchois); *R* fos. 17ᵛ–18ʳ (Bincoys)
4	3ᵛ–4ʳ	a) Par tous lez alans de par la b) Cheluy qui vous remerchira	2¹⁺¹	R		
5	4ᵛ–5ʳ	Puis que m'amour m'a prins en desplaysir	3¹	R	Jo. Dunstapel	(1) *Tr* 88 fo. 84ᵛ Cat. no. 248 (Dumstabl); (2) *MüBux* 61, fos. 33ᵛ–34ʳ; (3) *Tit* fos. 6ᵛ–8ʳ (T & Ct); Text: *Jard* CCLXXVII, fo. 87ᵛ
6	5ᵛ–6ʳ	Il m'est si grief vostre depart	3¹	R	(Vide)	*O* fo. 77ʳ (Jacobus Vide)
7	6ᵛ–7ʳ	Vostre tres doulx regart plaisant	3¹	R	(Binchois)	(1) *Mü* fos. 7ᵛ–8ʳ (Binchois); *R* fos. 16ᵛ–17ʳ (Bincoys); (2) *Rit* fo. 144ᵛ (T); (3) *Harl* fo. 2ʳ; Text: *Jard* CCCXXIV, fo. 92ʳ
8	7ᵛ–8ʳ	Tous desplaisirs m'en sont prochains	3¹	R		
9	8ᵛ–9ʳ	Se la belle n'a le voloir	3¹	R	(Binchois)	*Tr* 87 fo. 135, Cat. no. 115 (textless) (Binchois)

No.	Folios	Incipit	V	R/B	Attribution	Concordances
10	9ᵛ–10ʳ	Depuis le congié que je pris	3¹	R		*Mii* fo. 13ʳ (T & Ct)
11	10ᵛ–11ʳ	Vostre alée me desplait tant	3¹	R	(Binchois)	*Mii* fos. 13ᵛ–14ʳ (Binchois); Text: *Rob* 158, fo. 87ᵛ
12	11ᵛ–12ʳ	Je ne porroye plus durer	3¹	B		(1) *O.* fo. 5ʳ (G. Dufay); *Tr* 90 fo. 365ʳ, Cat. no. 1079 (anon.)
13	12ᵛ–13ʳ	Craindre vous veul, doulche dame de priz	3¹	R	(Dufay)	(2) *MiiEm* fo. 76ᵛ; 2¹ *contrafactum* 'Bone pastor' (anon.)
14	13ᵛ–14ʳ	Le tresorire de bonté	3¹	R	Binchois	*Tr 87* fo. 91ᵛ Cat. no. 61 (textless) (Binchois)
15	14ᵛ–15ʳ	Si j'eusse un seul peu d'esperanche	3¹	R	(Binchois)	*BU* 17, p. 18, fo. 52ᵛ (Binchois)
16	15ᵛ–16ʳ	Liesse m'a mandé salut	3¹	R	(Binchois)	*O* fo. 79ᵛ (Binchois); *Tr 87* fo. 166ᵛ, Cat. no. 152 (textless) (Grossin)
17	16ᵛ–17ʳ	Plains de plours et gemissements	3¹	R	(Binchois)	*O* fo. 66 (Binchois)
18	17ᵛ–18ʳ	Puis que Fortune m'est si dure	3¹	B		Text: *Jard* CXLIII, fo. 75ʳ; *Rob* 388, fo. 140ᵛ
19	18ᵛ–19ʳ	Bon jour, bon mois, bonne sepmaine	3¹	R	(Binchois)	*O* fo. 71ᵛ (Binchois)
20	19ᵛ–20ʳ	Or ne sçay je que devenir	3¹	R		Text: *Jard* CCCXX, fo. 91ᵛ
21	20ᵛ–21ʳ	Mon seul et souverain desir	3¹	R	(Binchois)	*Str* fo. 107
22	21ᵛ–22ʳ	Las! comment porraye avoir joye	3¹	R	(Nic. de Merques)	*O* fo. 71ᵛ (Guillermus Dufay)
23	22ᵛ–23ʳ	Lune tresbelle, clere lune	3¹	R	(Dufay)	*O* fo. 80ᵛ (Guillermus Dufay)
24	23ᵛ–24ʳ	Or pleust à Dieu qu'à son plaisir	3¹	R		*PR* fo. 97ᵛ (anon.)
25	24ᵛ–25ʳ	Porray je avoir vostre merchi	3¹	R	G du ✠ Y	*Str* fo. 77ᵛ (G. Dufay)
	25ᵛ	(Blank)				

No.	Folio	First Line	Voices	Form	Composer	Concordances	
26	26^r	Adieu, mes tresbelles amours	2^1	R	(Binchois)	(1)	Str fo. 53^r (Bynczoys) Tr 92 fo. 111^v, Cat. no. 1468 (3^1 anon.)
						(2)	MiiEm fo. 5^r (3^1 contrafactum 'Ave corpus Christi') (Wintzois) MiiBux 143, 144, fos. 77^v–78^r
						(3)	Jard CXCIV, fo. 79^v
27	26^v–27^r	Adieu, ma tresbelle maistresse	3^1	R		Text:	
						(1)	EscB fo. 14^r (C & T) (anon.) Tr 92 fo. 112^r, Cat. no. 1469 (anon.)
						(2)	MiiEm fo. 87^r (2 voc. textless contrafactum 'Deo Gratias') (anon.)
28	27^v–28^r	Adieu, adieu, mon joieulx souvenir	3^1	R	(Binchois)	Text:	Jard CCCLXIII, fo. 95
						EscB	fo. 7 (T & Ct.)
						MiiEm	fo. 45^v (textless) (Binchoys)
						O	fo. 56^v (Binchois)
						PC	fo. 64^v (T only) (anon.)
						R	fos. 5^v–6^r (C & T) (Bincoys)
29	28^v–29^r	Je n'atens plus de resconfort	3^1	R		Mii	fo. 10^v (C only) (Binchois)
30	29^v–30^r	Adieu, jusques je vous revoye	3^1	R	(Binchois)	Text:	Jard CCCXXVIII, fo. 92^v Rob 374, fo. 137^r
31	30^v–31^r	Al eerbaerheit weinsch ic voort an	3^1	St		Str	fo. 115^v
32	31^v–32^r	Adieu, mon amoureuse joye	3^1	B	(Binchois)	MiiEm	fo. 45^v–46^r (textless) (Bincoys)
						Tr 87	fo. 92^r, Cat. no. 65 (Binchois)
33	32^v–33^r	Belle, esse dont vostre plaisir	3^1	R		EscB	fos. 8–9^r
34	33^v–34^r	Bien viengnant, ma tresredoubtée	3^1	R		PC	fo. 62^r
35	34^v–35^r	C'est assez pour morir de dueil	3^1	R	(Binchois)	Text:	
						(1)	Jard CCCXLI, fo. 93^v MiiEm fo. 127^r (textless) (Egidius Prachoys)

No.	Folios	Title	Voices		Attribution	Concordances
						(2) MüEm fo. 129r (3^1 contrafactum 'Virgo rosa venustatis') (Wintzois) Text: Jard CCCLXIV, fo. 95v Rob 162, fo. 88v
36	35v–36r	Cuid'on que je poille castaingnes	3^1	R		
37	36v–38r	Dueil angoisseus, rage demeseurée	3^1; 4^1	R	(Binchois)	(1) EscB fos. 15v–17r (3^1 anon.) Luc fos. 1v–2v (3^1 Binchois) Mü fo. 20v (Prima pars only) (3^1 Binchois) MüEm fo. 107r (3^0 anon.) R fos. 6v–7r (3^1 Bincoys) (2) Tr 88 fos. 204v–205r, Cat. no. 345 (anon. contrafactum 'Rerum conditor' with incipit 'De Langwesus') (3) MüBux 59, 60, fos. 32v–33v Rob 22, fo. 33r Text: Tr 92
38	38v–39r	De ceste joieuse advenue	3^1	R		
39	39v–[40r]	De plus en plus se renouvelle	3^1	R	(Binchois)	O fo. 111v, Cat. no. 1467 (anon.) fo. 67v (Binchois)
40	[40v]–[41r]	En bonne foy vous estez belle	2^1	R		
41	[41v]–[42r]	Esclave puist yl devenir	3^1	R	(Binchois)	(1) EscB fos. 19v–20r (anon.) MüEm fos. 126v–127r (textless) (Egidius Prachoys) R fos. 15v–16r (Bincoys) Str fo. 109r (Binzoys) (2) MüBux 101, 102, fos. 57v–58v Text: Jard CXXV, fo. 73v
42	[42v]–[43r]	Fontaine, à vous dire le voir	3^1	R		

No.	Folio	First Line	Voices	Form	Composer	Concordances
43	[43ᵛ]–[44ʳ]	Helas! ma dame, qu'ay je fait	3¹	R		O fos. 9ᵛ–10ʳ (3¹ Binchois)
						Pr fo. 96ʳ (3¹ anon.)
						Text: Jard CCCXXIX, fo. 92ᵛ
44	[44ᵛ]–[45ʳ]	Helas! je n'ose descouvrir	2¹	R		
45	[45ᵛ]–[46ʳ]	Jamais ne quiers avoir liesse	3¹	R		
46	[46ᵛ]	Je n'ay quelque cause de joye	1¹	R		
47	47ʳ	[Jamais tant que je vous revoye]	1⁰	R	(Binchois)	
48	47ᵛ–48ʳ	J'ay mains espoir d'avoir joye	3¹	R		
49	48ᵛ–49ʳ	Je cuidoye estre conforté	3¹	R		
50	49ᵛ–50ʳ	J'ayme bien celui qui s'en va	3¹	R	(Fontaine)	BL 250, fo. 252ʳ (Fontaine)
						O fos. 17ᵛ–18ʳ (C & T) (Petrus Fontaine)
51	50ᵛ–51ʳ	La merchi, ma dame et amours!	3¹	R	(Binchois)	Str fo. 88ʳ
52	51ᵛ–52ʳ	Loez soit Dieu des biens de ly	3¹	R		
53	52ᵛ–53ʳ	Margarite, fleur de valeur	3¹	R	(Binchois)	Mü fo. 7ʳ (T & Ct) (anon.)
						R fos. 19ʳ–20ʳ (Bincoys)
54	53ᵛ–54ʳ	Mon coeur avoeque vous s'en va	3¹	R		
55	54ᵛ–55ʳ	Ope es in minnen groot ghenuecht	3¹	St		
56	55ᵛ–56ʳ	Soyés loyal à vo povoir	3¹	R		O fo. 67ᵛ
57	56ᵛ–57ʳ	Las! que feraye? ne que je devenray?	3¹	R	G. du Ⅎ—Y	O fo. 72ʳ (Guillermus Dufay)
						O fo. 89ʳ (C & T) (G. du Fay)
						Str
58	57ᵛ–58ʳ	L'onneur de vous, dame sans per	3¹	R		
59	58ᵛ–59ʳ	Bien viegnés vous, mon prinche gracieux	3¹	R		
60	59ᵛ–60ʳ	Estrinez moy, je vous estrineray	3¹	R	G. du Y	O fos. 20ᵛ–21ʳ (G. Dufay)
61	60ᵛ–61ʳ	Va t'en, mon desir gracieux	3¹	R		
62	61ᵛ–62ʳ	Jugiés se je doy joye avoir	3¹	R		
	62ᵛ	(3 empty 6-line staves)				

Appendix 2.

The Anonymous Songs, Escorial MS V.III.24

1. Songs attributable to Binchois

EscA No.	CMM 77 No.	Folio	Scribe	First Line
2	2	1ᵛ–2ʳ	B	Je vous salue, ma maistresse
8	4	7ᵛ–8ʳ	B	Tous desplaisirs m'en sont prochains
10	5	9ᵛ–10ʳ	B	Depuis le congié que je pris
12	6	11ᵛ–12ʳ	B	Je ne porroye plus durer
14	7	13ᵛ–14ʳ	B	Le tresorire de bonté
23	11	22ᵛ–23ʳ	B	Lune tresbelle, clere lune
27	12	26ᵛ–27ʳ	A	Adieu, ma tresbelle maistresse
29	13	28ᵛ–29ʳ	B	Je n'atens plus de resconfort
34	16	33ᵛ–34ʳ	A	Bien viengnant, ma tresredoubtée
38	18	38ᵛ–39ʳ	A	De ceste joieuse advenue
54	28	53ᵛ–54ʳ	A	Mon coeur avoeque vous s'en va
58	31	57ᵛ–58ʳ	B	L'onneur de vous, dame sans per
59	32	58ᵛ–59ʳ	B	Bien viegnés vous, mon prinche gracieux
61	33	60ᵛ–61ʳ	B	Va t'en, mon désir gracieux

2. Songs attributable to a 'school of Binchois'

EscA No.	CMM 77 No.	Folio	Scribe	First Line
33	15	32ᵛ–33ʳ	A	Belle, esse dont vostre plaisir
36	17	35ᵛ–36ʳ	A	Cuid'on que je poille castaingnes
46	24	[46ᵛ]	A	Je n'ay quelque cause de joye
49	26	48ᵛ–49ʳ	A	Je cuidoye estre conforté
52	27	51ᵛ–52ʳ	A	Loez soit Dieu des biens de ly

3. Songs attributable to a 'school of Dufay'

EscA No.	CMM 77 No.	Folio	Scribe	First Line
40	19	[40ᵛ–41ʳ]	B	En bonne foy vous estez belle
56	30	55ᵛ–56ʳ	B	Soyés loyal à vo povoir
62	34	61ᵛ–62ʳ	B	Jugiés se je doy joye avoir

4. *Unattributed songs*

EscA No.	CMM *77* No.	Folio	Scribe	First Line
1	1	1ʳ	B	Se mon cuer à hault entrepris
4	3	3ᵛ–4ʳ	B	*a*) Par tous lez alans de par la
				b) Cheluy qui vous remerchira
18	8	17ᵛ–18ʳ	B	Puis que Fortune m'est si dure
19	9	18ᵛ–19ʳ	B	Bon jour, bon mois, bonne sepmaine
20	10	19ᵛ–20ʳ	B	Or ne sçay je que devenir
31	14	30ᵛ–31ʳ	A	Al eerbaerheit weinsch ic voort an
42	20	[42ᵛ–43ʳ]	A	Fontaine, à vous dire le voir
43	21	[43ᵛ–44ʳ]	A	Helas! ma dame, qu'ay je fait
44	22	[44ᵛ–45ʳ]	A	Helas! je n'ose descouvrir
45	23	[45ᵛ–46ʳ]	A	Jamais ne quiers avoir liesse
48	25	47ᵛ–48ʳ	A	J'ay mains espoir d'avoir joye
55	29	54ᵛ–55ʳ	A	Ope es in minnen groot ghenuecht

Appendix 3

The Verse Structure of the Songs with French Texts

The French-texted poems of the Escorial MS V.III.24 have structures in keeping with the repertoire in general. The refrains of the *rondeaux* form the schemes ABBA, AABBA; the earlier paired rhyme ABAB appears in 'Las! comment porraye avoir joye' (*EscA* 22) by Merques and the AABB scheme in the English-influenced 'Loez soit Dieu' (*EscA* 52). The table of rhyme schemes found in the *EscA* repertoire may be compared to the following display of the evolution of the *rondeau*, derived from Poirion, *Le Poète et le prince*, 333:

Scheme	Froissart	Wenceslas	Deschamps	de Pisan	Garencières	Chartier
ABAB	—	2	2	—	—	—
AABB	—	—	2	—	—	—
ABBA	—	—	6	36	9	16
AABBA	—	—	1	—	2	8

Masculine rhymes predominate over feminine. It is interesting that the two *rondeaux* of exclusively feminine rhymes refer to the Lady in similar phraseology: 'La plus gratieuse de Franche' (*EscA* 34), 'En Franche n'en a point de telle | Ne plus digne d'être amoureuse' (*EscA* 40)—possibly a pair of songs addressed to a single guest of honour, since the poet makes the special point of mentioning her homeland. Forty-five *rondeaux* are octosyllabic. Six are decasyllabic (*EscA* 5, 57, 59: *rondeau quatrain*; 13, 28, 60: *rondeau cinquain*). The other four are as follows: 84848 (*EscA* 1), 88488 (*EscA* 35, 48), 848488 (*EscA* 46). Four of the ballades are octosyllabic (*EscA* 2, 12, 18, 32), one decasyllabic (*EscA* 37).

Rondeaux: Rhyme scheme

Type	Rhyme scheme	Total	EscA *Numbers*
Rondeau quatrain	ABAB	1	22
	AABB	1	52
	ABBA	23	4, 5, 9, 10, 15, 16, 17, 21, 23, 26, 27, 36, 38, 40, 41, 44, 45, 50, 53, 57, 58, 59, 62
Rondeau cinquain	AABBA	29	1, 3, 6, 7, 8, 11, 13, 14, 19, 20, 24, 25, 28, 29, 30, 33, 34, 35, 39, 42, 43, 47, 48, 49, 51, 54, 56, 60, 61
Rondeau sixain	AABBAB	1	46

Rondeaux: Masculine, Feminine Endings

Type	Scheme	Total	EscA *Numbers*
Rondeau quatrain	ffff	1	40
	mmmm	8	4, 17, 21, 26, 41, 57, 58, 62
	fmmf	6	15, 23, 27, 36, 38, 45
	mffm	8	5, 9, 10, 16, 44, 50, 53, 59
Rondeau cinquain	fffff	1	34
	mmmmm	9	1, 7, 11, 28, 35, 43, 54, 56, 60
	ffmmf	5	19, 30, 39, 47, 48
	mmffm	14	3, 6, 8, 13, 14, 20, 24, 25, 29, 33, 42, 49, 51, 61
Rondeau sixain	ffmmfm	1	46

Ballades

Rhyme scheme	EscA *Numbers*
ABABACAC	2
ABABBCBC	18, 37
ABABBCC	12, 32

Masculine, Feminine Endings

mfmffmm	12
fmfmmmm	32
fmfmmfmf	18
fmfmmmmm	2, 37

Appendix 4

Corrigenda

The following corrections and alternative readings should be noted when consulting the author's edition, *Anonymous Pieces in the Chansonnier El Escorial, Biblioteca del Monasterio Cod. V.III.24 (Corpus Mensurabilis Musicae,* 77).

A. MUSIC

1. Corrections

EscA No.	CMM 77 No.	Page	Measure	Voice	Correction
8	4	4	16³–17¹	T	
12	6	8	13²	Ct	
14	7	9	2³	T	
19	9	12	17³	Ct	
20	10	14	14²	C	
34	16	23	7¹⁻²	C	
42	20	29	4¹⁻²	C	
52	27	36	3	T	

2. Alternative Readings

The transcriptions by Thomas McGary offered in his dissertation ('Codex Escorial MS V.III.24: An Historical-Analytical Evaluation and Transcription') contain some interesting interpretations, assuming scribal error; four of these are particularly strong alternatives.

EscA No.	CMM 77 No.	Page	Measure	Kemp	McGary
2	2	2	21–22		
8	4	4	4–5		
20	10	14	16		
43	21	30	9–10		

B. TEXT

EscA No.	CMM 77 No.	Verse	Line	Correction
2	2	i	4	acuelle = acuel le
4	3	ii	1	scat = sçay
		ii	2	arrez = 'orrez
8	4	ii	2	me = me[s]
		iii	2–3	N'ay secours par elle, ou au mains, Ma vie soit recommandée,
10	5	i	4	cest = c'est
12	6	ii, iii		*not published*

Tant m'estoyt de vous raconter
La desplaysanche que j'avoye,
Ma dame, et de vous demander
De vous nouvelles à mon joye
Que sur toutes riens desiroye
Et ossy rayson le voloit
Tant fort long de vous m'ennooyt.

Mais, quant je sçus que retourner
Hastiement ver vous devoye,
Je commenchai à requierer
Une partie de ma joye
Pas encore à souffy n'estoye,
Car le chemin trop me tannoyt
Tant fort long de vous m'ennooyt.

18	8	ii		*not published*

Or est mon cuer en telle ardure
Qu'avoir ne l'en puist par effort,
Et saudez de telle saudure
Que cercher me fait la mort,
Car quant me vient l'ardent remort
De la chose toute assovie
Que veor ne puist, c'est trop fort
Quant soudanement me desnie.

19	9	i	1	Bon jour, bon mois
23	11	iii	2	scay = sçay
29	13	i	3	scay = sçay
		iii	3	Pour moy grever. Que vo diroye?
34	16	i	3	esperance,
36	17	i	1	Cuidon = Cuid'on
42	20	i	3	no semicolon
		ii	1	Car, pour vous à raison mouvoir,
		iii	4	neantment = neantmains

EscA *No.*	CMM *77* *No.*	*Verse*	*Line*	*Correction*
43	21	i		verse should read:
				Helas! ma dame, qu'ay je fait
				Encontre vous ne qu'ay meffait
				Qu'ainsy m'avez miz en oubly?
				Oncques de rien ne vous fally,
				N'envers vous ne me suis fourfait.
45	23	ii	1	qui a maistresse
49	26	iii	3	finée,
54	28	iii	4	Tous me lessent; pour moy servir
59	32		5	Scay = sçay
62	34	i	1	ce = se

Bibliography

A. ON MUSIC

Adler, G., Koller, O., Ficker, R., and Orel, A. (eds.): *Trienter Codices* (Denkmäler der Tonkunst in Österreich, Jg. vii Bd. 14/15 (1900), xi[1] 22 (1904), xix[1] 38 (1912), xxxvii[1] 53 (1920), xxxi 61 (1924), xl 76 (1933))).

Aldrich, Putnam: 'An Approach to the Analysis of Renaissance Music', *Music Review*, 30 (1969), 1–21.

Apel, Willi: *The Notation of Polyphonic Music* (Cambridge, Mass., 1953).

—— *French Secular Compositions of the Fourteenth Century* (*Corpus Mensurabilis Musicae*, 53), 3 vols. (Stuttgart, 1970–2).

—— (ed.): *French Secular Music of the Late Fourteenth Century* (Cambridge, Mass., 1950).

Apfel, Ernst: *Beiträge zu einer Geschichte der Satztechnik von der frühen Motette bis Bach*, 2 vols. (Munich, 1964).

*L'Ars Nova: Recueil d'études sur la musique du XIV*e *siècle. Les Colloques de Wégimont*, ii (1955) (Bibliothèque de la Faculté de Philosophie et Lettres de l'Université de Liège, fasc. 149 (Paris, 1959).

Aubry, Pierre: 'Iter Hispanicum . . . ii. Deux chansonniers français à la Bibliothèque de l'Escorial', *Sammelbände der Internationalen Musikgesellschaft*, 8 (1906–7), 517–34.

—— *Iter Hispanicum: Notices et extraits de manuscrits de musique ancienne conservés dans les bibliothèques d'Espagne* (Paris, 1908).

Bent, Margaret: *Dunstaple* (London, 1981).

Besseler, Heinrich: 'Musik des Mittelalters in der Hamburger Musikhalle, 1.–8. April, 1924', *Zeitschrift für Musikwissenschaft*, 7 (1924), 42–54.

—— 'Studien zur Musik des Mittelalters', *Archiv für Musikwissenschaft*, 7 (1925), 167–252; 8 (1926), 131–258.

—— *Die Musik des Mittelalters und der Renaissance.* (Bücken: *Handbuch der Musikwissenschaft*) (Potsdam, 1931–5).

—— *Bourdon und Fauxbourdon* (Leipzig, 1950).

—— 'Die Entstehung der Posaune', *Acta Musicologica*, 22 (1950), 8–35.

—— 'The Manuscript Bologna Biblioteca Universitaria 2216', *Musica Disciplina*, 6 (1952), 39–65.

—— 'Das Neue in der Musik des 15. Jahrhunderts', *Acta Musicologica*, 26 (1954), 75–85.

—— 'Dufay in Rom', *Archiv für Musikwissenschaft*, 15 (1958), 1–19.

—— 'Das Renaissanceproblem in der Musik', *Archiv für Musikwissenschaft*, 23 (1966), 1–10.

—— (ed.): *Drei- und vierstimmige Singstücke des 15. Jahrhunderts* (Capella, 1) (Kassel and Basel, 1950).

—— (ed.): *Guillaume Dufay, Zwölf geistliche und weltliche Werke zu 3 Stimmen* (F. Blume, ed., *Das Chorwerk*, xix) (Wolfenbüttel, 1951).

Besselev, Heinrich (ed.): *Guillelmi Dufay Opera Omnia.* (*Corpus Mensurabilis Musicae*, 1) *Tomus vi: Cantiones* (Rome, 1964).

Blume, Friedrich: *Renaissance and Baroque Music: A comprehensive survey* Trans. M. D. Herter Norton. (New York, 1967).

—— (ed.): *Die Musik in Geschichte und Gegenwart: Allgemeine Enzyklopädie der Musik*, 11 vols. (Kassel and Basel, 1949–79).

Bockholdt, Rudolf: *Die frühen Messenkompositionen von Guillaume Dufay (Münchner Veröffentlichungen zur Musikgeschichte*, 5) (Tutzing, 1960).

Boer, Coenraad L. Walther: *Chansonvormen op het einde van de XVde eeuw* (Paris and Amsterdam, 1938).

Boorman, Stanley: 'The Early Renaissance and Dufay', *Musical Times*, 115 (1974), 560–5.

—— (ed.): *Studies in the Performance of Late Mediaeval Music* (Cambridge, 1983).

Borren, Charles van den: *Guillaume Dufay: Son importance dans l'évolution de la musique au XVe siècle* (Brussels, 1926).

—— (ed.): *Pièces polyphoniques profanes de provenance Liégeoise (XVe siècle) (Brussels,* 1950).

Bowles, Edmund A.: 'Haut et Bas: The Grouping of Musical Instruments in the Middle Ages', *Musica Disciplina*, 8 (1954), 115–40.

—— 'Instruments at the Court of Burgundy (1363–1467)', *The Galpin Society Journal*, 6 (1953), 41–51.

—— 'Musical Instruments at the Medieval Banquet', *Revue belge de Musicologie*, 12 (1958), 41–51.

—— *Musikleben im 15. Jahrhundert (Musikgeschichte in Bildern*, iii. 8) (Leipzig, 1977).

—— 'Unterscheidung der Instrumente Buisine, Cor, Trompe und Trompette', *Archiv für Musikwissenschaft*, 18 (1961), 52–72.

Brown, Howard M.: *Music in the Renaissance* (Englewood Cliffs, NJ, 1976).

—— Review of recording by Page, *The Castle of Fair Welcome*, *Early Music*, 15 (1987), 277–9.

Bukofzer, Manfred: *Geschichte des englischen Diskants und des Fauxbourdons nach den theoretischen Quellen* (Coll. d'études Musicologiques, 21) (Strasburg, 1936).

—— 'The First English Chanson on the Continent', *Music and Letters*, 19 (1938), 119–31.

—— 'Fauxbourdon Revisited', *Musical Quarterly*, 38 (1952), 22–47.

—— *Studies in Medieval and Renaissance Music* (New York, 1950).

—— 'Dunstable: A Quincentenary Report', *Musical Quarterly*, 40 (1954), 29–49.

—— 'Changing Aspects of Medieval and Renaissance Music', *Musical Quarterly*, 44 (1958), 1–18.

—— (ed.): *Adrian Petit Coclico: Compendium Musices (1552) (Documenta Musicologica,* i, 9) (Kassel, 1954).

—— (ed.): *John Dunstable: Complete Works* (*Musica Britannica*, viii), 2nd. rev. edn. prepared by Margaret Bent, Ian Bent, and Brian Trowell. (London, 1970).

Burstyn, Shai: 'Power's *Anima Mea* and Binchois's *De plus en plus*: A Study in Musical Relationships', *Musica Disciplina*, 30 (1976), 55–72.

Bush, Helen E: 'The Recognition of Chordal Formation by Early Music Theorists', *Musical Quarterly*, 32 (1946), 227–43.

Cazeaux, Isabelle: *French Music in the Fifteenth and Sixteenth Centuries* (Oxford, 1975).

Charles, Sidney Robinson: 'The Provenance and Date of the Pepys MS 1236', *Musica Disciplina*, 16 (1962), 57–71.

—— (ed.): *The Music of the Pepys MS 1236* (*Corpus Mensurabilis Musicae*, 40) (Rome, 1967).

Clarke, Henry Leland: 'Musicians of the Northern Renaissance', in LaRue (ed.), *Aspects of Medieval and Renaissance Music: A Birthday Offering to Gustave Reese*, 69–81.

Clercx, Suzanne: *Johannes Ciconia: Un musicien liégeois, et son temps*, 2 vols. (Brussels, 1960).

Closson, E.: 'L'origine de Gilles Binchois', *Revue de Musicologie*, 8 (1924), 149–51.

Collaer, Paul and van der Linden, Albert: *Atlas historique de la musique* (Paris, 1960).

Coussemaker, C. E. H. de: *Scriptorum de musica medii aevi*, 4 vols. (Paris, 1864–76; reprint, 1931).

Crocker, Richard L.: 'Discant, Counterpoint, and Harmony', *Journal of the American Musicological Society*, 15 (1962), 1–21.

Dalhaus, Carl: 'Zu einer Chanson von Binchois', *Die Musikforschung*, 17 (1963), 398–9.

Dannemann, Erna: *Die Spätgotische Musiktradition in Frankreich und Burgund vor dem Auftreten Dufays (Sammlung Musikwissenschaftlicher Abhandlungen begründet von Karl Nef*, xvii (Leipzig, 1936).

Davis, Shelley: 'The Solus Tenor in the 14th and 15th Centuries', *Acta Musicologica*, 39 (1967), 44–64.

Davison, Archibald T., and Apel, Willi (eds.): *Historical Anthology of Music*, 2 vols., rev. edn. (Cambridge, Mass., 1954).

Dèzes, Karl: 'Der Mensuralkodex des Benediktinerklosters Sancti Emmerami zu Regensburg Bericht', *Zeitschrift für Musikwissenschaft*, 10 (1927–8), 65–105.

Downey, Peter: 'The Renaissance Slide Trumpet: Fact or Fiction?', *Early Music*, 12 (1984), 26–32.

Droz, E., and Thibault, G. (eds.): *Trois chansonniers français du XVe siècle* (Paris, 1928).

Fallows, David: 'English Song Repertories of the Mid-Fifteenth Century', *Proceedings of the Royal Musical Association*, 103 (1976–7), 61–79.

—— 'Words and Music in Two English Songs of the Mid-15th Century: Charles d'Orléans and John Lydgate', *Early Music*, 5 (1977), 38–43.

—— *Dufay (The Master Musicians Series)*, (London, 1982).

—— Review of Boffey, *Manuscripts of English Courtly Love Lyrics in the Later Middle Ages*, in *Journal of the Royal Musical Association*, 112/1 (1987), 132–8.

Finscher, Ludwig: Review of Rehm, *Die Chansons von Gilles Binchois*, in *Die Musikforschung*, 11 (1958), 113–15.

—— Review of Rehm, *Codex Escorial*, in *Die Musikforschung*, 13 (1960), 110–11.

—— and Mahling, Christoph Hellmut (eds.): *Festschrift für Walter Wiora zum 30. Dezember 1966* (Kassel, 1967).

Fischer, Kurt von: 'The Manuscript Paris, Bibl. Nat. Nouv. Acq. Frc. 6771 (Codex Reina = PR)', *Musica Disciplina*, 11 (1957), 38–78.

Fox, Charles Warren: 'Non-Quartal Harmony in the Renaissance', *Musical Quarterly*, 31 (1945), 33–53.

Funck, Heinz (ed.): *Deutsche Lieder des 15. Jahrhunderts aus fremden Quellen zu 3 und 4 Stimmen* (F. Blume, ed., *Das Chorwerk*, xlv) (Wolfenbüttel, 1931).

Gallo, F. Alberto: *Music of the Middle Ages*, ii, trans. Karen Eales (Cambridge, 1985).

Gastoué, A.: 'Note sur la facture instrumentale à la cour de Bourgogne au XVe siècle', *Revue de Musicologie*, 3 (1919), 193–7.

Gerber, Rudolf, (ed.): *Guillaume Dufay: Sämtliche Hymnen zu 3 und 4 Stimmen* (F. Blume, ed., *Das Chorwerk*, xlix) (Wolfenbüttel, 1937).

Gérold, Théodore (ed.): *Le Manuscrit de Bayeux: Texte et musique d'un recueil de chansons du XVe siècle* (Strasburg, 1921).

Glowacki, John (ed.): *Paul A. Pisk: Essays in his Honor* (Austin, Texas, 1966).

Goldthwaite, Scott: 'Rhythmic Pattern Signposts in the 15th-Century Chanson', *Journal of the American Musicological Society*, 11 (1958), 177–88.

Gombosi, Otto: Review of Bukofzer, *Studies in Medieval and Renaissance Music*, in *Journal of the American Musicological Society*, 4 (1957), 139–47.

Greene, Gordon: 'The Schools of Minstrelsy and the Choir-School Tradition', *Studies in Music from the University of Western Ontario*, 2 (1977), 31–40.

—— (ed.): *Polyphonic Music of the Fourteenth Century*, xviii, xix: *French Secular Pieces* (Monaco, 1981–2).

Gulielmus Monachus: *De preceptis artis musicae*, ed. Albert Seay (*Corpus Scriptorum de Musica*, ii) ([Rome], 1965).

Gülke, Peter (ed.): *Johannes Pullois: Opera Omnia* (*Corpus Mensurabilis Musicae*, 41) ([Rome], 1967).

Gurlitt, Wilibald: 'Burgundische Chanson- und deutsche Liedkunst des 15. Jahrhunderts', in *Bericht über den musikwissenschaftlichen Kongress in Basel, 1924* (Leipzig, 1925), 153–76.

—— (ed.): *Gilles Binchois: Sechzehn weltliche Lieder zu 3 Stimmen*. (F. Blume, ed., *Das Chorwerk*, xxii) (Wolfenbüttel, 1933).

Haar, James (ed.): *Chanson and Madrigal, 1480–1530* (*Isham Library Papers*, ii) (Cambridge, Mass., 1964).

Haas, Robert: *Aufführungspraxis der Musik* (Bücken: *Handbuch der Musikwissenschaft*) (*Potsdam*, 1934).

Hamm, Charles: 'A Group of Anonymous English Pieces in Trent 87', *Music and Letters*, 41 (1960), 211–15 (with correspondence, *ML* 42 (1961), 96–7, 295–6).

—— 'Manuscript Structure in the Dufay Era', *Acta Musicologica*, 34 (1962), 166–84.

—— *A Chronology of the Works of Guillaume Dufay, Based on a Study of Mensural Practice* (Princeton, 1964).

—— 'A Catalogue of Anonymous English Music in Fifteenth-Century Continental Manuscripts', *Musica Disciplina*, 22 (1968), 47–76.

Harrison, Frank Ll.: *Music in Medieval Britain* (Egon Wellesz (ed.), *Studies in the History of Music* (London, 1958).

—— 'Tradition and Innovation in Instrumental Usage, 1100–1450', in LaRue (ed.), *Aspects of Medieval and Renaissance Music: A Birthday Offering to Gustave Reese*, 319–35.

—— 'Faburden in Practice', *Musica Disciplina*, 16 (1962), 11–34.

—— and Rimmer, Joan: *European Musical Instruments* (London, 1964).

Hjelmborg, Bjørn, and Sørensen, Søren (eds.): *Natalicia Musicologica, Knud Jeppesen Septuagenario Collegis Oblata* (Copenhagen, 1962).

Höfler, Janez: 'Der "Trompette de Menetrels" und sein Instrument: Zur Revision eines bekannten Themas', *Tijdschrift van de Vereniging voor Nederlandse Muziekgeschiedenis*, 29 (1979), 92–132.

Hogwood, Christopher: *Music at Court* (London, 1980).

Hughes, Andrew: 'Some Notes on the Early Fifteenth-Century Contratenor', *Music and Letters*, 50 (1969), 376–87.

Hughes, Dom Anselm: *Medieval Polyphony in the Bodleian Library* (Oxford, 1951).

—— and Abraham, Gerald (eds.): *Ars Nova and the Renaissance, 1300–1450* (The New Oxford History of Music, iii) (London, 1960).

Hughes-Hughes, Augustus: *Catalogue of Manuscript Music in the British Museum*, 3 vols. (London, 1906–9).

Institut für Musikwissenschaft der Karl-Marx-Universität: *Festschrift Heinrich Besseler zum sechzigsten Geburtstag* (Leipzig, 1961).

International Musicological Society: *Report of the Eighth Congress* (New York, 1961) (Kassel, 1961).

International Musicological Society: *Report of the Twelfth Congress, Berkeley, 1977*, ed. Daniel Hearz and Bonnie Wade (Kassel, 1981).

International Society for Musical Research: *Report [Bericht] of the Fifth Congress (Utrecht, 1952)* (Amsterdam, 1953).

Le Jardin de plaisance et Fleur de Rhétorique, 2 vols., ed. E. Droz (Paris, 1924).

Jeppesen, Knud (ed.): *Der Kopenhagener Chansonnier: Das Manuskript Thott 291^8 der königlichen Bibliothek Kopenhagen* (Copenhagen, 1927).

Kemp, Walter H.: 'A Chanson for Two Voices by Cesaris, *Mon seul voloir*', *Musica Disciplina*, 2 (1966), 47–56.

—— 'The Burgundian Chanson in the Fifteenth Century, with special reference to the anonymous chansons in the MS Escorial V.III.24 and related sources', D.Phil. thesis, 2 vols. (Oxford, 1972).

—— 'The Manuscript Escorial V.III.24', *Musica Disciplina*, 30 (1976), 97–129.

—— 'Some Notes on Music in Castiglione's *Il Libro del Cortegiano*', in Clough, Cecil H. (ed.), *Cultural Aspects of the Renaissance: Essays in Honour of Paul Oskar Kristeller* (Manchester, 1976), 354–69.

—— '"Votre trey dowce": A Duo for Dancing', *Music and Letters*, 60 (1979), 37–44.

—— (ed.): *Anonymous Pieces in the Chansonnier El Escorial, Biblioteca del Monasterio, Codex V.III.24 (Corpus Mensurabilis Musicae*, 77) (Stuttgart, 1979).

Kenney, Sylvia W.: *Walter Frye and the Contenance Angloise* (New Haven, 1964).

Knust, Hermann: 'Ein Beitrag zur Kenntnis der Escorial Bibliothek', *Jahrbuch für romanische und englische Litteratur*, 9 (1868), 43–72.

Kottick, Edward L. (ed.): *The Unica in the Chansonnier Cordiforme (Corpus Mensurabilis Musicae*, 42) ([Rome], 1967).

Kristeller, Paul Oskar: 'Music and Learning in the Early Italian Renaissance', *Journal of Renaissance and Baroque Music*, 1 (1947), 255–74; reprinted in *Renaissance Thought*, ii: *Papers on Humanism and the Arts* (New York, 1965), 142–62.

Kultzen, Brigitte: 'Der Codex Escorial IV.a.24: Übertragung, Katalog, historische Einordnung einer Chansonsammlung aus der 2. Hälfte des 15. Jh', unpublished diss. (Hamburg, 1956).

Lang, Paul Henry: *Music in Western Civilization* (New York, 1941).

—— 'The So-Called Netherlands Schools', *Musical Quarterly*, 25 (1939), 48–59.

LaRue, Jan (ed.): *Aspects of Medieval and Renaissance Music: A Birthday Offering to Gustave Reese* (New York, 1966).

Laurencie, Lionel de la: 'La Musique à la cour des ducs de Bretagne aux XIVe et XVe siècles, *Revue de Musicologie*, 14 (1933), 1–15.

Leech-Wilkinson, Daniel: Review of Boorman (ed.), *Studies in the Performance of Late Medieval Music*, in *Early Music History*, 4 (Cambridge, 1984), 347–55.

Leichtentritt, Hugo: *Music, History and Ideas* (Cambridge, Mass., 1938).

—— 'The Renaissance Attitude toward Music', *Musical Quarterly*, 1 (1915), 604–22.

Lenaerts, R. B.: *Het Nederlands Polifonies Lied in de Zestiende Eeuw* (Amsterdam, 1933).

—— 'Nederlandse polyphonische liederen in de bibliotheek van el Escorial', *Revue belge de Musicologie*, 3 (1949), 134–9.

Leneerts, R. B.: 'Contribution à l'histoire de la musique belge de la Renaissance', *Revue belge de Musicologie*, 9 (1955), 103–20.

—— (ed.): *Die Kunst der Niederländer* (K. G. Fellerer, *Das Musikwerk*, 22) (Cologne, 1962).

Lerner, Edward R.: Review of Rehm, *Codex Escorial*, in *Musical Quarterly*, 45 (1959), 115–16.

Lesure, François: *Musicians and Poets of the French Renaissance* (New York, 1955).

Löpelmann, Martin (ed.): *Die Liederhandschrift des Cardinals de Rohan (XV. Jahrh.) nach der Berliner HS. Hamilton 674 (Gesellschaft für Rom. Lit.*, 44) (Göttingen, 1923).

Lowinsky, Edward E.: *Secret Chromatic Art in the Netherlands Motet*, trans. C. Bachman (*Studies in Musicology*, 6) (New York, 1946).

—— 'On the Use of Scores by Sixteenth-Century Musicians', *Journal of the American Musicological Society*, 1 (1948), 17–23.

—— 'Music in the Culture of the Renaissance', *Journal of the History of Ideas*, 15 (1954), 509–53.

—— *Tonality and Atonality in Sixteenth-Century Music* (Berkeley, 1961).

Mahrt, William Peter: 'Guillaume Dufay's Chansons in the Phrygian Mode', *Studies in Music from the University of Western Ontario*, 5 (1980), 81–98.

Marggraf, Wolfgang: 'Tonalität und Harmonik in der französischen Chanson zwischen Machaut und Dufay', *Archiv für Musikwissenschaft*, 23 (1966), 11–31.

Marix, Jeanne: *Histoire de la musique et des musiciens de la cour de Bourgogne sous le règne de Philippe le Bon, 1420–67 (Sammlung Musikwissenschaftlicher Abhandlungen*, 28) (Strasburg, 1939).

—— (ed.): *Les Musiciens de la cour de Bourgogne au XVᵉ siècle (1420–1467)* (Paris, 1937).

McGary, Thomas J.: 'Codex Escorial MS V.III.24: An unpublished Historical-Analytical Evaluation and Transcription', Ph.D. diss. (University of Cincinatti, 1973), U.M. 73-23846.

—— 'Partial Signature Implications in the Escorial Manuscript V.III.24', *Music Review*, 40 (1979), 77–89.

McGee, Timothy J.: 'Instruments and the Faenza Codex', *Early Music*, 14 (1986), 480–90.

—— *Medieval and Renaissance Music: A Performer's Guide* (Toronto, 1985).

Meech, Sanford B.: 'Three Musical Treatises in English from a Fifteenth-Century Manuscript', *Speculum*, 10 (1935), 232–9.

Morley, Thomas: *A Plain and Easy Introduction to Practical Music*, ed. R. Alec Harman, with a Foreword by Thurston Dart (New York and London, 1952).

Mueren, F. van der: 'École bourguignonne, école néerlandaise au début de la Renaissance', *Revue belge de Musicologie*, 12 (1958), 53–65.

Nagel, W: *Geschichte der Musik in England* (Strasburg, 1894).

Osthoff, Helmuth: *Die Niederländer und das deutsche Lied, 1400–1640* (Berlin, 1938).

Page, Christopher: 'Machaut's "Pupil" Deschamps on the Performance of Music: Voices or instruments in the 14th-century chanson', *Early Music*, 5 (1977), 484–91.

—— 'Music and Chivalric Fiction in France, 1150–1300', *Proceedings of the Royal Musical Association*, 3 (1984–5), 1–27.

Paris, Gaston (ed.): *Chansons du XVᵉ siècle*, 2nd edn.(Paris, 1935).

Parrish, Carl: *The Notation of Medieval Music* (New York, 1957).

Pincherle, Marc: *An Illustrated History of Music*, trans. Rollo Myers (New York, 1959).

Pirotta, Nino, and Li Gotti, Ettore: 'Il Codice di Lucca', *Musica Disciplina*, 3 (1949), 119–38; 4 (1950), 111–52; 5 (1951), 115–42.

Pirro, André: *Histoire de la musique de la fin du XIVᵉ siècle à la fin du XVIᵉ* (*Manuels d'Histoire de l'Art*) (Paris, 1940).
—— *La Musique à Paris sous le règne de Charles VI, 1380–1422,* 2nd edn. (Strasburg, 1958).
Plamenac, Dragan: 'A Reconstruction of the French Chansonnier in the Biblioteca Colombina, Seville', *Musical Quarterly,* 57 (1951), 501–42; 38 (1952), 85–117, 245–77.
—— (ed.): *Johannes Ockeghem: Complete Works,* 2 vols. (New York, 1947–).
—— (ed.): *Sevilla 5–1–43 and Paris N.A.Fr. 4379 (Pt. 1): Facsimile reproduction of the manuscripts, with an introduction* (*Publications of Medieval Music Manuscripts,* 8) (Brooklyn, 1962).
Powers, Harold (ed.): *Studies in Music History: Essays for Oliver Strunk* (Princeton, 1968).
Randel, Don. M.: *The New Harvard Dictionary of Music* (Cambridge, Mass., 1986).
Reaney, Gilbert: 'Fourteenth-Century Harmony and the Ballades, Rondeaux and Virelais of Guillaume de Machaut', *Musica Disciplina,* 7 (1953), 129–46.
—— 'John Dunstable and Late Medieval Music in England', *The Score,* 8 (Sept. 1953), 22–33.
—— 'The Manuscript Chantilly, Musée Condé 1047', *Musica Disciplina,* 8 (1954), 59–113.
—— 'The Manuscript Oxford, Bodleian Library, Canonici Misc. 213', *Musica Disciplina,* 9 (1955), 73–104.
—— 'Voices and Instruments in the music of Guillaume de Machaut', *Revue belge de Musicologie,* 10 (1956), 3–17, 93–104.
—— *Machaut* (London, 1971).
—— (ed.): *Early Fifteenth-Century Music,* 7 vols. (*Corpus Mensurabilis Musicae,* 11) ([Rome], 1955–).
Reese, Gustave: *Music in the Middle Ages* (New York, 1940).
—— *Music in the Renaissance* (New York, 1954).
—— and Brandel, Rose (eds.): *The Commonwealth of Music* (New York, 1965).
Rehm, Wolfgang (ed.): *Die Chansons von Gilles Binchois (1400–1460)* (*Musikalische Denkmäler,* 2) (Mainz, 1957).
—— (ed.): *Codex Escorial: Chansonnier* (*Documenta Musicologica,* i, 2) (Kassel, 1958).
Riaño, Juan F.: *Critical and Bibliographical Notes on early Spanish Music* (London, 1887).
Riemann, Hugo: *History of Music Theory: Polyphonic theory from the 9th to the 16th century,* trans. with commentary by Raymond Haggh (*Geschichte der Musiktheorie,* i and ii, compl. rev.) (Lincoln, Nebraska, 1962).
—— (ed.): *Gilles Binchois: Sechs bisher nicht gedruckte dreistimmige Chansons* (Wiesbaden, 1892).
—— (ed.): *Musikgeschichte in Beispielen,* 3rd edn. (Leipzig, 1925).
Riess, Josef: 'Pauli Paulirini de Praga Tractatus de Musica (etwa 1460)' *Zeitschrift für Musikwissenschaft,* 7 (1925), 259–64.
Robertson, Alec, and Stevens, Denis (eds.): *Renaissance and Baroque* (*The Pelican History of Music,* ii) (Harmondsworth, 1963).
Sachs, Curt: 'Die Besetzung dreistimmiger Werke um das Jahr 1500', *Zeitschrift für Musikwissenschaft,* 11 (1928–9), 389–9.
—— *The Commonwealth of Art: Style in the Fine Arts, Music and the Dance* (New York, 1946).
—— 'Chromatic Trumpets in the Renaissance', *Musical Quarterly,* 36 (1950), 62–6.
—— *Rhythm and Tempo* (New York, 1953).
Sadie, Stanley (ed.): *The New Grove Dictionary of Music and Musicians,* 20 vols. (London, 1980).

Sadie, Stanley (ed.): *The New Grove Dictionary of Musical Instruments*, 3 vols. (London, 1984).

Salop, Arnold: 'Jacob Obrecht and the Early Development of Harmonic Polyphony', *Journal of the American Musicological Society*, 17 (1964), 288–94.

Schering, Arnold: *Studien zur Musikgeschichte der Frührenaissance* (Leipzig, 1914).

—— (ed.): *Geschichte der Musik in Beispielen* (New York, 1950 (reprint of 1931 edition)).

Schrade, Leo: *Tragedy in the Art of Music (The Charles Eliot Norton Lectures, 1962–3)* (Cambridge, Mass., 1964).

Shipley, Donald Walter: 'Codex Escorial V.III.24.' (unpublished MA diss., University of West Virginia, 1969).

Société Belge de Musicologie: *Mélanges Ernest Closson: Recueil d'articles musicologiques offert à Ernest Closson à l'occasion de son soixante-quinzième anniversaire* (Brussels, 1948).

Southern, Eileen: 'El Escorial, Monastery Library, Ms. IV.a.24' *Musica Disciplina*, 23 (1969), 41–79.

—— (ed.): *Anonymous Pieces in the MS El Escorial IV.a.24 (Corpus Mensurabilis Musicae*, 88) (Stuttgart, 1981).

Sparks, Edgar: *Cantus Firmus in Mass and Motet, 1420–1520* (Berkeley, 1963).

Spruit, Jop: 'Speelmansrecht in de middeleeuwen', *Mens en melodie*, 15 (1960), 82–3.

—— 'De speelman in de Nederlanden van de 13e–15e eeuw', *Mens en melodie*, 15 (1960), 332–6.

Stainer, J. F. R., and Stainer, C. (eds.): *Dufay and his Contemporaries* (London, 1898).

—— —— *Early Bodleian Music*, 2 vols. (London, 1901).

Sternfeld, Frederick W: *Music in Shakespearean Tragedy* (London, 1963).

Stevens, John: *Music and Poetry in the Early Tudor Court* (London, 1961).

—— (ed.): *Mediaeval Carols (Musica Britannica*, iv) (London, 1952).

Strunk, Oliver: *Source Readings in Music History* (New York, 1950).

Szabolcsi, Bence: *A History of Melody* (London, 1965).

Thibault, Geneviève: 'Le Chansonnier Nivelle de la Chausée', *Annales Musicologiques*, 7 (1964–77), 11–16.

Tinctoris, Johannes: *Art of Counterpoint*, trans. and ed. by Albert Seay (*Musicological Studies and Documents*, 5) (American Institute of Musicology, 1961).

—— *Dictionary of Musical Terms*, trans. and ann. by Carl Parrish (New York, 1963).

Treitler, Leo: 'Tone System in the Secular Works of Guillaume Dufay', *Journal of the American Musicological Society*, 18 (1965), 131–69.

Trend, J. B.: 'Musikschätze auf spanischen Bibliotheken', *Zeitschrift für Musikwissenschaft*, 8 (1925–6), 499–504.

Trowell, Brian: 'Some English Contemporaries of Dunstable', *Proceedings of the Royal Musical Association*, 81 (1954–5), 77–92.

—— 'Faburden and Fauxbourdon', *Musica Disciplina*, 13 (1959), 43–78.

Trumble, E.: 'Authentic and Spurious Faburden', *Revue belge de Musicologie*, 14 (1960), 3–29.

Van, Guillaume de: 'An Inventory of the Manuscript, Bologna, Q. 15 (Olim 37)', *Musica Disciplina*, 2 (1948), 231–57.

Wathey, Andrew: 'Dunstable in France', *Music and Letters*, 67 (1986), 1–36.

Wienpahl, Robert W.: 'The Evolutionary Significance of 15th century Cadential Formulae', *Journal of Music Theory*, 4 (1960), 131–52.

Wilkins, Nigel: 'The Codex Reina: A Revised Description', *Musica Disciplina*, 17 (1963), 57–73 (with reply by Fischer, 75–7).

—— (ed.): *A 15th-Century Repertory from the Codex Reina* (Corpus Mensurabilis Musicae, 37) ([Rome], 1966).

—— (ed.): *One Hundred Ballades, Rondeaux and Virelais from the Late Middle Ages* (Cambridge, 1969).

Wolf, J.: *Geschichte der Mensural-Notation*, 3 vols. (Leipzig, 1904).

—— *Handbuch der Notationskunde*, 2 vols. (Leipzig, 1913–19).

Wolf, R. E.: 'The Aesthetic problem of the "Renaissance"', *Revue belge de Musicologie*, 9 (1955), 83–102 (with correspondence, 175–7).

Wolff, Hellmuth Christian: *Die Musik der Alten Niederländer (15. und 16. Jahrhundert)* (Leipzig, 1956).

Wright, Craig: 'Tapissier and Cordier: New Documents and Conjectures', *Musical Quarterly*, 59 (1973), 177–89.

—— 'Dufay at Cambrai: Discoveries and Revisions', *Journal of the American Musicological Society*, 28 (1974), 175–229.

—— *Music at the Court of Burgundy, 1364–1419: A Documentary History* (Henryville, 1979).

B. ON RELATED SUBJECTS

Abert, Herman: 'Die Musikästhetik der Echecs Amoureux', *Romanische Forschungen*, 15 (1903–4), 884–925.

Académie Royale des Sciences, des Lettres et des Beaux-Arts de Belgique: *Biographie Nationale* (Brussels, 1966–).

Andreas Capellanus: *The Art of Courtly Love*, trans. John Jay Parry (New York, 1959, (orig. 1941)).

Armstrong, C. A. J.: *England, France and Burgundy in the Fifteenth Century* (London, 1983).

Atiya, Aziz Suryal: *The Crusade in the Later Middle Ages* (London, 1938).

Barclay, Alexander: *The Eclogues*, ed. Beatrice White (Early English Text Society, 175) (London, 1928).

Beaucourt, G. Du Fresne de: *Histoire de Charles VII*, 6 vols. (Paris, 1881–91).

Beaulieu, Michèle, and Baylé, Jeanne: *Le Costume en Bourgogne de Philippe le Hardi à la mort de Charles le Téméraire, 1364–1477* (Paris, 1956).

Bennett, J. A. W.: *The Humane Medievalist: An Inaugural Lecture* (Cambridge, 1965).

Bloch, Marc: *Feudal Society*, 2 vols. (Chicago 1964 (orig. 1961)).

Brown, Carleton (ed.): *English Lyrics of the Thirteenth Century* (Oxford, 1932).

Brown, Elizabeth A. R.: Review of Vaughan, *Philip the Bold and John the Fearless*, in *Speculum*, 43 (1968), 554–50.

Boethius: *Philosophiae Consolatio*, ed. Ludwig Bieler (Corpus Christianorum, Series Latina, XCIV. i) (Turnholt, 1957).

Burckhardt, Jacob: *The Civilization of the Renaissance in Italy* (New York, 1954).

Burgess, Glyn S., and Taylor, Robert A. (eds.): *The Spirit of the Court: Selected Proceedings of the Fourth Congress of the International Courtly Literature Society, Toronto 1983* (Cambridge, 1985).

Calmette, Joseph: *Les Grands Ducs de Bourgogne* (Paris: Michel, 1949); Eng. trans.: Doreen
    Weightman, *The Golden Age of Burgundy* (London, 1962).

Cartellieri, Otto: *The Court of Burgundy* (London, 1929).

Chabod, Federico: *Machiavelli and the Renaissance* (Cambridge, Mass., 1958).

Champion, Pierre: *Le Manuscrit autographe des poésies de Charles d'Orléans: Étude*
    (*Bibliothèque du XVe siècle*, 3) (Paris, 1907).

—— *Vie de Charles d'Orléans (1394–1465)* (*Bibliothèque du XVe siècle*, 13) (Paris, 1911).

—— *Histoire poétique du quinzième siècle*, 2 vols. (*Bibliothèque du XVe siècle*, 27/28)
    (Paris, 1923).

Champollion-Figeac, M.: *Documents historiques inédits tirés des collections manuscrites*
    de la Bibliothèque nationale et des archives ou des bibliothèques des départements, iv
    (Paris, 1848).

Chapman, Seymour (ed.): *Literary Style: A Symposium* (London, 1971).

Charles d'Orléans: *The English Poems . . . from the Manuscript, Brit. Mus. Harl. 682*, ed. R.
    Steele, 2 vols. (Early English Text Society, 215, 220) (London, 1941–6).

—— *Poésies*, ed. Pierre Champion, 2 vols. (Paris, 1956).

Chartier, Alain: *The Curial made by maystre Alain Charretier, Translated thus in Englyshe*
    by William Caxton, 1484, ed. F. J. Furnivall (Early English Text Society e.s. 54)
    (London, 1888).

—— *Le Curial: Texte français du XVe siècle avec l'original latin*, ed. Ferdinand Heucken-
    kamp (Halle, 1899).

Chastelaine de Vergi, La, ed. Frederick Whitehead (Manchester, 1944).

Chastellain, Georges: *Chronique des ducs de Bourgogne*, ed. J. A. Buchon, 2 vols. (*Coll. des*
    chroniques nat. fr., 42–3) (Paris, 1827).

—— *Œuvres*, ed. by M. le baron Kervyn de Lettenhove, 8 vols. (Brussels, 1963–6).

Chaucer, Geoffrey: *The Complete Works*, ed. W. W. Skeat, 7 vols. (Oxford, 1894).

Chrétien de Troyes: *Arthurian Romances*, trans. W. W. Comfort (*Everyman's Library*)
    (London, 1914).

—— *Le Chevalier au Lion (Yvain)*, ed. Mario Roques (Paris, 1957).

—— *Cligés*, ed. Alexander Micha (Paris, 1957).

Christine de Pisan: *Œuvres poétiques*, ed. Maurice Roy, 3 vols. (Paris, 1886–96).

—— *The Treasure of the City of Ladies*, trans. Sarah Lawson (Harmondsworth, 1985).

Chronique du religieux de Saint-Denys, contenant le règne de Charles VI, de 1380 à 1422,
    ed. M. L. Bellagnet, 6 vols. (Paris, 1839–52).

Cohen, Gustave: *Histoire de la chevalerie en France au moyen âge* (Paris, 1949).

—— (ed.): *Recueil de farces françaises inédites du XVe siècle* (Cambridge, Mass., 1949).

Cornish, F. W., Postgate, J. P., and MacKail, J. W. (eds.): *Catullus, Tibullus and*
    Pervigilium Veneris (*Loeb Classical Library*) (Cambridge, Mass., 1962).

Cosneau, E.: *Le Connétable de Richemont* (Paris, 1886).

Cressot, Marcel: *Vocabulaire des Quinzes Joyes de Mariage, d'après le texte de la seconde*
    édition de la Bibliothèque elzéverienne de 1857 (Paris, 1939).

Crow, Joan: 'A Little-known Manuscript of the *Quinze Joyes de Mariage*', E. A. Francis
    (ed.), *Studies in Medieval French Presented to Alfred Ewert in Honour of his*
    Seventieth Birthday (Oxford, 1961).

Curtius, Ernst Robert: *European Literature and the Latin Middle Ages*, trans. Willard R.
    Trask (London, 1953; New York, 1963).

Deschamps, Eustache: *Œuvres complètes*, ed. by Le Marquis de Queux de Saint-Hilaire and
    Gaston Raynaud, 11 vols. (Paris, 1878–1903).

Deschaux, Robert: *Un Poète bourguignon au XVe siècle: Michault Taillevent* (Geneva, 1975).

Desplanque, M. A.: *Projet d'assassinat de Phillippe le Bon par les Anglais (1424–1426)* (Brussels, 1967).

Devillers, Léopold (ed.): *Cartulaire des comtes de Hainault, de l'avènement de Guillaume II à la mort de Jacqueline de Bavière* (1337–1436), 6 vols. in 7 (Brussels, 1881–96).

Dickinson, Jocelyn Gledhill: *The Congress of Arras, 1435* (Oxford, 1955).

Dodd, W. G.: *Courtly Love in Chaucer and Gower* (Gloucester, Mass., 1959 (orig. 1913)).

Doutrepont, Georges: *La Littérature française à la cour des ducs de Bourgogne (Bibliothèque du XVe siècle*, 8) (Paris, 1909).

Dudek, Louis: *The First Person in Literature* (Toronto, 1967).

Dyggve, Holger Petersen: *Gace Brulé, trouvère champenois: Edition des chansons et étude historique* (*Mémoires de la Société Néophilologique de Helsinki*, 16) (Helsinki, 1951).

Ehler, Sidney Z.: 'On Applying the Modern Term "State" to the Middle Ages', in J. A. Watt, J. B. Morrall, and F. X. Martin (eds.), *Medieval Studies presented to Aubrey Gwynn, S.J.* (Dublin, 1961).

Escouchy, Mathieu d': *Chronique*, ed. G. Du Fresne de Beaucourt, 3 vols. (Paris, 1863–4).

Evans, Joan: *Magical Jewels* (Oxford, 1922).

—— *Life in Medieval France* (London, 1957).

—— and Serjeantson, Mary: *English Mediaeval Lapidaries* (Early English Text Society, 190) (London, 1933).

Fenin, Pierre de: *Mémoires, comprenant le récit des événements qui se sont passés en France et en Bourgogne sous les règnes de Charles VI et Charles VII (1407–1427)*, ed. L. M. F. Dupont (Paris, 1837).

Ferguson, Wallace K.: *The Renaissance in Historical Thought* (Cambridge, 1948).

—— *Europe in Transition, 1300–1520* (Boston, 1963).

—— *The Renaissance: Six Essays* (New York, 1963).

—— *Renaissance Studies* (*Studies in the Humanities*, ii) (London, Ont., 1963).

Fiske, Christabel Forsyth (ed.): *Vassar Mediaeval Studies* (New Haven, 1923).

Fleming, John V.: *The Roman de la Rose: A Study in Allegory and Iconography* (Princeton, 1969).

Fowler Kenneth: *The Age of Plantagenet and Valois* (London, 1967).

Fox, John: *The Lyric Poetry of Charles d'Orléans* (Oxford, 1969).

Froissart, Jean: *Chronicles*, ed. Geoffrey Brereton (Harmondsworth, 1968)

Gachard, L. P.: *Collection de documents inédits concernant la Belgique* (Brussels, 1833–5).

García de la Fuente, Fray Arturo: *Catálogo de los manuscritos franceses y provenzales de la Bibliotheca de El Escorial* (Madrid, 1933).

Garnier, Joseph: *La recherche des feux en Bourgogne aux XIVe et XVe siècles* (Dijon, 1976).

Gautier, Léon: *Les Epopées françaises*, 3 vols. (Paris, 1865–8).

—— *La Chevalerie* (Paris, 1884).

Godefroy, Frédéric: *Dictionnaire de l'ancienne langue française et de tous ses dialectes du IXe au XVe siècles*, 10 vols. (Paris, 1881–).

Gower, John: *Confessio Amantis*, ed. G. C. Macaulay, 2 vols. (Early English Text Society, e.s. 91–2) (London, 1900–1901).

Green, Richard Firth: *Poets and Princepleasers: Literature and the English Court in the Late Middle Ages* (Toronto, 1980).

Guillaume IX: *Les Chansons de Guillaume IX, Duc d'Aquitaine (1071–1127)*, ed. A. Jeanroy (Paris, 1927).

Guillaume de Lorris and Jean de Meun: *Le Roman de la Rose*, ed. Felix Lecoy, 2 vols. (Paris, 1965); trans. Harry W. Robbins (New York, 1962).

Harsgor, M.: 'L'Essor des bâtards nobles au XVe siècle', *Revue historique*, 253 (1975), 319–54.

Hauser, Arnold: *The Social History of Art*, ii (New York, 1957).

Hay, Denys: *The Renaissance* (London, 1963).

Highet, Gilbert: *The Classical Tradition* (Oxford, 1949).

Hill, R. H. and Bergin, T. G. (eds.): *Anthology of the Provençal Troubadours*, 2 vols. (New Haven, 2nd. rev. edn. 1973).

Huguet, Edmond: *Dictionnaire de la langue française du seizième siècle*, v (Paris, 1973).

Huizinga, Johan: *The Waning of the Middle Ages* (Harmondsworth, 1955 (orig. 1924)).

Hunt, R. W., Pantin, W. A., and Southern, R. W. (eds.): *Studies in Medieval History presented to F. M. Powicke* (Oxford, 1948).

Imbs, Paul (ed.): *Trésor de la Langue Française*, xii (Paris, 1986).

Jacob, E. F.: *Essays in the Conciliar Epoch* (Manchester 1943).

—— The Fifteenth Century, 1399–1485 (Oxford History of England, vi) (Oxford, 1961).

—— *Essays in Later Medieval History* (Manchester, 1968).

—— (ed.): *Italian Renaissance Studies: A Tribute to the late Cecilia M. Ady* (London, 1960).

Jehanno, C.: 'Boire à Paris au XVe siècle: Le vin à l'Hôtel–Dieu', *Revue historique*, 276 (1986), 3–28.

José, Marie: *La Maison de Savoie: Amédée VIII*, 2 vols. (Paris, 1962).

Keen, Maurice: *Chivalry* (New Haven, 1984).

Kilgour, Raymond Lincoln: *The Decline of Chivalry as shown in the French literature of the Late Middle Ages* (Cambridge, Mass., 1937).

Kingsford, C. L.: *Prejudice and Promise in Fifteenth Century England* (London, 1962 (orig. 1925)).

Kristeller, Paul Oskar: *Renaissance Thought, ii: Papers on Humanism and the Arts* (New York, 1965).

—— and Wiener, Philip P. (eds.): *Renaissance Essays from the Journal of the History of Ideas* (New York, 1968).

Kultenbacher, Robert: 'Der altfranzösiche Roman Paris et Vienne', *Romanische Forschungen*, 15 (1904), 321–688.

Kunz, George Frederick, and Stevenson, Charles Hugh: *The Book of the Pearl* (London, 1908).

Laborde, Le Comte de: *Les Ducs de Bourgogne: Etudes sur les lettres, les arts et l'industrie pendant le XVe siècle . . . Seconde partie . . . Preuves*, 3 vols. (Paris, 1849–52).

La Curne de Sainte-Palaye, Jean Baptiste de: *Mémoires sur l'ancienne chevalerie*, new edn., 3 vols. (Paris, 1781).

La Marche, Olivier de: *Mémoires*, ed. Beaune and d'Arbaumont, 4 vols. (Paris, 1883–8).

Lavaud, René: *Les Poésies d'Arnaut Daniel* (Geneva, 1973 (orig. Toulouse, Périgueux, 1910)).

Lawlor, John (ed.): *Patterns of Love and Courtesy: Essays in Memory of C. S. Lewis* (London, 1966).

Lazar, Moshé: *Amour courtois et 'Fin Amours'* (Paris, 1964).

—— (ed.): *Bernard de Ventadour: Troubadour du XIIIe siècle. Chansons d'Amour* (Paris, 1966).

Lewis, C. S.: *The Allegory of Love* (London, 1933).

—— *The Discarded Image* (Cambridge, 1964).

Littré, Emile: *Dictionnaire de la langue française*, v (Paris, 1962).

Lowes, J. L.: 'The Prologue to the *Legend of Good Women* as related to the French Marguerite Poems and to the *Filostrato*', *Publications of the Modern Language Association*, 19 (1904), 593–683.

Luchaire, Achille: *Social France at the Time of Philip Augustus* (New York, 1967 (orig. 1912)).

Lydgate, John: *The Minor Poems*, ii, *Secular Poems*, ed. H. N. MacCracken (Early English Text Society, 192) (London, 1934).

Martin, Alfred von: *Sociology of the Renaissance* (New York, 1962, (orig. 1944)).

Mathew, Gervase: *The Court of Richard II* (London, 1968).

Meyer, Paul: *Girart de Rousillon* (Paris, 1884).

Migne, Jacques Paul (comp.): *Patrologiae cursus completus . . . Series Latina* (Paris, 1844–64).

Morrall, John B.: *Political Thought in Medieval Times* (New York, 1962 (orig. 1958)).

Morris, Colin: *The Discovery of the Individual, 1050–1200* (London, 1972).

Myers, A. R. (ed.): *The Household of Edward IV: The Black Book and the Ordinance of 1478* (Manchester, 1959).

Olson, Glending: 'Deschamps' *Art de Dictier* and Chaucer's Literary Environment', *Speculum*, 48 (1973), 714–23.

Oudemans, A. C.: *Bijdrage tot een middel- en oudnederlandsch Woordenboeck*, 7 vols. (Arnhem, 1870–80).

Ovid: *The Art of Love, and Other Poems*, ed. and trans. J. H. Mozley (*Loeb Classical Library*) (Cambridge, Mass., 1962).

Pannier, Leopold: *Les Lapidaires françaises du moyen âge* (Paris, 1882).

Paris and Vienne: Translated from the French and printed by William Caxton, ed. MacEdward Leach. (Early English Text Society, 234) (London, 1957).

Paterson, Linda M.: *Troubadours and Eloquence* (Oxford, 1975).

Pearl, ed. E. V. Gordon (Oxford, 1953).

Pearsall, Derek, and Salter, Elizabeth: *Landscapes and Seasons of the Medieval World* (Toronto, 1973).

Petit, Ernest (ed.): *Itinéraires de Philippe le Hardi et de Jean sans Peur, ducs de Bourgogne, 1363–1419, d'après les comptes de dépenses de leur hôtel . . .* (*Collections de documents inédits sur l'histoire de France*) (Paris, 1888).

Piaget, Arthur: '*La Cour amoureuse* dite de Charles VI', *Romania*, 20 (1891), 417–54; 31 (1902), 597–603.

Pirenne, Henri: *Early Democracies in the Low Countries* (New York, 1963 (pub. 1915 as *Belgian Democracy*)).

Planche, Alice: *Charles d'Orléans ou la recherche d'un langage* (*Bibliothèque du XVe siècle, 38*) *(Paris, 1975)*.

Pliny [the Elder]: *Natural History*, 10 vols., ed. and trans. H. Rackham (*Loeb Classical Library*) (Cambridge, Mass., 1938–63).

Pocquet du Haut Jussé, B.: *La France gouvernée par Jean sans Peur: Les dépenses du receveur général du royaume* (Mémoires et documents publiés par la société de l'école des Chartes, 13) (Paris, 1959).

Poirion, Daniel: *Le Poète et le prince* (Paris, 1965).

Pope, M. K.: *From Latin to Modern French: With Especial Consideration of Anglo-Norman* (Manchester, 1934).

Postan, M. M., Rich, E. E., and Miller, Edward (eds.): *Economic Organization and Policies in the Middle Ages* (*Cambridge Economic History of Europe*, iii) (Cambridge, 1963).

Potter, G. R. (ed.): *The Renaissance, 1493–1520* (*New Cambridge Modern History*, i) (Cambridge, 1961).

Quarré, Pierre: *La Sculpture en Bourgogne à la fin du moyen âge* (Fribourg, Paris, 1978).

Raby, F. J. E.: *A History of Secular Latin Poetry in the Middle Ages*, 2 vols. (Oxford, 1934).

Rasmussen, Jens: *La Prose narrative française du XVe siècle: Étude esthétique et stylistique* (Copenhagen, 1958).

Raynaud, Gaston (ed.): *Rondeaux et autre poésies du XVe siècle publiés d'après le manuscrit de la Bibliothèque Nationale* (Paris, 1889).

Reiffenberg, F. A. de: *Enfants naturels de Philippe le Bon* (Brussels, 1846).

René, duc d'Anjou: Livre du Cuer d'Amours Espris, ed. O. Smital and E. Winkler (Vienne, 1927).

Robbins, Rossell Hope (ed.): *Secular Lyrics of the XIVth and XVth Centuries* (Oxford, 1955).

Robertson, D. W., Jr.: *Essays in Medieval Culture* (Princeton, 1980).

Le Roman en prose de Gérard de Rousillon, ed. L. De Montille (Paris, 1880).

Runciman, Steven: *The Fall of Constantinople, 1453* (Cambridge, 1965).

Rutherford, C.: 'The Forgeries of Guillaume Benoit', *English Historical Review*, 30 (1915), 216–33.

Rychner, Jean: *La Littérature et les mœurs chevaleresques à la cour de Bourgogne* (Neuchâtel, 1950).

Scheludko, D.: 'Ovid und die Trobadors', *Zeitschrift für romanische Philologie*, 54 (1934), 129–74.

Schirmer, Walter F.: *John Lydgate: A Study in the Culture of the XVth century* (London, 1961).

Schofield, William Henry: 'Symbolism, Allegory, and Autobiography in *The Pearl*', *Publications of the Modern Language Association*, 24 (1909), 585–675.

Seznec, Jean: *The Survival of the Pagan Gods*, trans. Barbara F. Sessions (New York, 1961 (orig. 1953)).

Shirley, Janet (trans.): *A Parisian Journal, 1405–1449: Translated from the Anonymous Journal d'un Bourgeois de Paris* (Oxford, 1968).

Stephen, Leslie, and Lee, Sidney (eds.): *Dictionary of National Biography*, 63 vols. (London, 1885–1901).

Struder, Paul, and Evans, Joan: *Anglo-Norman Lapidaries* (Paris, 1924).

Sypher, Wylie: *Four Stages of Renaissance Style: Transformations in Art and Literature, 1400–1700* (New York, 1955).

Taylor, Davis: 'The Terms of Love: A Study of Troilus's Style', *Speculum*, 51 (1976), 69–90.

Theocritus: *Works*, ed. with a translation and commentary by A. S. F. Gow, 2nd edn., 2 vols. (Cambridge, 1952).

Tilley, Arthur: *The Dawn of the French Renaissance* (Cambridge, 1918).

—— *Medieval France: A companion to French studies* (Cambridge, 1922).

—— *Studies in the French Renaissance* (Cambridge, 1922).

Topsfield, L. T.: *Troubadours and Love* (Cambridge, 1975).

Toynbee, Arnold J.: *A Study of History*, ix (London, 1954).

Vale, M. G. A.: *Charles VII* (Berkeley and Los Angeles, 1954).

—— Review of Vaughan, *Valois Burgundy*, *Times Literary Supplement*, 5 Sept. 1975, 1005.

Valency, Maurice: *In Praise of Love* (New York, 1961 (orig. 1958)).

Vaudin, Eugène: *Gérard de Roussillon: Histoire et légende* (Paris, 1884).

Vaughan, Richard: *Philip the Bold* (London, 1962).

—— *John the Fearless* (London, 1966).

—— *Philip the Good* (London, 1970).

—— *Charles the Bold* (London, 1973).

—— *Valois Burgundy* (London, 1975).

Verwijs, E. and Verdam, J.: *Middelnederlandsch Woordenboek*, 9 vols. (The Hague, 1885–1929).

Waddell, Helen: *Mediaeval Latin Lyrics*, 5th edn. (London, 1948).

Werkmeister, William H. (ed.): *Facets of the Renaissance* (New York, 1963).

Wilkinson, L. P.: *Ovid Recalled* (Cambridge, 1955).

Willard, Charity Cannon: '"Nobility" as a Humanistic Problem in Burgundy', *Studies in the Renaissance*, 14 (1967), 33–48.

Williams, E. Carleton: *My Lord of Bedford: 1389–1435* (London, 1963).

Woledge, Brian (ed.): *The Penguin Book of French Verse*, i (Harmondsworth, 1961).

Wolffe, Bertram: *Henry VI* (London, 1981).

Ziegler, Philip: *The Black Death* (Harmondsworth, 1970).

Index of Songs

A. Songs in Escorial MS V.III.24

'Adieu, adieu, mon joieulx souvenir'
    (Binchois) 5, 6, 7, 20, 21–2, 24, 61;
    Exx. 2*a*, 17*d*
'Adieu, jusques je vous revoye'
    (Binchois) 5, 7 f., 18, 19 f., 56 f.;
    Ex. 15*a*
'Adieu, ma tresbelle maistresse'
    (anon.) 30–1, 35, 60, 61, 112; Ex. 34
'Adieu, mes tresbelles amours'
    (Binchois) 60–1
'Al eerbaerheit weinsch ic voort an'
    (anon.) 57–9, 105 n. 70

'Belle, esse dont vostre plaisir' (anon.) 7,
    29, 35–8, 62; Exx. 37, 41
'Bien viegnés vous, mon prinche gracieux'
    (anon.) 98, 105 n. 70
'Bien viengnant, ma tresredoubtée'
    (anon.) 9, 20, 23, 34, 41, 61, 98, 105
    n. 70; Ex. 21
'Bon jour, bon mois, bonne sepmaine'
    (anon.) 99

'C'est assez pour morir de dueil'
    (Binchois) 18, 19 f., 60, 90, 93;
    Ex. 15*b*
'Craindre vous veul, doulche dame de priz'
    (Dufay) 31, 34
'Cuid'on que je poille castaingnes'
    (anon.) 29, 31, 34, 35, 41, 62, 87
    n. 42, 96, 111; Exx. 32, 35*b*

'De ceste joieuse advenue' (anon.) 20, 61,
    98, 105 n. 70
'De plus en plus se renouvelle'
    (Binchois) viii, 20, 21, 27, 61, 116
    n. 12; Exx. 17*b*, 26
'Depuis le congié que je pris' (anon.) 4
    n. 5, 22–3, 39, 60; Ex. 20
'Dueil angoisseus, rage demeseurée'
    (Binchois) viii, 9, 15, 16, 46 and n. 33,
    54, 61, 112, 116; Exx. 13*g*, 52*b*

'En bonne foy vous estez belle'
    (anon.) 53–5, 62, 105 n. 70, 112;
    Exx. 51, 52*a*, 53
'Esclave puist yl devenir' (Binchois) 112
'Estrinez moy, je vous estrineray'
    (Dufay) 5–6, 31, 34, 82 n. 43, 99;
    Ex. 2*b*

'Fontaine, à vous dire le voir' (anon.) 99,
    105 n. 70

'Helas! je n'ose descouvrir' (anon.) 54–5,
    92
'Helas! ma dame, qu'ay je fait' (anon.) 7

'Il m'est si grief vostre depart' (Vide) 12 f.,
    77; Ex. 8

'Jamais ne quiers avoir liesse' (anon.) 11,
    34, 113 n. 30
'Jamais tant que je vous revoye'
    (Binchois) 21, 117; Ex. 17*c*
'J'ay mains espoir d'avoir joye' (anon.) 34,
    38 and n. 9; Ex. 42
'J'ayme bien celui qui s'en va'
    (Fontaine) viii, 46 n. 31, 47*f*, 113
    n. 30, 117
'Je cuidoye estre conforté' (anon.) 4 n. 5,
    31, 62, 90–1, 96–7, 99
'Je n'atens plus de resconfort' (anon.) 9,
    29, 30, 39–41, 112; Exx. 5*a*, 33*a*, 45*a*
'Je n'ay quelque cause de joye' (anon.) 52,
    62; Ex. 50
'Je ne fai tousjours que penser'
    (Binchois) 7, 57
'Je ne porroye plus durer' (anon.) 56–7;
    Ex. 56
'Je vous salue, ma maistresse' (anon.) 55–
    6 and n. 4, 87, 90; Exx. 54, 55

B. Other Songs

152 *Index of Songs*

General Index